John Stolz, William Henry Ryder

Murder, capital punishment, and the law

John Stolz, William Henry Ryder

Murder, capital punishment, and the law

ISBN/EAN: 9783337229184

Printed in Europe, USA, Canada, Australia, Japan

Cover: Foto ©Suzi / pixelio.de

More available books at **www.hansebooks.com**

MURDER,

CAPITAL PUNISHMENT,

AND

THE LAW.

IN THREE PARTS.

By JOHN STOLZ, M. D.,

AUTHOR OF A "TREATISE ON THE HUMAN FIVE SENSES," PRACTISING PHYSICIAN AND SURGEON, LECTURER ON PHYSIOLOGY, HYGIENE, MENTAL TRAINING, &C., &C.

PUBLISHED BY SUBSCRIPTION ONLY.

UNION PUBLISHING COMPANY,
335 WABASH AVENUE, CHICAGO, ILLINOIS; 179 WEST FOURTH STREET, CINCINNATI, OHIO.

A. L. BANCROFT & CO.,
SAN FRANCISCO, CAL.

1873.

PREFACE.

After writing a book, it seems as necessary for the author to solicit the courteous attention of the reader to its pages, in a few prefatory remarks, as it is when forming the acquaintance of a stranger to be introduced by one already acquainted with the person whose society is sought. In this duty I take great pleasure, hoping that those who peruse this volume may realize much profit, as thus my object will be attained.

The prevalence of crime in general, and the many murders in particular, at the present time, was the actuating motive which induced me to attempt an inquiry into the cause and effect of this sad grievance, and, if possible, to point out a more successful treatment, a sure means of preventing crime, and a better, more humane method of treating the criminal than has hitherto been employed. The idea that the infliction of the death penalty for capital crime is either a preventive measure or a protection to society is fully discussed, and shown to be utterly false, unnatural, and an incentive to crime, and its speedy abolition strongly urged. I have also endeavored to point out correct principles, by which the laws of man may be made to harmonize with those of God and nature; and have striven to create a popular sentiment with a view to bring about a general reform.

The work which I have undertaken is an attempt only to defend the truth, and to fill a certain vacancy, which at the present epoch seems to be widely felt. I offer no excuse for a murderer, or in any manner shield crime, but, on the contrary, am in favor of a rigid enforcement of the law. So long as capital punishment is the law, let it be enforced; but I contend that the law is wrong, and should therefore be repealed. I have labored studiously to set forth in clear and pointed language the natural causes which induce men to commit crime, and the just punishment and rational means of prevention which have never before been presented to the public in the same light.

For my standpoint of reasoning, I have selected the science of physiology, which, doubtless, is the starting-point of all human action. The moral, the intellectual, and the emotive natures of man are governed by, and must, therefore, be studied in connection with, the laws which govern physical existence. Man is a creature of education, governed wholly by circumstance; his surroundings make him what he is. The law of pliancy is as much a law of the mind as of the body, and is fully discussed in this volume. It is held in these pages that mind is a physical force; that all knowledge is derived from the external world; that crime is the result of an unbalanced condition of the mental and physical constitution, either hereditary or acquired; that the treatment of crime, to be right, must be reformative and reparative; that man's laws must agree with the laws of physiology, which are also laws of nature; that all corporal punishment is contrary to the laws of nature; that society is largely responsible for the many crimes committed, and that it is in duty bound to enforce the principles set forth in this volume; that education must be made compulsory; that all wrong actions on the part of man are the fruit of ignorance, moral and physical depravity, and the only remedy is in the universal education of the people, and the certain enforcement of the laws; that it is a duty of the state to establish reformatory prisons and educational institutions; that it costs the people more to try and punish criminals than to educate and reform them, to be successful in which we must understand and obey first principles. These are some of the topics which are discussed in this volume.

I have endeavored to avoid all sectarian ideas, or such as are inclined to a weak sentimentalism. I have studiously labored to follow the teachings of science upon the subject in hand, believing that the matter has never received that unbiased attention which it strenuously calls for, and which an appeal to reason, and a right use of the knowledge we have of human nature, will afford.

The book, to be appreciated, must be carefully read, chapter by chapter; and, to be understood well, it must be studied.

Whatever criticisms may be offered by the public, I hope will be given in the most liberal sense, and in as kindly a spirit as that which actuated the author in its composition.

JOHN STOLZ, M. D.

TABLE OF CONTENTS.

PART FIRST.

MURDER AND CRIME.

CHAPTER I

CAUSE OF CRIME.

	PAGE.		PAGE
Opening Lines	15	Parents	25
Primary Laws of Nature	16	Is Man a Free Agent?	26
Different Ages or Epochs of Time	17	The Author's Position Sustained	27
Progress of Events	18	Feeble-Minded Persons	28
The Child a Blank at Birth	19	Why we Seek the Society of One Another	29
Color of Hair and Eyes	20	What Distinguished Writers Say	30
The Advanced Thinker or Philosopher	21	An Explanation Easily Understood	31
Definition of Crime	22	Our Surroundings and Conditions, and the Story of a Barber	32
Wonderful Observations	23		
A Reasonable Conclusion	24		
The Child a Counterpart of the			

CHAPTER II.

ORGANS OF THE BRAIN AND THEIR FUNCTION.

On the Activity Called Life	33	men and Men	39
No Traces of Mind in the Lower Forms of Creation	34	Inattention to Bodily Health—Anger	40
Mind a Physical Manifestation	35	Torture of a Wife—A Little Broth	41
On the Mysterious Operations of God	36	If a Man Breaks his Leg	42
Harmony Among the Faculties	37	A Physiological Maxim	43
Woman—The Heart—The Brain—The Causes of Discord	38	A Well-Balanced Education	44
Unhappy Associations with Wo-		Principles with which we have no Right to Interfere	45

CONTENTS.

CHAPTER III.

CONSTITUTIONAL PREDISPOSITION TO CRIME.

	PAGE.		PAGE.
Our Trip to New York—Two Happy Men	46	The Morris and the Gill Family.	51
Conversation Between a Lawyer and A Doctor	47	Two Years After—Conversation with a Lady	52
The Murderer Williams	48	Three Classes of Persons who Commit Crime	53
The Family that had a Predisposition to Steal	49	He Fixed on a Night	54
Physical Laws—Depravity—The Monomaniac—The Clergy	50	A Little Instruction Required	55
		One who would have Stolen the Money	56

CHAPTER IV.

THE TWO PATHS OF THE CHILD.

Two Boys of Equal Rights	57	Black-legs—The Literature of To-day	64
The Boy on the Left-hand Path	58	The History of a Man on an Adjoining Farm	64
The Boy on the Right-hand Path	59		
How to acquire a Second Nature	60		
Every Step you Take	61	Our Hero on the Left-hand Path	66
One Step in Advance	62	The End of the Two Boys	67
Behold a Man!	63		

CHAPTER V.

ON MAN'S SOCIAL NATURE.

How we are Disappointed	68	—Farmers—Mechanics, etc	71
What Money can Buy—Respectable Society	69	Social Propensities and How to "Get a Little More"	72
Fifty or a Hundred Dollars per Month	70	Law and Order—The Physician	73
The Social "Rings"—Statesmen		Where we Lay Crime	74

CHAPTER VI.

THE WORKING MAN.

Capital and Labor	75	Legal Persuasion	81
It is a Physiological Truth	76	What we Said in a Lecture	82
What is a Day's Work?	77	The Death Drink	83
What Science has Revealed	78	Shall we Compromise with Vice?	84
The Eight-Hour System	79	New Kind of Associations	85
Eight O'clock, P. M.—Places where Criminals are Made	80	Woman's Reform—A Child Six Years Old—A Little Group	86
Change of Tactics—Moral and			

CONTENTS.

CHAPTER VII.
ON ACCIDENTAL CRIME.

	PAGE.
Voluntary and Involuntary Crime	87
Those who Never Commit Crime,	88
Things in Nature—What is it that will Restrain?	89
A Temporary Fit	90
A Train of Cars—Post-mortem	91
The Man and his Peach	92
What is it that Overshadows the Present Era	93
The Gentleman of Forty—Brains—The Doctor—Books—Health and Wealth	94
The Man and his Dirk	95
Chicago—Intrinsic Virtue—Men and Electricity	96
The Wickedest Demon of Our Day	97
"Heigh-ho! Captain, Whither are you Going?"	98
"Mind your Business! I can Stem the Tide."	99
The Majority of the Present Generation among the Breakers	100

CHAPTER VIII.
ON THE PRINCIPLES WHICH GOVERN THE ACTIONS OF HUMAN BEINGS.

How Life and Mind are Created	101
"It is not by Bread alone that we Live"	102
On the Faculties and Propensities of the Mind	103
Knowledge impels toward the Right	104
On the Innate Principle which desires to be Happy	105
Those who follow Horse-racing understand, etc.	106
The Straight Road	107
How men use their Best Arguments	108
How Thousands are Persuaded	109
Early Traits of Depravity	110
Story of a Little Six-year-old and his "Ma"	111
Modern Science and Marriage	112
The Human Race—What Rev. H. W. Beecher says	113
Nature is ever True	114

PART II.

CAPITAL PUNISHMENT.

CHAPTER IX.
HISTORY AND PROGRESS OF CAPITAL PUNISHMENT.

	PAGE.
The only Divine Command ever given on the Subject	115
Pagan Nations and the Death Penalty	116
The Most Painless Manner of Killing Men	117
What it was Fifty Years Ago	118
The Progressive Ages and Capital Punishment	119
Conditions which have Existed from all Time	120
Chaos and Order	121
What the Masses can be Made to Believe	122

CONTENTS.

CHAPTER X.

ON PUNISHMENT OF CRIME IN GENERAL.

	PAGE.		PAGE.
An Evident Daily Observation	123	A Reformatory Prison	129
How to obtain an Average Expression of the Conscience of Men	124	Punishment to be Reformative and Reparative	130
How Happiness is obtained by Man	125	The question, How to Prevent Crime?	131
The Primary Object of all Law	126	The Criminal and the Lawyer	132
Different Modes of Punishment	127	Effect of the Uncertainty of the Punishment	133
The Criminal on his Return from Prison	128	The End of the Chapter—Read It	134

CHAPTER XI.

STATE PRISONS AS A MEANS OF REFORMATION.—WHAT WE UNDERSTAND BY A REFORMATORY PRISON.—HOW IT SHOULD BE CONSTRUCTED, AND HOW CONDUCTED.

Rigid Legislation, Crime, Depravity, etc.	135	After the sound of the "Gavel," all are required to say "Amen," aloud	141
Nature's Laws, Crime, Pardon, and Punishment	136	Music and Prayer in Prisons	142
Qualities Common to those who Mingle in Good Society	137	Woman and her Powers in giving Moral Instruction	143
Story of a Prisoner	138	Murderers' Prisons	144
After the Day's Work	139	Educators, Lecturers, Clergy, and Men of Science who visit Prisons	145
Prof. Tyndal and his Proposed Prayer Test	140	A Deplorable Condition	146

CHAPTER XII.

REFUTATION OF THE DEATH PENALTY.—HAVE WE A RIGHT TO INFLICT PUNISHMENT BY DEATH?—REASONS IRREFUTABLE.—NOT A SINGLE RATIONAL ARGUMENT LEFT WHY WE SHOULD KILL TO PUNISH.

Our Argument	147	While they were yet Smoking the Trap Fell	157
The Heathen Mother and the Christian Hangman	148	Whence the Authority for a Judge or Jury, to say to a Condemned Man, "Make your Peace with God, for in so many Days thou wilt be Hanged"	158
"He ought to be Hanged by the Heels"	149		
Hanging a Legal Murder	150		
Each Point in Law, How Analyzed	151	Is Capital Punishment an Act of Christian Duty?	159
Other Reasons why we should Banish the Barbarous Practice of Hanging	152	The New Testament and the Death Penalty	160
Life and Death	153	Heaven a Condition—Hell a Condition	161
Statement of Daniel O'Connell	154		
The Great Faith in Man and Victor Hugo	155	Probationary Time, Conversion, Sentence, and Execution	162
Discussion of a Strange Question	156		

CHAPTER XIII.

ON THE DEATH PENALTY AS A PREVENTIVE MEASURE OF FUTURE CRIME.—IS SOCIETY THEREBY PROTECTED, AND SHALL WE CONTINUE TO KILL?

	PAGE.
The Only Possible Justification of the Death Penalty	163
A Mere Possibility	164
The Gallows, the Public, and the Elixir of Terror	165
We are all under the Sentence of Death,—How does this Effect Mankind?	166
While writing a Paragraph, at One O'clock p. m., Friday, March 14th, 1873, an Important Lesson was Administered to the People	167
Opinions of Distinguished Authors	168
Interesting History of the Effect of Hanging	169
Words of a Murderer, just before being Swung into Eternity	170
He began the Work of Murder.— The Death Penalty, and the Policeman	171
Thousands of the Best Minds are with us	172
Quotation of Opinions	173
The Death Penalty Cheapens Human Life	174
The Rev. W. H. Thomas, of Chicago, on Capital Punishment	175
What the Public Good Demands	176
How the Lawyers Wrangle and Quarrel	177
A Family of Six Children Uneducated and Unsupported	178
Stokes' Case, Justice, Dollars and Cents	179
Capital Punishment and the Press	180–181
The Insanity Dodge	182
Great Excitement and a Cry of Help	183
Two Hundred Policemen required to Hang Foster	184
The Reader's Question, "Will it Do?"	185
A Relic of Heathen Nations, and Christian Glory	186

CHAPTER XIV.

ON COMPULSORY EDUCATION.—SUGGESTIONS HOW TO PREVENT CRIME.—PUBLIC EDUCATIONAL INSTITUTION FOR THE FRIENDLESS, ETC., ETC.

The Great Problem Solved	187
The Old Sore Leg—A Flag of Distress	188
Crime, Symptoms, and the Rational Treatment	189
Can the Healing Potion be Successfully Administered?	190
Crime, Depravity, and a Universal Fact	191
Murderers, Physiology and the Common Branches of Education	192
Obligation of Parents, Paupers, Orphans, and Vagabonds	193
The Tribune and Our Mode of Treating Criminals	194
Statistical Cost of Trying our Criminals in Large Cities and the United States	195
A State Institution	196
How Constructed and how Conducted	197
Quotation on Compulsory Education	198
The Girl of Sixteen and the Boy of Eighteen	199
The Child—Factories and the School	200
The Parents and a Few Dollars More	201
Marriage, Vocation, and Money	202
Prof. Huxley, Public Halls and Law	203
Moral Suasion and Legal Persuasion	204
"Will this then be a free Country?"	205
What we would have Remembered	206
Physicians, Lawyers, Clergymen, and their Use	207
The Terrible Disease which Pervades Society, and how it may be "check-mated"	208

CHAPTER XV.

WHAT WE KNOW ABOUT INSANITY:—WHO ARE THE INSANE? AND SHALL WE MAKE INSANITY AN EXCUSE FOR CRIME?

	PAGE.
Insanity Physiologically Considered	209
What an Insane Man Thinks of	210
How the Brain is Exhausted	211
Different Forms of Mental Impairment	212
Hallucination, Illusion, and Delusion	213
Emotional Insanity	214
Doctor Maudsley gives an Illustration	215
What it is that makes one Commit Suicide	216
Mania, either Chronic or Acute	217
Report of a Strange Man; what he declared himself to be	218
Melancholia, Paralysis and Women	219
Dementia, Idiocy, Imbecility	220
Massachusetts Reports of the Insane	221
A Source of Criminality and Insanity no one can doubt	222
Overtasking the Intellect	223
A Serious Error	224
Religious, Political and Reformatory Gatherings	225
What a Single Idea may do for a Person	226
Those who Jump into the River or Put a Bullet through their Heart	227
What shall we do with the Insane?	228

CHAPTER XVI.

ON CORPORAL PUNISHMENT IN SCHOOLS.—IN FAMILIES AND BY THE STATE.

Can we "Put" Goodness into the Child by the Free Use of the Rod	229
What a Little Three-year-old said to its Mother	230
The Child can Reason.—The First Study of Parents	231
What Sort of a Lesson a Child is Taught by Whipping it	232
The Result of Striking a Man or Woman in the Face	233
A New Method—What we were asked by a Lady while lecturing in Indiana	234
We Heard it Whispered, "The Doctor must give it up"	235
How "Mamma" should Act when her Child is Angry	236
Our Visit to the Schools in Ohio	237
A Paper from a Medical Journal	238
"I love it, I love it, so merry and wild, the artless and innocent laugh of the child"	239
What we Think will be admitted	240
The Clergyman, the Rod, and his Bible	241
A Thousand Efforts and Parental Correction	242
A Heartrending Narrative of a Christian Father in Boston	243
The Unhappy Father and his Little Boy	244
"A big tear had stolen down his cheek, but he was sleeping calmly and sweetly"	245
The Little Coffin, a Playmate, the Father's Hell, his Little Boy, and the last Smile	246
The Words that always Sounded in the Father's Ears	247
Alas! who would not Weep Tears of Blood?	248
A Moral View of the Case	249
Another Inexcusable Folly	250
A Physiological View of the Case	251
Eleven Maxims which Every Adult person should Commit to Memory	252
Eleven Suggestions from the Ladies' Sanitary Association of London, Eng.	253
Why we Need not Provide a Halter for the Adult	254

CHAPTER XVII.

ON WEALTH, HEALTH, CRIME, AND THE LABORING CLASSES.—ORGANIZED CAPITAL AND THE EFFECT IT HAS ON SOCIETY.

	PAGE.		PAGE.
Subsistence and Preservation	255	of Man	259
Men of Capital have Variously Organized	256	Conflicting Opinions	260
		Wealth, and the Chicago Police Force	261
Mental Culture. Compared with Money	257	A Brave Hand	262
How Society Becomes Unbalanced	258	The "Hod-Carriers"	263
Ten Millions—Intellectual Work		The Faculty which Rules Society	264

CHAPTER XVIII.

OUR PRESENT JURY SYSTEM.—PROPOSED REFORMATION.—MURDER TRIALS.—WOMEN AS JURORS.—CONCLUSION OF PART II.

Reasons why the Grand Jury should be Discontinued	265	How Men spend their Last Dollar	271
A Reformed Jury System	266	Those who Fear Hell Less than Men	272
Opinion of the Attorney General of England	267	Recapitulation	273
		"The Chief End of Man"	274
How True Justice is Attained	268	Aspirations of a Young Man	275
Qualifications of Jurors	269	A Melancholy Sight—"The Silver Spoon"	276
Women in the Jury-Box, and Why Not?	270	One Great Drawback	277

PART III.

THE LAW.

CHAPTER XIX.

ON THE LAWS OF NATURE.

Definition of the Laws of Nature	279	Certain Faculties of the Mind Considered	287
The Written and the Unwritten Law	280	The Ultimate Object of Human Action	288
What we See when we Open our Eyes	281	The High-Road to Happiness	289
The Faculty of Intuition	282	Future Generations	290
The Intentions and Secrets of Nature	283	Human Laws	291
The Customs of Society	284	Human Actions—Physical Existence—Physiology	292
Pleasure and Pain	285	Speaking from a Moral Standpoint	293
How the Body is Protected	286		

CONTENTS.

	PAGE		PAGE
How we Decide between Right and Wrong	294	Excessive Emotion	302
Story about a Red-hot Iron	295	The Youth and the Grandeur of his Hopes	303
Does Nature Teach that we shall not Steal?	296	Innate Powers, Spirit and Body	304
How Men Differ in Organization	297	What Nature says through a Certain Philosopher	305
Sensibility the Source of all our Greatness	298	Intelligence a Ruling Force	306
Laws of Nervous Sensibility	299	The Elevation and Compass of Thought	307
Cromwell and Napoleon	300	How Men Differ in Organization	308
A Multitude of Inferences	301	Laws Established by Man	309

CHAPTER XX.

THE LAWS OF PHYSIOLOGY THE ONLY RELIABLE STARTING-POINT FOR THE ENACTMENT OF HUMAN LAWS.

Governmental Laws Based on the Teachings of Physiology	310	Physiology of Man	329
On the Commandments	311	Physiology Defined	330
A False God	312	On that which Composes our Bodies	331
Impressions on Mind and Body	313	Water and its Use in the System	332
A Certain Cause of Disease	314	The Best Kind of Food	333
Savans in Smoky Laboratories	315	The Quantity of Food Required by a Healthy Man Daily	334
A Delicate Organization	316	On Nutrition	335
Affections of the Brain	317	The Digestive Apparatus	336
A Death Warrant	318	How the Different Elements of Food are Digested	337
Misanthrope and Hypochondria	319	How Blood is Formed	338
Those who Extract Poison from Every Event of Life	320	Sounds of the Heart	339
That which Leads to the Marvelous	321	Respiration	340
Tasso Heard Voices Whispering his own Thoughts	322	The Growth of the Body	341
The Virgin, Beautiful and Young	323	The Natural Temperature of the Body	342
Of Organs Especially Affected by Excessive Labor	324	Nitrogenized and Non-Nitrogenized Elements of the Food	343
How Thoughts Absorb the Life	325	A Brief Statement of Facts	344
The Poet Santenil	326	What Should be a Law of the Land	345
Orators, Musicians, Actors, Physicians, etc.	327	When we may Expect to Enjoy the Glory of Heaven	346
The Kind of Poison that Killed him	328		

CHAPTER XXI.

MENTAL CULTURE, OR THE LAWS WHICH GOVERN MENTAL TRAINING.

The Store House of the Soul	347	Spontaneous Growth	352
The Blockhead and the School Room	348	From Dr. Burrows' Lecture	353
The Young Mind	349	The Boy of Fourteen and His Teacher	354
Basis of a Strong Mind	350	"I See It." How Beautiful! A Great Event	355
The Boy and His Horse	351		

	PAGE.		PAGE.
What is of Immense Importance.	356	In Passing Through a Crowd, etc.	365
College Graduates—The Piano. Greek—Latin	357	Power of the Press	366
How Should It be Done	358	City News-stands, Bar-Rooms, The Novel, etc	367
The Richest Man that Walks the Earth	359	Delusions of Mortals	368
A Sad Time—The Garden of the Mind	360	Why Married Men Run Away With Young Girls	369
The Whipped Dog—The Pet Bird	361	The Unguarded Household	370
The Child that is too Good to Live	362	What Novel-Reading can Produce	372
The Farmer—Interesting Reflections	363	The Mind and Barrel of Powder	373
The Maniac—Why are We not All There	364	Poetry, Music, Stories, Games, etc	374
		A Glorious Sight	375
		When Once the Day of Probation is Past	376

CHAPTER XXII.

ON THE LAWS OF PHYSICAL CULTURE—TEMPERAMENTAL HARMONY THE BASIS OF PHYSICAL PERFECTION.

Temperaments and Physiology	377	A Man of Genius	395
Human Temperaments Defined	378	Phrenologist and the Human Brain	396
The Most Scientific Classification ever Given	379–380	What of the Forty-Two Pairs of Nerves	397
The Vital, Mental and Motive Temperaments	381–382–383	The Tabernacle of the Soul	398
How the Temperaments May be Studied	384–385–386	A Work of Three Thousand Years	399
How to Read Character by Temperamental Indication	387–388–389	On the Advantages of the Temperament in which the Nervous System Predominates	400–401–402
Important Hints by George Comb	390	A Vigilant Sentinel	403
How to Cultivate, and How to Restrain the Different Temperaments	391	An Amazing Tenacity of Life	404
		Certain Literary Character	405
Daily Observation	392	How to have great Enjoyment	406
Temperamental Condition When Variously Compounded	393	A Remarkable Youth	407
		The daily Practice of Physicians attests to a truth	408
Characteristics of a Vast Intellect	394	Those who rouse the world	409
		A Happy Ending of All	410

APPENDIX I.

HANGING AS A MEANS OF GRACE.—ELOQUENT DISCOURSE BY W. H. RYDER, D.D.—DOES HANGING QUALIFY A MURDERER FOR HEAVEN?—IF IT IS A MEANS OF GRACE, THE MORE OF IT THE BETTER.—HOW THE CONDEMNED SHOULD BE TREATED.—THE MATERIAL IDEA OF HEAVEN AND HELL.

His Bible Text	419	Pity, but not Sympathy	414
What he says on the side of Humanity	412	Repentance of Criminals	415
		Interesting Opinions of a Condemned	416
The Clergyman and the Gallows,	413		

CONTENTS.

	PAGE.		PAGE.
What is meant by the word "Paradise"	417	What of Heaven and Hell	419
		Where is God	420
How the Gallows may be made a means of Grace	418	A Walk toward Zion	421

APPENDIX II.

TO HANG OR NOT TO HANG.—FROM THE CHRISTIAN UNION.

An Anticipated Horror	422	Laws of a number of Different States	424
Interesting Statistical Statement	423	Murder Will not Walk Abroad	425

APPENDIX III.

PAUPERISM AND COMPULSORY EDUCATION.—FROM THE NATIONAL INDEPENDENT, OF PHILADELPHIA, PA.

What of Disreputable Parents	426	Mourn	429
A Main Pillar	427	Rescue and Reformatory Schools	430
Official Corruption	428	Jack Sheppard and other Criminals	431
Our Rulers, and the People who			

PART FIRST.

MURDER AND CRIME.

CHAPTER I.

CAUSE OF CRIME.

Take heed, erring man, and learn of those who by experience have been taught;
Erase from the mind "the written troubles," crime, murder, and every evil thought,
And cure thy brain of that dreadful malady, which now weighs down upon thy soul.

We are living in an age of the world's history which requires every individual to live in obedience to "law and order" established by civilized and Christian governments. Laws, like other institutions of human construction, have changed from time to time, and were improved as rapidly as the human family progressed in their understanding of human nature, the laws of nature, science, circumstances, and the surroundings which govern men in their actions.

Each amendment in governmental, and criminal

laws was thought to be right and strictly in harmony with the laws of nature, at the time of enacting such amendment or law. But if found, after a few years' experiment, that such was not the case, farther amendment was made, and all clauses which were thought to be too harsh, unnatural, impractical,—doing injustice to those who were found guilty of crime, —were thrown out or modified, according to the judgment and conscience of a majority of the population of the community, state, continent, or country.

And I am of the opinion that this great work of perfecting human institutions will thus continue, until ultimate principles are arrived at. All laws, to be successful and of benefit to those whom it is intended to correct and govern, must agree with ultimate and primary laws of nature. In proportion, then, as we understand those primary laws, are we enabled to construct correct laws by which to govern men in their intercourse with each other.

Science, observation, and experience of the past, have established one great truth, and that is, that whenever an ultimate principle is arrived at, in the construction of any doctrine or law, it will stand the test, and always bring happiness to the human family. The laws of any country, which have for their object the correction and regulation of human action, and to determine between the right and the wrong, are progressive in their nature, like other institutions of the world. Few of the sciences are known to be perfect; still the work of progress is going on steadily, year after year. Events follow each other, and since the dawning morn of human intelligence, reformation, inventions, discoveries in mechanics, agriculture, navigation, and the various branches of science, medicine, and surgery, the wonderful operations of the human mind and the natural relations that one human being sustains to another are gradually becoming more perfectly understood, and consequently human happiness is this day greater than even a century ago.

The entire human family have, collectively and individually, labored in this work of discovering ultimates, primates, and laws governing the coporeal and the phenomena, both in physical nature as well as in the realm of mind.

Each age or epoch of time has furnished its philosophers—persons of a high susceptibility, mental and moral impressibility, which enabled them to take a step in advance of the masses, and see in advance of them the incoming of scientific and moral reform.

Each improvement was recognized as a truth at the time of its advent; but after experience, and a few years' practice, all that was found to disagree with the laws of God and Nature was discarded and allowed to take its place among the things that were. Not so with ultimate principles or laws. The actions, discoveries, and legal enactments, as long as they are in harmony with the fixed laws of nature, and are intrinsically a truth, ever have stood, and will continue as long as eternity may roll.

The present era will take its place in human history marked by every nation of the globe as having made greater progress in scientific investigations, discoveries, moral and political reformation, than any other period since the advent of man on the earth. To sustain this statement, I will simply cite to the reader a few leading facts. Never before was the road to knowledge more clear, and advantages better for all classes of men and women to acquire, if they choose, even scientific knowledge. Ecclesiastical and canonical laws are almost entirely banished. Men have greater freedom of thought. Scientists can now give an opinion without being restricted by some tyrant king or priest. Even religion is allowed a geater field, and men are permitted to worship God according to the dictates of their own conscience, which never was so extensive as now. There never was a time when the world contained so many scientists,—so many great men and women who were distinguished on the farm, in machinery, in commerce, in the various professions, on the rostrum, in the schools, in reformatory efforts, and in statesmanship, as now. The world never before was linked together by a cable of cold, inanimate matter, sunk to the bottom of the ocean, and caused to hold conversation between men at a remote distance, carrying messages from continent to continent in one moment of time. Mountains are pierced, valleys are bridged, and the country traversed by the locomotive with almost lightning speed. Oceans, rivers, and lakes are navigated by steam. That great disseminator of human thought and recorder of human actions, the printing press, made its advent on this earth, with its improvements, within the present period of the nineteenth century. The sewing machine, suspension bridges tunneling of rivers, chloroform in surgery, new discoveries in physiology, in medicine, and other sciences, are wonderful to relate, and are sufficient proof that the world is moving.

The time was when the world believed that persons who transgressed the laws of the land were possessed of devils, and that the best thing that could be done with such individuals was to kill them. Persons were believed to be bewitched, and were put to death. Even now some of our religionists believe and teach that man by nature is "desperately wicked," and that he has no good within him, a doctrine, however, which is fast becoming extinct; for science has revealed to us that mankind comes into life a

BLANK,

and has no character so long as the senses are not acted upon, and so long as the young being is yet uneducated. The child is, therefore, only a rudimetary man or woman, neither good or bad at birth, and whatever he or she becomes in after life depends upon the conditions of birth, or, in other words, the prenatal existence. At the time when the being is conceived in the mother's womb a certain impulse is given to the faculties, which, in after life, become the leading propensities, especially when they are fostered by the surroundings, habits, associations, and moral and intellectual education. This is a question which long has furnished points of dispute, but now is almost universally admitted to be a truth. Physiology teaches that the offspring partakes of the peculiarities and character of its parent, not only in physical strength and goodness or physical weakness and disease, but also of the mental and moral predisposition, as is universally demonstrated in every-day life.

Even in stature, physiognomy, refinement of texture, color of hair, eyes, and complexion, temperamental conditions, and mental and intellectual powers, a striking similarity exists between the child and the parent. It is a maxim that the rising generation is simply a counterpart of the present, and whatever improvement is made, or whatever reformatory achievement attained, must be made in the present generation; then the next will be far better, and so continue generation after generation, until in one thousand years, crime and murder will sink into oblivion. It is not now a mooted question that longevity runs in families. Lung consumption, scrofulous diseases, delicate constitution, and shortness of life are hereditary. I have known even a goitre or thick neck to be peculiar to certain families. Insanity, epilepsy, and many of the diseases afflicting families are transmitted from parent to child; sometimes in a modified form; sometimes in an aggravated form. Greater will be the sufferings of your child if you violate the laws of nature to-day, and to-morrow become a father or mother of the future man and woman—a counterpart of yourself. And thus we find that it is a scientific truth "that the sins of the parent shall be visited upon the children until the third and fourth generation." The diseased conditions of your offspring will be modified providing you live strictly according to physiological laws which, in the third or fourth generation, may result in the production of a perfect man and woman,—beautiful in figure, healthy in body and mental and moral harmony. Individuals make up families; families, the community, state, or country. Society is made up of individuals and families. Now, as we find physical depravity and inharmonious operations of the bodily forces in the individual, so will we find a corresponding depravity and inharmonious operation of the mental, moral, and spiritual forces of that individual. Society being made up of the individual, rules and laws of society will correspond to the exact degree of the depravity and goodness of its individual members. Laws of cities, countries, or states are enacted by the people, and it is evident that the perfection or imperfection of these laws correspond to the imperfection or perfection of the people that create and enforce such laws. Whenever it so happens that a law is enacted by the instrumentality of a superior person,—an advanced thinker or philosopher, as we may justly call him,—such enactments being many years in advance of the comprehension of the masses, they become a dead letter on our statute books until the masses can be educated up to that standard of advanced thought.

Now, before we can consistently suggest any change in our laws, or improve our present manner of punishment of crime and murder, it is well first to understand the different causes of crime. For whenever we fully comprehend the real and various agencies which induce men to commit criminal actions, we can easily understand the indications as to the proper means to be employed in the prevention and cure of criminal conditions. This is our present undertaking, and the first part of this volume is mainly devoted to the origin and nature of crime. Before we proceed to a consideration of the mental and moral action of mankind, we will call attention to a proper

DEFINITION

of crime. By crime we understand any action or deed perpetrated against the laws of the country by sane persons, who are in the full exercise of their faculties, of proper age and responsibility. This is a popular definition, and for short is well enough; but we shall show that no person in the natural and full exercise of the faculties will ever commit crime, having knowledge of the law. A further definition may be interesting and useful. We copy from Webster the following definition:

"Crime is an act which violates a law, divine or human; an act which violates a rule of moral duty; an offence against the laws of right, prescribed by God or man, or against any rule of duty plainly implied in those laws. A crime may consist in *omission* or neglect as well as in commission, or positive transgression. The commander of a fortress, who suffers the enemy to take possession by neglect, is as really criminal as one who voluntarily opens the gates without resistance. But, *in a more common or restricted sense*, a crime denotes an offence, or violation of public laws of a deeper and more atrocious nature; a public wrong,—or a violation of the commands of God, and the offences against the laws made to preserve the public right; as treason, murder, robbery, theft, arson, etc. The minor wrongs committed against individuals or private rights, are denominated *trespasses;* and the minor wrongs against public rights are called *misdemeanors*. Crimes and misdemeanors are punishable by indictment, information, or public prosecution; trespasses, or private injuries, at the suite of the individuals injured. But, in many cases, an act is considered both as a public offence and a trespass, and is punishable both by the public and the individual injured."

With this explanation of crime, we proceed to consider the actuating principles which induce or force men to commit crime. When men and women of Christian and civilized birth and education, with the law before them and the sure punishment which is to follow any violation or disobedience to the law, still continue in the commission of crime, there must be in existence some force that impels them to commit such crime, which is stronger than the law or the punishment.

In our investigation of this subject, we wish to be understood that we are dealing wholly with the physical existence of man, and the laws and actions, therefore, which govern human physical life may be studied the same way that we study and learn any of the different branches of science. During our investigation of the various and mysterious operations of nature we have also extended our

OBSERVATIONS

and examinations into the field of mental and psychological phenomena, which operate through the human organization. The ultimate object of all learning centers in the mind; what it is, whence it is, and how we may enlarge our knowledge in regard to its wonderful operations or manifestations, is the work of mankind and the great desire of every thoughtful person. We have reason to believe from our knowledge of the mind, that it is dependent for its generation, or its creation, upon conditions similar to those that electrical, vital, and other forces in nature are dependent upon for their generation, and like them, is a physical force.

Certain conditions evolve electricity; others, light; others heat; and, as we ascend the scale, other conditions produce vital manifestations. When the conditions under which these forces act no longer exist, they all cease their action. Prevent oxygen from uniting with carbon and hydrogen, and the heat and light, which by such combination has been evolved, now ceases its action. Place a zinc plate into a copper vessel containing sulphuric acid, and water, and electricity is generated. Remove the acid, and one of the conditions producing it being taken away, it becomes extinct. So with the mind. Let the conditions on which it is dependent for existence be withheld, and its manisfestations will cease. If only partial destruction of the conditions producing these forces, then a disturbance of the harmony or perfect manifestation is immediately evident. As in demented persons and others. When the conditions producing mentality are interfered with in their proper action, intellectuality proceeds improperly. Pressure applied to the brain, will derange thinking, feeling, remembering, and a general discord among all the mental operations will be the result.

It is a reasonable conclusion, then, the mind emanating from the corporeal system, that its manifestations are physical, and its characteristics derived from the constitution of the body. All peculiarity belonging to the mind—its capacity to reason, to make deductions, to analyze the mysteries of nature and grasp subjects of highest magnitude for contemplation—

mainly depend on that organ termed the brain. The brain, being the great center of the nervous system, also imparts energy and strength to the intellectual faculties, such as perception, memory, conception, reasoning, etc., as well as the emulative part of man; feelings and impulses which mark his character, controlling and directing his moral actions are derived from the same source—the brain. Impressions, intended to educate the faculties, which come from outer nature, are conveyed to the mind through the five senses. The senses all centering in the brain, it is evident that intellectuality and mental phenomena operate wholly through that organ, and also mainly depend for a proper and harmonious manifestation on the healthy condition of the brain, in discharge of its function as a vital organ.

The intimate relation which exists between the mind and the brain, leads us, then, to conclude that the first is but the result of certain conditions fulfilled in the latter, from the fact, also, that mental traits and dispositions are hereditary to a large extent. From this, our readers may understand that we claim that distinguished talents in parents are transmitted alike to their children. Of course, this does not always follow, on account of a want of strict reciprocation, or perfect blending of all the forces necessary for a perfect counterpart, between the father and the mother; still, we find that great and distinguished men and women—minds of strong capacity—often fall in families of like powers, and do not run out until a number of unfavorable intermarriages; as in the Lincoln family, Henry Clay, Washington, and hundreds of others which might be cited. Healthy and robust parents, who live to a ripe, old age, usually transmit the elements of longevity to their children. Let this be decided as it may, sufficient analogy has been observed by our most distinguished physiologists, psychologists, and scientists, to enable us to pronounce with certainty, that the constitution of the mind is affected by the constitution of the body; as is also the intellectual, moral, and social nature. Observe the children of depraved parents. Unless carefully guarded, they will live a life of depravity. There is an old proverb that, "the apple does not fall very far from the stem." It is even claimed by eminent authors, that an infant born of depraved parents may be brought up under the influence and training of a pious family, and no pains be spared to develop its moral feelings and to restrain its natural ones; that frequently the result will be, notwithstanding its culture, unmistakable indications of depravity when it arrives at adult age, though not so great as if these had been nurtured through youth, still, often bringing disappointment to those who have fostered such children.

After having said these things, our readers may raise the question: To what extent is man a

FREE-AGENT?

Cannot man control and make his own fortune? Is he wholly subject to circumstances acting upon him? Or can he not live, act, and do as he pleases, independent of his surroundings and external influences?

Can man truly say, "this good thing have I done because I chose to do it, and this evil thing for the same reason;—in all that I do, I follow my own volition, and could have done otherwise if I had willed it"?

These are questions of great importance, and should be settled among men, for much depends on our understanding whether a man is a "free moral agent" or whether he is not, as to the actions and government of the moral relation one human being sustains to another. These are questions, however, which we do not propose to discuss in our present undertaking, only to notice well-established facts in regard to the actions of men and women in general. We leave our readers to answer these questions after our task has been completed.

To sustain our position, we might quote many of the best authors of this country, as well as Europe, had we the space; but as it is, we recommend our readers to read Lock on "Human Understanding," or any more modern and scientific work on the philosophy of the mind, and you will find it a well settled fact, admitted by all who have given the subject any thought, that, as we have already said, as to the origin of mind, man has nothing to do as to the capacity of his mind. He did not have the making of himself, nor was he consulted under what peculiar circumstances he should be forced into life, consequently his reasoning powers, his quickness, and the conditions of his faculties, which, either on account of their natural strength, enable him to canvass space and measure other worlds, master the sciences and construct new systems of government, and discern order where there seems to be choas, or, on account of their feebleness, unfit him for any profound reflection, and merely adapt him to occupy himself with those things which administer to his animal propensities. Man had not the say whether he should possess the one or the other of these conditions, and yet they have everything to do with his actions. Those individuals who look beyond the mere circumstances of their immediate surroundings—who trace effect to cause, and contemplate and grasp profound subjects—are far different in organization, from the fact that by culture and education they cannot improve their condition so as to stand equal in mental power with those who have by nature a highly refined organization. How different the conduct of these individuals. However much they may differ in organization, or in their general behavior in life, it cannot be said that the results are the consequence of any volition on their part.

A feeble-minded person may think that groveling to be its own choice, still we know that it is in accordance with the degree of power of the faculties and functions received at birth. Some one said:

"The man of great intellect aspires, even as the bird soars aloft, because the air is its natural element. He cannot grovel whose mind impels to great undertakings."

Though it is our object to make this volume strictly original, it is well enough to give some of the views of others; yet our space will not allow us to give elaborate references, therefore we simply say that what we teach in this volume is well supported by our best thinkers, writers, physiologists, psycologists, and scientists in this and the old country.

To understand clearly human actions, and further consider mental operations, we are pleased to give the views of Prof. J. A. Thacker, who is good authority, and is the doctrine which will entirely overthrow, by and by, our present mode of punishing criminals. This author divides the mind into two departments: the intellectual, or understanding, and the emotive, or effective faculties, consisting of the emotions, or sensibilities. The order of movement is the order in which they have been mentioned. He says that "the intellect first presents an object which arouses some one or more of the emotive faculties, and they, in turn, call into action the movements which follow —the will, as it is termed, being but the response to that emotion which is in the ascendency.

" If we give the subject any consideration, we perceive that there can not be any action without an excitement first of the sensibilities, without some emotion, desire or inclination having been aroused. We seek food and drink to allay the sensations of hunger and thirst and preserve life. We seek the society of one another to minister to the gratification we receive from social intercourse. In brief, we are impelled in all that we do to perform an object which has its origin in the emotive part of our nature. The intellect, then, being antecedent in its operation, in the feelings or sensibilities, we have the causes of all men's actions. But we have demonstrated that the emotions arise in the brain—in the body—the same as the other department of the mind, the intellect, and their character is fixed; for as the constitution of the body is, so must their constitution be.

"It follows from what we have said that every act of the individual has its motive, which has had its antecedent in some previous intellectual operation; that, knowing the disposition of a person, and the causes which have been brought to bear upon him, we can state with certainty his course of conduct in any given matter. When the result is different from what we had anticipated, we must attribute it to having been deceived, either in the emotive functions of some of his feelings in comparison with others, or having been mistaken in the antecedents, or both. But as a distinguished writer says, 'we never can know the whole of any man's antecedents, or even the whole of our own; but it is certain that the nearer we approach to a complete knowledge of the antecedent, the more likely we shall be to predict the consequent.' It is this confidence of uniformity of conduct in one another, under given circumstances, upon which we rely in all our associations. Without it there could be no society.

"But if we pass from the study of the individual to the contemplation of human actions in societies, we will be further rewarded in our researches; and we will find in our examinations that the conduct of men, as they make up communities, under particular circumstances, is always the same. As, for instance, the crimes of murder and suicide occur with such regularity that, in any country, it can be predicted from year to year, with very slight error, how many of each will take place. Mr. Buckle, in mentioning this fact, states that, in London, about 230 persons annually make way with themselves; the number oscillating, from the pressure of temporary causes, between 266, the highest, and 213, the lowest. When, in these offences, we consider how accidental, in the majority of them, the circumstances seem which lead to them, we are filled with astonishment at the result. M. Quetelet, the greatest statistician of his day, also makes mention of the great regularity which takes place annually in the number of the commissions of crime. Mr. Buckle's explanation of these phenomena is as follows: 'In a given state of society a certain number of persons must put an end to their own life. This is the general law, and the special question as to who shall commit the crime depends, of course, upon special laws; which, however, in their total action must obey the large social law to which they are all subordinate. And the power of the larger law is so irresistible, that neither the love of life nor the fear of another world can avail anything toward even checking its operation.'

"An explanation more easily understood, would be, we think, that in every country from food, soil, climate and other physical causes, a certain general character is begotten among all the inhabitants, and in different communities or large aggregated masses of people in the same country, there are a certain proportion endowed with similar characteristics or affective faculties. Now, since certain causes, exterior to the individual, are acting continually to arouse particular traits or propensities in every member of a community possessing them, these, brought into action, must produce certain results."

From the facts we have stated in this connection, we think sufficient has been said to make it evident that the conduct of men is controlled by laws—is not left to chance, but is governed by law as well as everything else in nature.

Before closing this chapter, we would say that as man is wholly governed by circumstances, surroundings, and conditions, which effect him from all sides, as well as those constitutional characteristics over which he has no immediate or absolute control, it may be well to suggest that persons as soon as they learn that they have an inclination to steal immediately discontinue all business which may give an opportunity to carry out such inclination.

We once knew a barber who never could shave a man and not think of cutting his throat. This feeling grew so strong that he became alarmed, and one day made this statement to us. Our advice was that he should quit the business, which he did in a few weeks. I believe this saved the man from becoming a murderer. When it is found that persons in any community have a disposition to commit crime, we think that after we have so conclusively shown how men are governed in their actions, that it is evident that all punishment should be mainly reformatory, with a view to cure our unfortunate criminals, and thereby also protect society.*

---

* See Part Second, Chapter II.

CHAPTER II.

ORGANS OF THE BRAIN AND THEIR FUNCTION.

Life is an activity manifested upon the corporeal plane of action only through an organized body, composed of organized and inorganized matter. This organization becomes more and more perfect and more complicated as we ascend in the scale of creation. From the lowest form of the sea-mosses to the most beautiful flowers of our garden, and from the creeping worm of the dust beneath our feet on up to the human mind, where the most perfect and most powerful manifestations of life force in the universe exist.

Whenever we find that activity called life, we find an organization through which it operates. In the lowest forms of the grasses and mosses, life is scarcely apparent for the reason that their organs are few, and mostly single, through which it acts. As we ascend the scale of development in our observations among plants, we find an increase of organs, also refinement in texture, and a greater activity of life. So in the animal creation. In some of the lowest forms of animals, a single organ of vitality exists through which life is manifest. Here the life phenomena are very short in duration, but as we trace this force in its progressive development through the various species and phases of animal creation, we find an increase of organs, a greater complication and combination of principles through which life is manifested upon the physical plane of action. In the human organization we have a greater number and more perfect organs of vitality than in other animal organizations, and consequently a greater activity of life. It is evident that the human brain and nervous system is susceptible of greater activity and admits of a wider field of action, aside from the intellectual operations of the mind, than any other being of which we have any knowledge.* Now, we can easily perceive that, as life depends upon corporeal organization for its physical manifestation, the human mind, as it is of itself an organization, requires an organ or organs as a media through which it may act or manifest its existence upon the physical plane of action. We may therefore, also, reasonably conclude that the more perfect the brain,—which all scientists now admit to be the organ of the mind,—the more perfect the manifestations of the mind and the more powerful is its action.

In the lower forms of creation, mind is but faintly manifest. As we descend in the scale of beings, we find the brain decreasing in size, also in the number of convolutions and different departments, until entirely lost, the same as other organs of the body, less in number, less in size, and less important in function, until all traces of mind and life are lost among the crude corporeal matter of the earth. That animals have not a mind is not now a mooted question; only it is not a human mind. The horse has a mind

---

* See the author's work on the "Human Five Senses."

peculiar to himself, which we may call with propriety a horse's mind.

So every other living creature on earth differs in degree of manifestation as the brain differs in its relative size, refinement in texture, and perfectness in organization. If, then, it is admitted, as by every thinking person it must be, that life is an agency or activity, operating only through bodily organizations, the brain being the organ of the mind, we may further reason correctly that the mind is an organization of faculties, these various faculties together constituting and producing the various intellectual operations, and establishing also a moral character. This is a force or agency which mainly controls men's actions in their intercourse one with another, although it may be traced far down in nature; yet, as it mainly concerns us, we will confine our investigations to mankind. The faculties of the mind, in their combined action producing intellectual and moral characteristics, lead in the direction of moral action; and by experience in the result of such actions, we are enabled to know as to the right and the wrong, These faculties are evidently of a physical nature, for they are governed by circumstances, or, in a word, by our corporeal surroundings. Mind being a physical manifestation it will follow that physical laws control it in the same manner that physical laws govern the physiological operations of the brain, or the stomach, or the food that is prepared for our use by nature. If this is a correct position we may deal with the mind as with other human physical existences. But our reader may say that the mind is a psycological phenomena, and that it is a reflection of the mysterious operations of the soul, and that it is too mysterious a subject for us to understand. So we may further argue that it is a great mystery why all foliage and grasses come forth and appear in the primitive color, green; and that it is a mysterious operation of God through nature far beyond our comprehension, and yet we do know something about it, for the chemistry and physiology of plants, and the natural sciences, have given us great light on the subject. We have stated that physical laws govern the action of the human mind, as well as other physical manifestations.

In the perfect manifestations of life phenomena throughout all nature, we find that concert of action of all the organs of any body is necessary; and let there be the slightest discord, we soon see a fading away of the life activity, and unless harmony is restored, the body will die. Withhold any of the lifegiving or life-sustaining agencies, and the same disastrous result will follow. So in the human organization; let any of the vital organs become deranged, from disease or accident, and discord of the vital phenomena are immediately manifest. If this is allowed to continue, the body will soon decay and die; also, if the necessary means to sustain life is withheld, the effect will be the same. The brain being the organ through which the mind acts, and mind being a physical manifestation, it will follow as a natural consequence that concert of action of all the organs of the brain is necessary to a perfect mental manifestation. Let the slightest discord take place in the brain, from whatever cause, and immediate disarrangement of the mental phenomena will be the natural result. The brain being thus deranged, and being intimately connected with other organs of vitality,—in truth, it may be classed as one of the organs of vitality,—will, if harmony is not restored, soon end in death, or lead to insanity, which is equally disastrous. Thus far, we think we have reasoned logically, and if we cannot apply our manner of reasoning to the brain and other higher natures of mankind, we would consider what has been said a failure. We do not fear that, however, though we may have undertaken more than we bargained for. We have stated that the mind is an organization composed of faculties. These faculties require concert of action, in order to manifest mental harmony and correct moral actions in life. Let there be discord and disagreement among the faculties, and the result would be disease of the mind, which if allowed to go on, and not corrected, will end in wrong doing —violations of physiological laws or the laws of the land, bringing sorrow to the individual and injury to others. Discord of action among the organs of the body and brain, we have stated, will, if harmony is not restored, lead to disease, and eventually end in death.

Diseased conditions of the brain and nervous system, if not cured, are liable to end in death, or what is worse—insanity. Discord of action among the moral and intellectual faculties, if not corrected, and allowed to go on, does not only produce disease of the mind, but is liable to end in crime, murder, or self-destruction.

Our readers may now naturally inquire how this moral and intellectual disagreement or discord among the faculties takes place. The causes are various, and this volume does not admit of space to enumerate them. In the first place, however, we will state that the immediate cause or causes are of two kinds, the one is slow and insidious; the other sudden and accidental. The reader is, perhaps, familiar with some of the causes which produce disease of the physical organism. They are of two kinds, the same as those affecting the faculties of the mind. They are slow, insidious, accidental, and having their starting-point in ignorance, contrary habits, and evil associations. By inattention to the proper selection of food, the body gradually becomes unbalanced in the natural chemical constituents, and diseased action will take place; or, by disobedience to the physiological laws of digestion, that terrible disease, dyspepsia, may gradually be superinduced, or consumption, heart disease, disease of the brain, and a consequent disarrangement of the mind, and a perversion of the intellectual and moral faculties, is the result of wrong-living. Thus we see that physical goodness is necessary to mental, moral, and intellectual goodness, and is also a great source of mental disturbance, and often ends in the commission of a terrible crime. Let a woman, who by means of tight dresses, or by strapping around her chest that hideous monster called *corset*, compress her lungs, and she will soon find herself becoming not only physically diseased, but also mentally; she becomes fretful, and, in a word, terribly inharmonious, and where it will end no one can tell. If her son does not commit crime, her grandchild may end its days on the gallows or in prison. The subject of extreme mental labor, continuous thought on one subject, disappointments in the affections, long continued, unhappy associations with women or men, is very liable, if the difficulty is not corrected, to end in disease of the mind, to unbalance the physical organization, also the moral, character, and is in every way a subject of legislation long before crime is committed.

A man affected with hydrophobia once came under my care. While the paroxysm was on him, it became necessary to tie him hand and foot to the bedstead, in order to prevent him from doing injury to himself and others. After a few times, he could tell when the paroxysm was approaching, and would call at the top of his voice, "Tie me! tie me, or I must bite you!" So many persons are now at liberty, not cared for in the proper way to cure their malady, who, no doubt, often feel like crying aloud, "Tie me! tie me, before I bite you!" The reader is here referred to the third chapter in part second of this book. In chapter fourth, we trace the various causes which pervert the moral faculties, under the head of the "Two Paths of the Child," which the reader should study carefully.

Among the accidental causes of discord among the faculties, we refer first to the injuries of the body. Wounds, bruises, fractures, surgical operations, have in many instances produced such a powerful mental shock that discord of action of many of the faculties became almost irreparable. This condition is of longer or shorter duration. I have known it to last only a few minutes, and, in a number of cases, two and three months. One lady, I remember, I was called to treat a few years ago, who, by accident, in trying to split some wood, split her great toe wide open. The wound, in itself not very dangerous, gave such a terrible shock to the brain and nervous system, that though by the proper treatment entire constitutional reaction was restored, the wound healed by what surgeons call first intention, and in every sense good bodily health, yet the discord among the faculties lingered a long time, and it was nearly four months before perfect reason was fully restored.

Anger may be classed among the sudden causes. Though a disposition to anger is gradually acquired by habit, yet it may be provoked by circumstances over which the person has no acquired ability to control, and often terrible derangement of the moral and intellectual powers is the immediate result, and before the difficulty can be arrested a hideous crime is committed. Many cases may be cited where persons were not aware that they were guilty of any crime for weeks after such a mental debauch as simply a fit of anger. Persons who become enraged, no matter what the exciting cause may be, are very liable to commit crime, and also liable to become permanently deranged. There never is a fit of anger without a mental and physical prostration following, which sometimes lasts for hours. It produces a shock to the brain and nervous system the same as a physical injury, and a reaction sometimes leaves the person in a terrible condition. A Mr. Symonds who came under my notice in the city of Philadelphia, Pa., in the year 1860, had a regular bar-room fight. Though not injured by his antagonist in the least, he became so infuriated that it was a long time before he could be quieted, and about the time of reaction, he had a genuine epileptic fit. His reason never was fully restored; for nearly one year he was a hopeless maniac, and is still confined to the insane asylum. Habitual anger, if it does not lead to crime, will bring on diseased conditions and shorten life. I further affirm that all persons who become enraged at everything that does not please them, on causes most trivial, are dangerous persons of society, and are subjects of legislation, in order to prevent crime. A German of this city gradually contracted such a habit to anger at everything that went slightly contrary to his wishes, that at times he would become almost furious, throw things about in his shop, and break the dishes for his wife, until he was nearly half of his time in an enraged condition. One day he threw a hammer at his own son's head, but fortunately, for the boy, missed him; and frequently would torture his wife and children. By this means, he brought on an incurable disease of mind and body, aside from the malady that weighed down his soul. He is now a hopeless invalid, his poor wife giving him her entire attention, feeding him a little broth, and nursing him to the best of her ability, only to prolong his miserable life a few days longer. Whenever she happens to put the spoon a little edgeways into his mouth, he will swear and damn everything that is great and good, and I have heard him say things to his wife and children too hideous to relate. To briefly recapitulate, we will remind the reader that the mind, moral, and intellectual faculties, are physical manifestations, operating through a physical organism, and are subject to and controlled by physical laws. Now, as the moral and intellectual faculties may be and are mainly disturbed through physical causes, so may the difficulty be corrected through physical agencies or means by which to arrest the tendency to crime and wrong-doing. If a man by accident breaks his leg, the surgeon will apply splints, and give the parts rest until nature heals the fracture; or, let any of the organs of vitality become diseased, the physician will use such remedials of cure as, by experience and the study of physiological laws, enables him to correctly prescribe and cure his patient. The disease is of a physical nature, a disturbance of the vital forces, which may be local or constitutional. The means of cure must correspond to the nature of the disease, and be strictly in accordance with nature's laws. The physician cannot cure his patient, or the surgeon heal a fracture, by the use of means that will inflict greater injury, instead of means that will soothe, calm, and control diseased conditions. The same course of reasoning will apply to the faculties; let any of them become discordant with the others, and we have mental disturbance—in a word, diseased conditions of the mental or moral nature. To cure such persons the same laws will have to be observed as when the body is diseased, viz., rest, proper selection of food, hygienic and remedial means by which to stay the "devouring flame," and save the individual from crime and premature decay. We will take a person with whom the faculty to acquire money and property has become uncontrollable by conscience, caution, reason, and other faculties, and this person is lead in this manner to rob his neighbor. The natural treatment should be rest, in a house of correction, the proper exercise of other faculties, exercise of the body, the proper selection of food, and the proper education of this faculty, which may be considered in a diseased condition, by such means as the indications of the case may require, bearing always in the mind that the means of cure is cooling, soothing, calming, and restorative, rather than depleting and trying to cure one disease by creating another, often rendering the means of cure worse than the disease.

The faculties also come under physical laws in regard to their function; in fact, they are almost wholly dependent upon the objective and corporeal surrounding for their exercise; consequently, all educational means must be of a tangible or physical character, and, like the body, may be strengthened and very fully developed by obeying physiological laws. If we would strengthen a certain muscle, we must give it the requisite exercise and rest. This is a physiological maxim, and will hold good throughout all nature. Any of the bodily organs may be made stronger by the same rule—the brain, the nervous system, or any of the senses admit largely of cultivation, and thus may be made stronger and perform their functions more perfectly. The brain becomes stronger by exercising the mind in intellectual pursuits so that each faculty, or all the faculties collectively, may be enlarged in capacity, in concert of action, and all brought into perfect working order by a well-balanced education.

The immediate means of education to be mainly considered are: first, our immediate surroundings and conditions in life; second, associations; and thirdly, vocation. The reader here is referred to Chapter IV, on the "Two Paths of the Child."

All education and knowledge is acquired in two ways: first, by experience; second, by learning the experience of others; in other words, by being taught, by conversing, reading, and attending schools instituted for that purpose. The first is positive; the latter, negative, but becomes positive as it is brought into practice. The first means of acquiring knowledge should be encouraged, and the latter should be made compulsory, by which means, at least, a theoretical foundation is laid, and if strictly correct, in accordance with the laws of nature, the laws of conscience, reason, and a combined support of all the faculties, will stand when brought into practice, prove to be good, and bring untold happiness to every individual and society in general.

As to the accidental causes of crime, no law can be enacted to prevent such. The perpetrator can be tried as to the cause, intent, and motive. The slow and insidious causes of crime may be controlled by legal enactment, the tendency averted, and our present prevalence of crime very much decreased by observing the suggestion in Part Second of this book. From what has been said under this head, we can easily perceive that crime, murder, and all wrong-doing is the result of a diseased condition of the body, deranged brain, and a perversion of the moral and intellectual faculties, brought about by wrong education, habits, association, unfavorable surroundings, conditions of the parents before being born, and the influence of society in general.

If this is not correct reasoning, then I ask this question: whence the cause of crime? is crime innate or acquired? If acquired, we have a right to take hold and correct the person guilty; but if an innate principle, then we have no right to interfere with what God has seen fit so to create.

The question, I think, has been settled long since by our best thinkers, that faculties are innate, but not principles; organs, brain, nervous system, vital phenomena, and faculties of the mind are innate, but the various intellectual operations of the mind, the moral sense and character, are acquired, and hence the poor unfortunate criminal cannot be held alone responsible for his crime. Perhaps fifty, a hundred, or more persons were accessory to the crime with which he is charged.

CHAPTER III.

CONSTITUTIONAL PREDISPOSITION TO CRIME.

In March, eighteen hundred and seventy-one, I made a visit to the great city of New York for the first time in my life. After a short stay, I seated myself in the cars, for Buffalo. About one hour's ride from the great metropolis, the train made a stop at a station, and two well-dressed gentlemen entered the cars, and were seated just in front of me. They were busily engaged in talking, and continued a spirited conversation. From their conversation, I could know that one was a lawyer by profession and the other a physician. I was especially interested in their conversation, for both were evidently of a highly refined, mental and physical organization; men of culture, correct habits, and liberal education, about forty years of age; the lawyer of the vital and the physician of the mental temperament; both possessing great psycological powers; in a word, appearing to be happy, congenial, and living in the very sunshine of health. All these conditions, my dear readers, have some bearing, with me at least, as to the truth of a doctrine advanced by men and women, and I give weight to the ideas advanced by persons of a well-balanced, healthy organization more than when I find people in an opposite state or condition. I never knew a dyspeptic that was not fretful, fault-finding, hateful, with never a smile for any one,—not even for themselves,—and such a person is disqualified to think on subjects of vital importance, or to teach mankind the way to health and happiness. Those men whose conversation I am about to relate, were, so far as I am able to judge of a man's health, entirely clear of dyspepsia and mental depression, as there was not the slightest evidence of disease written upon their physiognomy. After a few minutes, their conversation turned upon the seeming prevalence of crime and murder; for it seemed but recently an outrageous murder had been committed in their town, also a number of daring robberies. For the benefit of our readers, we here reproduce the leading ideas advanced by those men, from notes taken at the time, but unobserved by them. We will call the one Lawyer Jones, and the other Doctor Newton.

Lawyer Jones said he was very sorry to see that young man James Gill arrested for breaking in, and robbing Mr. Johnston's store the other night; "for this," he said, "is the only boy of four brothers out of the penitentiary, and it was always believed he was honest; but circumstances are so strong against him that he cannot escape conviction. It is singular, indeed, in regard to the Gill family, for it is known that nearly all of them will steal. The old man, a few years ago, you remember, was convicted for robbing Mr. Rollins of a considerable sum of money. He broke in the house during Sunday afternoon, while the family were at the Sabbath school. He was induced to refund the money, and was afterward reprieved by reason of his extreme old age."

Doctor Newton.—Yes. I have kept track of that family for a number of years, and have also inquired into their previous history. It seems that they have all been industrious, and very saving, by which means they have accumulated a handsome fortune. Still, they would all steal, and even the women are strongly suspected. The mother of these boys, I am credibly informed, has admitted that from a child she had a strong propensity to take little things while visiting her neighbors, but thinks she has overcome that inclination in after years. .

L. J.—Do you think, then, doctor, that a predisposition to steal, lie, etc., may be transmitted from parent to child, and become an inherent principle, untimately and finally ending in some terrible crime, like that of the murderer Williamson, who, it seems, had an irresistable mania for thieving, from a little boy.

Dr. N.—I have not the slightest doubt on the subject, for I have given the matter considerable attention, and inquired into the subject, as well as into the history of many of our criminals; and as a general thing I find nearly every case traceable to a disreputable ancestry, who, previous to propagating their offspring, have lived in open violation of the laws of physiology, and moral and religious principles. I am, further, of the opinion that such parents continue to feed those organs by their examples in life, and instead of all the faculties being simultaneously acted upon, the child hears and sees nothing but wrong-doing on the part of his parents and associates, and consequently a constitutional inclination to steal, etc., is created, and those organs of the brain, and those faculties of the mind, which have the greater activity become the stronger, and in time they become the predominating or controlling power of the man or woman thus created and educated.

L. J.—It would seem that your position is correct, for I cannot recall in my mind a single instance of our most noted criminals where the previous history was anything but favorable. In nearly every instance, the parents of our murderers, and criminals of lesser magnitude, were terribly depraved. The children of such parents, being begotten and raised under the influence of vice, crime, physical, moral, and social depravity, of course obey their nature; and what but crime can be expected of them?

Dr. N.—If you are correct,—which I believe you are,—then, why not make provision for the prevention of crime, restraining the liberty of such persons as are found possessing a predisposition to steal, etc., and placing them in a house of correction, until they outgrow such disposition? For example: the Williamson murderer had a perfect mania for stealing, and it was generally known. He also stated in court that he only wanted the man's money, and was very sorry that he had to kill him; for the man fought desperately, and in the struggle was killed. I do not believe that this man Williamson is constitutionally a murderer, for he feels very sorry. Others, I believe, have a natural desire for blood, as Williamson had only for thieving. I think such persons are subjects of legal attention, long before they become uncontrollable and commit some outrageous crime.

L. J.—It is a fact. This subject is rapidly being investigated, and men are changing their views as to the real cause of crime, and I think we are standing on the threshold of a radical change in our criminal laws. It also seems that something more is necessary to stay the present tendency to crime; for all our punishment, and efforts aiming merely to protect society and bring every criminal to justice, does not mitigate crime, but seems to increase it.

Dr. N.—I am glad that the legal profession is beginning to see this subject in its true light. Some of our most eminent clergymen are also investigating the philosophy and causes of wrong-doing, crime, and murder. The most eminent of the medical faculty, physiologists, and professors of mental science, now nearly all agree that mind is a physical manifestation, that it is governed by physical laws, and that all crime is the result of an organic or constitutional condition, favoring or producing discord among the faculties of the mind, and criminal action is the result.

It is a settled truth that crime is the result of depravity, both physical and mental, and may be considered a species of insanity. Long-continued thought in a certain direction, long practice of certain habits,—say swearing, lying, stealing,—is a species of insanity. The miser, who worships his gold above every thing else, is a monomaniac; and such conditions will doubtless lead to further commission of crime.

L. J.—Doctor, you do not presume to say that all crime is an outgrowth of an organic or constitutional predisposition? I will cite a case. Ned Morris, a man of forty-five, was caught stealing corn from the crib of Mr. Nelson, the other day, and it seems, from the evidence elicited in the case, that he was forced to do so, or beg, or starve. His family was greatly in need of subsistence, and this was evidently the first attempt to steal in his life.

Dr. N.—We divide criminals into two kinds: those who lie, steal, etc., from necessity, and those who do so from choice. The first commit crime to keep from starving, and the last do so merely to obey a natural propensity. Ned Morris simply erred in judgment. His pride would not allow him to beg, so he tried stealing. He also made frequent efforts during the winter to earn a subsistence, but his neighbors refused to employ him. The actuating causes to steal, in Ned Morris's case, and the Gill family are widely different, and I think the mode of punishment should differ as much as the forces which caused either to commit crime. The one should be compensatory, and the other reformatory. Ned Morris should be supplied with subsistence and something to do, and the Gill boy placed in a house of correction, until he entirely outgrows his disposition to steal.

The conversation of these two gentlemen was suddenly brought to a close by the conductor announcing a certain station, which, it seemed, was their destination. I was sorry to part with them, for the subject which they were discussing was very interesting to me. The conversation of these two gentlemen reminds me, however, of observations of my own, which I take the liberty to state in connection with this subject. It is a well-attested fact that persons acquire a sort of mania to lie, steal, etc., brought about by circumstances most insidious, and over which they have no control; among which we mention parental transmission, associations, bodily habits, and influence of society in general. While lecturing in Southern Illinois, I was consulted by the parents of a little girl about fourteen years of age, in regard to her uncontrollable desire to steal. She could not be allowed to visit the neighbors without bringing disgrace upon herself and her family. My prescription was to make her carry back any article stolen by her to the owner, and ask their pardon. Two years after, I received a letter stating that my suggestion almost entirely cured the child. The parents were in the habit of punishing the little girl severely by whipping her until she would promise never to do so again, thus forcing her to lie, for neither the punishment nor her promise was strong enough to counteract the mania to steal. This, of course, I strictly forbid, and in place of the parents carrying back the stolen goods of the little girl, as they were in the habit of doing, require her to do so herself, and only reason with her, and never punish the child in a a corporal manner; also never to force her to make a promise unless sure she could keep it. I also required the mother to visit the neighbors frequently with the child; for seclusion from society would have made matters worse. In conversation with the lady, —and she was a woman of more than an ordinary mind,—the mother admitted that when young she was nearly as bad as her daughter; and not until after she had given birth to this child did she entirely overcome this inclination. Even now, she thought, if her condition in life were unhappy,—if she were in want,—she could be easily induced to exercise that inclination. But her husband was a very good man, and loved her, and did everything to make his family happy. I might relate hundreds of similar cases of different shades and degrees of the mania to steal, lie, etc., and also, were it necessary, give many statements elicited from convicts on this subject. Dr. Buckley, who is one of our best authorities on this subject, even states that there is a condition which creates a mania for burning buildings, torturing and destroying animals and men, poisoning persons—and taking the greatest delight in doing so. Another class, who commit crime from necessity, are not to be classed among those who are constitutionally so inclined, and require different treatment at the hands of the law. It is a common proverb that "necessity is the mother of invention." So necessity is often the mother of crime. One person is stronger and constitutionally better qualified to resist temptation, and overcome circumstances of necessity, than another.

These persons may be divided into three classes. The first are by force of necessity acted upon so as to at once begin to plan, and soon are enabled to carry out their desire successfully. The second, think and lay plans how to steal money or property in order to help themselves, but their conscience will not allow them to carry them into execution. An acquaintance of mine positively made this statement to me, and I have reason, from his candor, to believe that he made a truthful disclosure of his experience, which might have ended in years of toil in the penitentiary. He stated that a few years ago he was greatly in need of four hundred dollars, to pay the balance due on his farm. His neighbor had just received six hundred dollars, and he knew, from conversation he had with him, where it was kept. An idea struck him very forcibly that his neighbor was rich and had no use for that money, while he was so much in need of it. This lead him to think that he could steal the money, and no one would even know it,—a thought which, he said, never before entered his mind. He fixed on a night when he should perform this act. He had gone about half the distance on his errand when his remorse was so great that he returned. He discussed the pros and cons, the ifs and ands, in his mind for one week, when he made the second attempt. This time he arrived at the gate of the neighbor's house, and was again forced to abandon the job; not from fear of detection, for everything was in his favor to perpetrate a successful robbery; but the various faculties of caution, reason, conscientiousness, and others argued the right and wrong and the consequences so strongly with the faculty of acquisitiveness that they became masters of the situation, and held in subjection a power that was about to force this man to commit a crime. All was quiet for two weeks, he making every endeavor to hire money; but he failed, and the force of necessity became so great that he was induced to make the third attempt, and this time pried open the window with a crow-bar, and got quite into the room where the money was, but abandoned the job as before. The next morning he called on this neighbor, and without any trouble obtained the requisite loan. He said he was glad, for had the old gentleman refused, he believed he should have attempted it another time, and been successful. Thus we see that to commit crime requires some practice, some training, even where the disposition is naturally strong. This man was not a good robber,—he did not understand his business. A little instruction, however, would have made him successful. For example, had he taken a glass of whisky before he started, he would have had no such trouble as he related. Thousands of our criminals first deaden their moral sensibilities with some narcotic,—most generally whisky,—before they undertake to carry out their criminal designs. The third class are equally acted upon by force of necessity; but never think of lying or stealing to help themselves out of trouble. They use means to accomplish ends, and endeavor to make the best of life. These persons are honest, and would not lie or steal, to make a cent more. While traveling with a friend, we had occasion to remain over night at a hotel in Lincoln, Ill. My friend had three hundred dollars, which he placed under his pillow for safety. The next morning he forgot it, and we left the town. It was not until the afternoon that he discovered the loss. He immediately returned to the hotel, with a hope of recovering his money. The chamber-maid had found the money and returned it to the clerk, who locked it up until the owner should call for it. The clerk and the maid both were properly rewarded for their honesty. This maid was only receiving three dollars per week for her labor, and had also very poor clothing. Why did she not attempt to keep this money, which she could have done as easy as not? Simply for the reason that she was naturally honest. One not so would have stolen the money That no one is strictly honest is not true, for we could cite hundreds of similar circumstances that show conclusively that there are persons strictly honest, who are naturally and constitutionally inclined to do right—to render unto all men that which belongs to them. Such persons do right because it is right to do right, and not from policy, but for that reason also it brings happiness to themselves as well as others.

> "Then be thou to thyself true,
> It will follow, as does night the day,
> Thou canst not be false to any man."

No. 1.

No. 2.

No. 3.

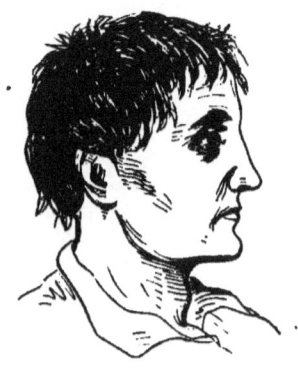

No. 4.

CHAPTER IV.

THE TWO PATHS OF THE CHILD.

The subject of this chapter is the child, in its career through life. To bring the subject clearly before the mind of our reader, we will suppose two boys begin existence at the same time, both born of healthy parents. Each of these boys has equal rights, so far as subsistence is concerned. The same sun that shines on the one shines on the other; the same atmosphere supplies both with oxygen; and each have equal claims upon their parents and society. Both have a just claim to a correct education, a proper training of their faculties, and in every way being fitted to take their places, each, respectively in his proper station in life, becoming a useful member of society. The original design of nature in the creation of human beings, doubtless, is their own ultimate happiness. But in these two boys we find it is quite contrary, the one going astray on the left hand path, while the other continues on the right hand path,—the one leading to destruction and sorrow; the other, to life and happiness. Why this is so is our present object of inquiry. Let us, then, follow the one upon the right hand path, and the other upon the left hand path of life. The subject of prenatal condition and prenatal transmission of constitutional predisposition to human offspring is fully discussed in other parts of this book. We take these boys, supposing that they are equal in organization, and still the end is so dissimilar. And why? The wood-cuts Nos. 1 and 2 represent health and intelligence; and, as rudimentary human beings, divinity and holiness. No one can consistently argue that there is any depravity here, or that by nature they spring into life "desperately wicked." No; it is a pleasure to look upon them. Every line marks perfection upon the "face divine." They are both now on their way to the ultimatum of life. Action is a law of nature, and these two boys must act; there is no standing still. They take a step in advance. And this brings us to the wood-cuts Nos. 3 and 4. How different in appearance! What a wonderful improvement in the one on the right; and how different the other, on the left! Let us inquire into the reason of this change. We have stated that both must act. Both are now growing, though very tender, as the little sprout that makes its first appearance in your garden in the spring of the year. Like the tender sprout, they are affected and mainly controlled by their surroundings. The young plant requires proper cultivation. The weeds must be pulled up around it, and all obstacles to a natural growth removed. If the husbandman allows the weeds to grow up with the good seeds sown, nine chances to one the tender twig becomes crippled and deformed; and thus by neglect a crooked, homely, uncouth, and worthless tree in after life is the result. So with our two boys. No matter how pure the germ, by neglect of the proper cultivation of the germinal faculties, and the physiology of the body, depravity soon stamps itself upon the physiognomy, and it is apparent to every one acquainted with human nature, that this boy is on the high road to disease, sorrow, and crime.

The boy on the right hand path has thus far received proper cultivation of the faculties; his surroundings are more favorable; the example of his parents is better; and he is growing under the sunshine of right training, correct associations, and happy surroundings. His mother does not tell him a lie every time she goes away from home. The father does not every day make the boy great promises which he does not keep. He does not use profane language, nor chew tobacco, nor drink intoxicating drinks, nor allow himself to become angry in the presence of his child. He never leaves home without a kiss and a "by-by, Johnny." He awards his boy for the good he does, and explains the right in contrast to the wrong. Instead of applying the, rod he reasons with his boy, and by example teaches him to return good for evil. The mother co-operates in this great work, and if she is a true mother she will take the lead. These good parents select proper associations for their child, and always know where he is, and what he is doing. They will teach him correct habits of life; how to divide his time,—a time to play, a time to work, a time to eat, a time to read, a time to go to school, a time to sleep. They will select the proper kinds of food, and prepare it in a healthful manner. They will teach him how to bathe and keep clean, how to exercise, and how to rest. They will also provide the proper kind of literature, and in every way see that their boy receives a well-balanced education—physically, morally, intellectually, and socially. They will also provide him with some employment.

The boy on the left hand receives the opposite attention, and we find opposite results. He grows up among the weeds of unfavorable surroundings, and we behold the effects in his face. He is a "crooked stick" at best; and what shall we do with him? By practice and cultivation, human depravity may be changed from bad to worse or from depravity to goodness. This boy, if allowed to go on under the thus far unfavorable training, and neglect of proper cultivation, will continue to become more and more degenerated; but, like the little plant in the garden, which the weeds may have almost smothered, by careful cultivation may become revived, improved, and end in a moderately fine growth. By removing all unfavorable influences, correcting the daily habits, setting a good example, and giving both body and mind the proper exercise, this boy may also pass upon the right hand path. But while this work of reformation is accomplishing, the first boy has steadily progressed; consequently, the boy who has spent say five years in the wrong direction is just thus far in the rear; so much of his life is lost to him. But we are safe in asserting that the boy who has moved five years upon the left hand path has lost ten years; for it will take five years to get back to the first position. To acquire a second nature will require considerable time, and I am of the opinion that it will take longer to overcome a second nature, than it did to acquire it; hence all reformation is slow. The application of principles of cure must be strictly natural. The young are easily lead out of the right path, but are also more easily set right again. A boy can contract the habit of chewing tobacco in from one to two weeks, and in about the same time can cure himself again. But if the habit is continued to adult age, it will be difficult to reform. So in regard to any of the vices.

Parents, and men and women in general, you cannot be too careful in setting a good example before children; for the child observes and copies

EVERY STEP YOU TAKE.

Thence we can justly hold parents and society responsible, to a great extent, for the deeds of the rising generation. The boy whom we picture upon the right path would not thus remain in the right were there no inducements, or if he were not assisted and guided by his parents, associates, teachers, and persons who live by the precepts which they teach. Neither would the boy whom we picture upon the left, pursue so unnatural and unhappy a course were he not stimulated in that direction. It is a maxim that you must bend the tree while it is yet young, for when old it is almost impossible. "Train up the child in the way he should go, and when he is old he will not depart from it." In our story of these two boys, we have divided human life into four stages: childhood, youth, manhood, and old age. The most important of these four stages is childhood; hence here is where we must begin our work of correcting, educating, and drawing out the principles of goodness originally implanted in place of the evil; for—as we hold—either good or evil principles may, by education, become the ruling power through life. Napoleon once said, "Give me the children of any nation, and I will overthrow the government of that nation in ten years." We will be more reasonable, and say, take the children for the next twenty years, and we can banish whisky from the land, or reconstruct our entire government, if it be necessary for the happiness of our people. To accomplish this, it will simply be necessary to so instruct the faculties and powers of the child as to keep it upon the right-hand path of life. If we would increase our drinking shops, give lawyers and physicians plenty of work, fill our poor houses, insane asylums, and prisons, all that is required is to stimulate and foster the propensities, faculties, and passions of the child tending to keep it upon the left-hand path of life. And in twenty years this nation will be sufficiently miserable, even so as to open direct communication with the great city of destruction, sending its victims upon the left-hand path as it were with lightning speed, the child making its journey in a few years.

Let us now take a step in advance, and follow our two boys through the second stage of life—from youth to manhood. Here, as before, our illustrations speak for themselves. Behold wood-cuts Nos. 5 and 6. What a wonderful change has been wrought in the constitutions of these two boys! No. 5 shows evident improvement. See how cleanly and tidy he appears in his dress; his hair properly combed; his

No. 5.

No. 6.

No. 7.

No. 8.

form straight and comely; his figure attractive; his forehead massive; his eyes lively and bright. In a word, his face bespeaks intelligence, refinement, and a moral and religious character, which makes everybody love him, speak well of him, and, in the language of the poet,

"Behold in him a man."

He was taught all the liberal branches of education, and not only caused to speak his pieces, but by precept daily, step after step, to bring into practice all the requisite qualifications necessary to make an exemplary man; enabling him to take his place in life as parent, teacher, preacher, lawyer, physician, statesman, or to pursue any other honorable vocation in life equally necessary to make up what we truly may term good society.

Now, let us behold for a moment wood-cut No. 6. We see that a wonderful change has been wrought since we saw him in youth. His tilting hat, his cigar in his mouth, scars upon his face, roguish eyes, uncouth appearance, filthy, shabby clothing, deformed figure,—in a word, his face and general appearance, —bespeak depravity. Physically, mentally, and morally he is almost a wreck. He did not "usure with his talents," he did not make use of every opportunity to improve his powers in the right direction. It may have been that he learned to speak his piece in school, but was not taught by precept. His mother sent him to school to get him out of her way; allowed him to play on the street till ten o'clock in the night, to keep him out of her way. His father spent his evenings down town. The boy received attention only when a bad report was brought to the father or the mother, when he was punished with a rawhide. He learned to hate his parents. The faculty of combativeness was strongly stimulated at home, and fighting with other boys, and being naturally intelligent,—"made of good grit,"—was soon called a "jocky fellow," took his glass with ease, threw the dice skillfully, and won at games of cards. His vocation was that of a vagabond, liar, robber, and "black-leg," in general; he was well trained in his profession, understood every turn and sharp hit calculated to make him a successful pilgrim upon the left-hand path of life. He possessed every qualification to make him distinguished among his fellows,—the elements necessary to make up what we may call "very bad society."

I must beg to be indulged here, and revert again in this boy's history to one prevalent cause which leads its thousands upon the wrong path, where the majority end their life in disgrace—perhaps in prison, perhaps on the gallows; or, at least, live an unhappy life, die broken-hearted, and prematurely end a life which otherwise might have been prolonged. I refer to the literature

OF TO-DAY,

which is so extensively circulated throughout the land,—such as the *Police Gazette*, New York *Ledger*, New York *Weekly*, *Saturday Night*, sporting papers, dime novels, and higher-priced novels, tragical literature, unnatural love stories, robber books, tragical theatrical performances, nude and immodest exhibitions of women in theaters, and illustrations in papers and books, all only intended to draw out, or act upon the passions and faculties of the lowest order of men and women. This sort of literature we term light reading, and literature of easy virtue. This kind of reading feeds the mind the same as pork, coffee, and tobacco would feed the body, and will produce discord among the faculties. The person so educated searches after the enjoyment of those unnatural conditions with which the mind is impressed. The subject of this chapter, the boy on the left-hand path, was mainly fed on this kind of literature—sustained by gaming for money, " bad whisky," and worse than all, evil associations.

I am well acquainted with the history of a man who was born on an adjoining farm. We grew up together until we were fifteen years of age, he being one year my senior. He was not a bad boy. His mother was a very good woman. His father was a man of easy virtue, yet no one could speak aught of him. The father, however, indulged the boy in many things, such as an occasional fight at school, which was well enough in self-defence, but this boy brought on quarrels, and his father did not reprove him, but always spoke of his "smart boy." At the age of fourteen, some one in the little town, within one mile of our homes, loaned him the History, Life and Death of that noted robber and murderer, John A. Murrel. He read and studied that book until he could almost repeat it from memory. This was the beginning of his ruin. He bought and borrowed all this sort of literature that was at his command, and I often heard him say that some day he should be distinguished as a highway robber. This was all kept from his mother, but the father gave him money to buy novels. At the age of sixteen, he ran away from home, following the Ohio river. He served a time in the Tennessee penitentiary, and now is learning the cooper trade in the penitentiary, at Jeffersonville, Indiana. His mother died in great sorrow, lamenting to her last moments the loss of her son, who was once a noble boy.

Our hero upon the left-hand path possessed an extraordinarily strong constitution, or he would have died long before he even reached middle age. It is a physiological law that those who live a life of debauchery, and in violation of nature's laws, do not live out half the days allotted them by nature. An unbalanced education of the moral and intellectual nature, and disobedience to the health-giving principles of the body, create conditions well illustrated in wood-cut No. 8. Contrast this with wood-cut No. 7, and we see the end of our two boys, who started in life at the same time and under similar conditions. How different is the end! Our boy on the left contracted gradually, through life, such habits, and acquired such conditions as are now lashing him even unto death. His own vagabond friends have forsaken him, society despises him, though, to a great extent, he is the workmanship of its own hands. The good people of the church give him but little attention; the day of reformation is passed. Retribution surely follows sin. Nature is "true to herself." Diseased in soul and body, what shall we do for him,—kill him, nurse him, teach him, or doctor him? (See Part Second of this book.) He would prefer death, if he could die. He calls aloud for some healing balm—for some one to cool his parched lips. Earth has no charms for him; all his joys have been engulfed in the sea of vice; the world has forsaken him, and now, an inmate of a prison cell, chained and condemned to death for crime.

> The boy originally pure and divine,
> The most miserable now of human kind;
> Every act of life wrote upon his face
> That the good *was* there, but vice now took its place.

Wood-cut No. 7 represents our boy on the right-hand path in old age. Here we behold the marks of a well-spent life. The opposite represents a life of depravity; but this, purity and good intentions. He has labored for himself; he has labored for others. His heart beats for all mankind; he is the good old grandfather, giving good advice to the rising generation. His mind is well stored with knowledge; all of his faculties have been well trained through life, and consequently he is as happy as life can make him. Such a man is not afraid to die; he is prepared for death,—happy in life, happy in death,—and the future can bring nothing but happiness. A healthy body, healthy mind, and healthy character are the best qualifications to enable us to pass into that happy state called Heaven.

CHAPTER V.

ON MAN'S SOCIAL NATURE.

Man is an intellectual, moral, and social being. In this only is he distinguished from, and rises above all other created beings. The intellectual gives him understanding, the moral a sense of right and wrong, and the social a desire to associate with his fellows, which makes him friendly, happy, and is that 'which forms society. The first object or desire with all human beings is to be happy. This he seeks in various channels; if he fail in one, he will try another; sometimes he lays his plans and labors for a lifetime in a certain direction, overcoming all obstacles in the way, and often at the end of life finds it all a failure. He seeks congenial associations in the various organizations of society, and only to renew his search when he finds himself disappointed. He will labor and study how to accumulate wealth, all to gain social position, and each year he adds to his "glistening store;" still the desired end has not been reached. He leaves his rural vocation for some petty office in a crowded city, and only regrets his step when too late. While young he aspires to some profession; he enters it with great expectations, and only sees his folly in after life. He soon finds there is no royal road to professional distinction. So, in every vocation and channel of human life, men and women are daily discouraged at finding the road to social, political, and professional position and fame beset with thorns on all sides, and happiness is not to be found in that direction.

Men and women in their social intercourse with each other are mainly attracted and repelled, to or from each other, by two forces, which are antagonistic, and bring untold misery and unhappiness to individuals, communities, and society in general. These two forces are wealth and poverty; wealth attracts and poverty repels. Those who are poor are constantly striving to gain wealth, at least a home, and as the common expression is, appear moderately well in society. Those who have wealth are constantly afraid that the poor will rise and become their equals. The mistress is terribly chagrined if Bridget should manage, by industry, to treat herself to a dress nearly as good as her mistress, especially if she has it made fashionably. The capitalist has all that money can buy; he lives in a fine house, drives his fine horses, keeps his servants, wears fine clothing, gets into office, makes our laws, and is said to be respectable. He is the center of attraction, and people will spend their last dollar to keep up appearances in society. The poor man, the laborer, the mechanic, the clerk, the student, have social organs, as well as the rich, which demand social position. Yet he thinks the rich are happy, and the poor only miserable. They are excluded from the social intercourse of what is called respectable society, and happiness comes not to them.

They are forced to associate with those in equal financial circumstances; and thus the mechanic, the laborer, or what is termed, in the language of society, the "irrepressibles," the non-respectable class, become the center of repulsion. There is a constant effort on the one hand to establish a social line of demarcation, and on the other hand, a terrible strife to tear it down, to blot out, if possible, all such distinction. Here is a prolific source, which furnishes the majority of our criminals. It killed Fisk; it kills its thousands; it grinds the poor; it jeopardizes the rich man's wealth; it enters all stations of life, and furnishes its victims; it fills our prisons, the gallows, with its culprits, the asylum with its inmates, the county-house with its paupers, and throws little orphans upon the cold charities of the world, without a guiding star, whither to steer their little bark upon the life current of the world. Man is a social being, and often uses wrong means to satisfy the social nature. This he is forced to do nine times out of ten by society. The fifty or hundred dollars a month is not sufficient to pay rent, or pay on a little home, to feed and clothe the children, and buy silk dresses or velvet cloaks for the wife, in order to appear well in society. Now, if the lie is not told to make the dollar, or, under cover of the night, property unlawfully appropriated, they withdraw from society, and live a life of comparative seclusion, which is almost as sure to lead to crime as if the first inclination had been indulged. By and by, they become dissatisfied with life, and soon misunderstandings between husband and wife end in an unhappy manner, for which they are severely censured by society, and receive not the slightest sympathy. The children imbibe from their parents' bad example an unhappy disposition, and if the difficulty is not cured, and they do not commit crime, their offspring, almost as a rule, end in the commission of some terrible crime, to which, I hold, society is accessory, and should be held responsible as well as the poor victim.

Society has not provided a place of amusement for the working class to attend once a week for a mere nominal sum, where the social nature and other faculties of the mind can have an hour's relaxation from the cares and labors of the day. There are no lecture halls where the working man with his family can attend once a week free, or at least, for a small sum, where our lecturers, physicians, clergymen, lawyers, statesmen, scientists, teachers, farmers, mechanics, and business men, should be invited to lecture, in the course of the year, on all subjects pertaining to man's education, reformation, and cultivation of the various faculties, and thus tend to improve the condition of all classes. Other public institutions of learning should be erected in every community, as we shall show in another part of this work, where the social as well as the intellectual and moral faculties may receive proper attention. The social "rings," as they now exist in society, I think, are productive of evil. Like many "rings," monopolies, and associations which combine their efforts in order to gain the controlling power, society has gradually been organized into "rings," monopolizing power, which should be discouraged. The social faculties require careful training the same as the intellectual and moral. These faculties are blind, and rush headlong in the pursuit of happiness, irrespective of right and wrong, or consequences; that is, a man or woman unacquainted with physiology will, under the influence of the social nature alone, indulge in the social glass, and while having a "jolly good time," circumstances over which their intellectual and moral faculties have lost all control, will force them on, and before they have regained their equanimity, have committed some terrible crime. The condition or end of such persons is brought about generally by a slow process; gradually indulging uncultivated inclinations; ignorantly, or by circumstances over which, as individuals alone, they have no control, contracting a sort of mania, and becoming dangerous members of society.

Another, uninformed and unbalanced, fosters his social propensities, and labors from morning till night, year in and year out, in accumulating a few dollars more, mainly to gain a high social position. The intellectual and moral is called into requisition, mainly to aid the social inclinations, irrespective of the right or the wrong, so the end is attained. If this course be persisted in, or unrestrained, it will end in crime. Society is the actuating principle; wealth the attractive, and poverty the repelling force. Such persons are living in constant fear of becoming poor, and, if so, they would be forever in discord; consequently we find a wonderful struggle among men and women to rise and "get a little more."

The affections and the sexual passions, unrestrained and uncultivated, lead thousands into criminal channels, secret vices, and social discord. Society has a thousand and more allurements to entrap and seduce those who have by nature, or by virtue of birth, these faculties large, and are otherwise unbalanced in their intellectual, moral and social nature. Men and women disguise their true nature by art, dress, and "putting on style." The little girl is dressed *a la mode* by exposing her legs, regardless of modesty and physiological laws, ruining her health, and perverting her social nature, all to be in style, and appear well in fashionable society. Society—what a word! who knows what it is, and what it means? How little attention is given by the people to the wonderful influence that society exerts upon the moral and social nature of the individual. Attention is only given to the unfortunate one who is caught stealing, or in the commission of any other crime, and society cries aloud, " Protection, protection against such fiends !" No one ever suggests the idea of inquiring into the cause of a murder or any other crime. It is true, the *immediate* provocations are sufficiently investigated at the time of the trial. This is simply treating the wound inflicted upon society; and the constitutional, predisposing cause, which permeates the very soul and body of society, of which the poor criminal is simply a slight eruption, is lost sight of; and thus we are only treating the effect, instead of removing the cause. Law is only instituted to reach the criminal; lawyers deal only with the criminal; physicians prescribe only for the sick; and society makes no real provision for the prevention of crime. Let the lawyer lecture upon the philosophy of "Law and Order;" the physician, on physiology, natural laws, and how to be healthy;

the teacher, on the understanding; the clergyman, on moral philosophy; and the scientist, on science, etc. And I apprehend, when we open these various channels of education, in addition to those that are now in operation (and, I hope, are in good working order), that the time is not far hence when society will be so reformed that comparatively few crimes will be perpetrated. We, then, lay crime at the door of society; and to eradicate it from among us, more attention must be given to the cultivation of the social, as well as the moral and intellectual faculties of the rising generation.

CHAPTER VI.

THE WORKING MAN.

The working men and women constitute the only foundation upon which we can base the perpetuation of our civilized and republican form of government. Capital has been said to be superior to labor, and to control it. This I do not credit, however. A man can till the soil, and grow potatoes, wheat, and corn, thus maintaining a subsistence independent of capital. Therefore, I hold that labor should be honored, and capital made subordinate, or better, be co-operative, as either is almost indispensable; but we cannot admit that capital is the superior. By the working men and women, we mean all those people who labor for a living. The men and women who labor with their hands in the shop or field to maintain an honorable subsistence, are,—other things being equal,—in my judgment, the respectable classes. So long as society judges men by the clothes they wear, the amount of money and property they own, so long will true merit, honesty in motive, intellectual and moral acquirements, go unrewarded, and will not be considered necessary qualifications to attain an honorable position in society.

> "If I were tall to reach the pole,
> Or grasp the ocean in my span,
> I must be measured by my soul,
> For the mind's the standard of the man."

True merit of character, honest motives, educational attainments, dignified deportment, etiquette strictly based upon the laws of nature, truth, love, and friendship, are qualifications which society should hold at a high premium, rather than at a discount. To acquire these requisite individual attainments, and reconstruct society so that the greatest amount of happiness may come unto all classes of men, and thereby prevent future commission of crime, the condition of the working classes must be so improved that greater facilities are given for the expansion and development of the higher nature of mankind.

In the condition in which we now find the working man, he has but little time, and much less opportunity, to attend to the exercise of his natural faculties. The majority of the working classes are comparatively short lived, the average longevity of the men and women of our factories and shops, the mechanic and common laborer, being only about twenty-eight years, while those who carry on business, the professional, and the wealthy, attain an average longevity of about forty; proving conclusively that the physical condition of the working classes is not so favorable to length of days as that of the last class mentioned.

It is a physiological truth that a man laboring incessantly for ten or twelve hours out of twenty-four expends each day a greater amount of vital force than nature is enabled to restore during the few hours of rest and sleep which he is permitted to enjoy, especially if he should set apart three or four hours for mental improvement—reading, conversing, attending lectures or places of amusement. By this means he becomes physically and mentally unbalanced. His body becomes diseased, and, of course, the mind sympathizes,—he is made unhappy; life has lost its pleasures, and if he does not commit crime, his offspring will; and he succumbs to the destroying force that prematurely ends his sorrowful life, which otherwise might have been prolonged and made happy. A man performing what is called "a good day's work" of ten hours' hard labor requires, if he complies with physiological laws, at least three hours to attend to his toilet and other little matters about his home (for working men, as a rule, cannot keep body servants), before the bodily forces react and become moderately well balanced—before he is really in a condition to give the brain-work the necessary attention. We would give him three or four hours for mental improvement, and the time required to come and go to and from his place of labor. Thus, altogether, at least, eighteen hours of his daily life are spent in a state of activity, expending a greater amount of vital force than is re-accumulated.

To say nothing of the restless hours spent in bed, trying to go to sleep, and the many hours during which the various faculties of the mind receive no attention, we still find the majority of the working class in a very deplorable condition, viewing the subject, as we do, from a physiological standpoint. Life itself is an expenditure of the original vital capital transmitted by parental creation, and if we in an unnatural manner call an extra amount into use, without attention given to the necessary restorative means, we cut short our existence, and render our days most miserable. So long, then, as men disobey physiological laws in their various corporeal exercises, in their daily vocations, and in the exercise of the mind, so long will we have need for courts of justice, and prisons.

Science has revealed many truths, as well as Divine revelations, and among those revelations is the now established maxim that physical depravity creates intellectual as well as moral and social depravity. To avert the present tendencies of crime, bring about a general regeneration of each individual member of society, and establish new institutions of learning, and additional methods of developing that divine and more noble nature of man. All have a common interest in the work, and all should take a part. I will state here a firm conviction, formed from long observation, that too much one-sided education has been given to the rising generation in times past; *i. e.*, the churches have hitherto mainly given their whole time to the cultivation of the moral and religious nature alone, while the laws governing the corporeal are almost wholly neglected. I will illustrate my idea. A celebrated clergyman in Brooklyn, N. Y., receives a salary of twenty thousand dollars. Fifteen thousand dollars of that money is invested in a corn farm. The products of that farm are gathered and sold to the distillers, and that fiery liquid, alcohol, which all nature universally abhors, is bottled and sold at the highest market price to the very class of men, whom, by his previous labors, he sought to reform, to convince of their sins, and, if possible,

"To render happier a cheerless lot."

But by this means all is counteracted, and if any difference in the condition of men, they are worse than if the first effort had not been made. By this illustration I wish to convey this idea: in the cultivation of man's capabilities, by an effort in one direction, and total neglect in another, a counteracting force is created, and the opposite force is just as liable to become the controlling power of the being as the one which is correct, and hence such education is really worse than no education, and, no doubt, is a great source of crime.

To revert to the working classes, and further inquire into their conditions and well-being, if possible, to fully understand the real causes of crime, I will say that I am strongly in favor of the

EIGHT HOUR SYSTEM,

which, if rightly understood, and diligently applied, will doubtless much improve the physical condition of the laboring man; and I can not see that capital, which employs labor, is not also much the gainer thereby. On the principle that "an ounce of prevention is better than a pound of cure," we claim that it is much cheaper to prevent crime than it is to maintain courts, jails, prisons and poor-houses. This being the case, it would seem quite reasonable that a universal effort should be made, for it is quite easy to establish the fact that too much occupation predisposes to physical, moral, and intellectual depravity Let a universal decree go forth that every working man cease his labor at five P. M., and every store, shop, or other place of business, be closed at seven P. M., and I affirm that the present condition of all classes will be vastly improved; and where we now have loafers, vagabonds, and criminals, respectable men and women will take their places. All classes will then get through with their work during the day, —do their shopping, buying, and selling,—so that the evening may be spent in rest, amusement, music, social enjoyment, and mental recreation, which should always, however, have for its object progress and improvment in divine humanity. As it is now, men keep open their stores, shops, and places of business, most generally until late hours of the night, attracting around their counters a certain class, with a hope of making a "few cents more." Go into any of our towns, and announce a lecture on physiology, and at eight o'clock P. M., you will find the majority of people shopping or loitering about in their usual places of resort—saloons, stores, etc. These places hatch out a majority of our criminals. The lecturer will have a few of the righteous ones who "require not salvation." By too much occupation, and not a proper division of our time, manifold evils follow as a natural consequence. Eight hours of well applied industry will insure to every person a vine-clad home and a pleasant little spot of ground, and we are safe in saying also a competency to leave for those dependent on them to enjoy. Eight hours for our daily vocation, eight hours for rest and mental improvement, and eight hours for sleep. This seems to be the most natural division of time that we can have, unless our object is to work men and women like beasts of burden, and traffic with the life and souls of men. Who will take the lead in this great work? Of course some one must make an effort. The good people in every community should call a convention, and hold adjourned meetings once every week, until the necessary laws can be passed, establishing the eight-hour system, closing every shop, saloon, store, or other place of business, at six, or at least at seven, P. M.

Consider the construction of public halls for lecturing and other educational purposes. Let society change its tactics, and let every body co-operate in the accumulation of bodily health, brain capital, moral and social worth, rather than to accumulate mere earthly wealth, which is any day liable to "take to itself wings and fly away."

For the present, our churches, and county courthouse, and school-house may be occupied one night each week, at least until appropriations can be made, and provisions for the great work of prevention of crime in reality, by the proper education of a class of people who are woefully neglected, and who furnish the majority of our criminals. Moral suasion, it may be argued, is all that is necessary. We believe in moral suasion, but

LEGAL PERSUASION

is the only hope, in controlling those whose moral faculties are almost entirely dormant. The man or woman who can not see the right, and will not obey the right, when it is made self-evident to every reasoning mind, it is necessary to control by legal persuasion. We spoke as follows, in a lecture in Ohio, a few years since, though our remarks were directed merely in a temperance point of view; still, what was said is applicable to all conditions which we hope to reform, mentioned in this chapter.

The question, "How may the temperance cause be successful?" is, no doubt, interesting to every temperance man and woman. It has been the theme for many years. Various plans have been adopted; and in course of time, each, in turn, has done some good. The success was in proportion as these plans, or temperance institutions, were based upon natural and fundamental principles. For any institution or organization having man's higher development for its object, grounded upon these principles, must and will finally succeed. A truth can never be annihilated; it may be retarded in its progress for a time, but finally it will rule. Truth, like the fixed laws of nature, is an emanation from God, and, like himself, is all-powerful. Man in his undeveloped state is not prepared to recognize it; yet by sad experience and careful research he is often brought to light, and oh! how bright and beautiful.

The first work that occupied the attention of educated men in the temperance cause was to ascertain how spirituous liquor affects the human system. These investigations were suggested, in the first place, by the manifest results it produced upon those who drank it. It was evident that those who imbibed this "fiery liquid" were soon disqualified to attend to their daily avocations, or the ordinary duties of life;

and that many of the evils that afflicted mankind were the result of intoxicating drinks, even capable of producing death,

At first it was thought that a moderate use of it would be healthful; but even this was found to be incorrect. By experiments made on animals and men, it is now an established truth that alcohol absolutely acts as a poison on the tissues of both man and animals. In view of these facts, philosophic minds soon began to advocate the total abstinence of the use of so deadly a drink, as a beverage, and in a very short time, became quite a power, in persuading many of the best minds of the country to advocate the total abolition of this huge monster from among us.

Various plans were suggested, from time to time, and all in turn have, thus far, been unsuccessful. And why? Moral persuasion has ever been persevered in, and all that has been accomplished, including the work of the temperance orders, is simply establishing a line of demarkation between the man that drinks and he that is strictly sober and temperate. There is no more association with each other. This is an important point attained. In this we boldly recognize the foe to human improvement, and know where to find him.

Now, notwithstanding the general diffusion of scientific knowledge, on the deleterious effect of whisky on the human system, and the positive demonstration to our senses every day, we find that it is distilled, bought, sold, and drank, delivering up its thousands annually to *delirium tremens* and **death**.

No one can consistently plead ignorance at this stage of human progress; therefore, it may be considered a willful and malicious violation of the laws of nature and the laws of humanity, sinning against light and knowledge. I believe that no man has a moral right, and should not have a legal right, to consign himself under the influence of any force that may, for a time, cause him to forget his moral obligation to his fellow-man, and to assist him to carry out some fiendish end, thus disgracing humanity.

In the hope of success, I recognize at this stage of the temperance work, first, *rigid and thorough legal action.* This will hold the rum-traffic and the drunkard in check, while general diffusion of scientific knowledge will so prepare the future man that he will be a law unto himself. But some one will say, "This has been tried and failed." Yes, and always will, so long as we aim only to regulate the excessive use of it. If we would dry up a stream, we must stop the fountain. Hence, the only hope is to regulate by law the indiscriminate distillation of rum. Place it wholly under the control of properly-qualified physicians, the same as other poisons and medicines. A rigid license law, as in some states, might be useful. But this would be simply palliating; the disease would still exist.

Shall we compromise longer with vice? or shall we advocate true principles, and stand aloof from every contaminating influence of the low, undeveloped brute, man, who will not hear the truth? Is it not more noble to prevent the commission of crime than to punish the perpetrators after the hideous deed has been consummated? Is it not reasonable that a thing capable of doing so much mischief in the land should be made a subject of positive legislation, or even a topic as a political issue? Do we not often spring issues of much less consequence? I apprehend that the question of abolishing negro slavery in this country was of no greater importance than the question before us now; for it underlies all evil, or all reformation.

However, before legislation can be enforced, the public mind must be educated up to the proper point. And here I recognize the *second* most important thing to be done, which is, if we would be successful in educating the masses, to organize our forces. The time for pleasing temperance orations, music, and young men and ladies flirting with each other in lodges, has gone by. Action is what the true temperance public wants, and the whisky ring is looking for it. They are getting a good ready, for they know that their days are short; and nothing deters them more than a thorough organization.

United effort is sure of success, and to educate the public mind up to this standard—which implies action—I would suggest the organization of the following associations, in addition to the present church and temperance organizations:

First, a "*Young Men's Physiological Association*" should be organized in every city, town, or precinct, where all sorts of subjects, pertaining to health, sobriety, and consequent happiness are debated and taught. These should meet once a week, and every young man should belong to it. In these associations physicians should make themselves useful.

Our women should be thoroughly organized into "*Women's Health Reform Associations*," where all subjects pertaining to their development could be taught and debated, and in a very short time she would have all the rights that her mission in life demands. Here, again, physicians should take an active part; then, instead of prescribing a few powders for the sick, the more noble part of the profession would be brought into use; that is, of being health-educators, thus preventing sickness, suffering, and often premature death.

Then, "*Children's Health and Temperance Lyceums*" should be established all over our great country, and in ten years thirty millions of new voices will speak in thunder tones. The drunkard, the rumseller, the distiller, will not object to their children being educated "in the way they should go." Every child six years old should be induced to attend a lyceum once a week. Each lyceum should be known by some motto, inscribed upon a banner; then its little members should be divided into groups, each having its little banner and motto, or name, and each child be furnished with a little flag inscribed with an appropriate motto. This work, I believe, should be conducted by the ladies. Every young lady should have charge of one of these little groups. Let us give the ladies something to do, and I believe they will work.

CHAPTER VII.

ON ACCIDENTAL CRIME.

The various causes of crime and murder which we have noticed in other chapters, are, as we have also stated, of two kinds, and of different origin, the one originating in a hereditary predisposition, and the other in an acquired condition, which predisposes to crime. Sufficient explanation has been given, and the facts successfully established, to enable us to introduce a third kind of crime, the origin of which is purely accidental. Crime is divided by some into voluntary and involuntary. Those who have by creation a natural and irresistible impulse to commit crime, it is claimed, do so *involuntarily*, and those who have acquired a disposition, commit a *voluntary* crime. The last statement is not true, for both the acquired and the hereditary condition, is forced on the individual, as we have shown, and hence all actions are involuntary. Since the first condition, which is the actuating power, is not assumed by any voluntary act of theirs, it cannot be reasonably argued that the results or actions are voluntary. Again, no person of a sound mind, highly developed perceptive and reflective powers, well educated, with good habits, good associations, and a harmonious physical and mental organization, can ever commit crime. Doubtless a certain degree of depravity is necessary for any one to lie, steal, and murder. Now, if a depraved condition is necessary to perpetrate crime, can you consistently claim and prove your position, —that people voluntarily take upon themselves physical, moral, intellectual, and social depravity, in order that they are enabled to carry out wicked designs? No one would voluntarily assume the life of a drunkard, and none ever do, for all such conditions gradually grow and overpower men before they are aware.

If it is true that the good, the wise, the religious, and those that are pure in heart, never commit crimes such as lying, stealing, murdering, etc., then it will follow that such deeds are never the result of wisdom, reason, pure motives, and due consideration of consequences, or the fruit of knowledge and a refined intellectual organization. If crime could be the result of wisdom and purity of heart, then we might call such a deed a voluntary act; but so long as it cannot be proven from either Divine revelation, science, or nature, that man ever performs a voluntary act of life, we are not willing to admit that it is possible for a man to commit a voluntary crime or murder. For any person to perpetrate a willful crime, more than ordinary depravity is required, and depravity is generally the result of ignorance, neglected culture, and unfavorable surroundings of the young, and persons even in after life may acquire such conditions.

We do not believe, then, in voluntary crime, and so long as science will sustain this idea, we do not hesitate to assert it.

We therefore class all such as hitherto were thought

to be voluntary crimes with those which we denominate accidental.

We have, then, only involuntary and accidental crime to deal with. The reader here may propound the question, if all crime is only involuntary and accidental, then, who is responsible? and how can we hold any one accountable for their wrong deeds? In answer, we say, that for the very reason that such a force exists, which in an involuntary manner causes men to commit hideous crimes, are they accountable, and subjects of legislation, in order to restrain all such conditions or dispositions until the difficulty is entirely overcome.

No one need ever fear those who have no involuntary feeling in the direction of committing crime; but it is this involuntary power which has insinuated itself into the human family, that is so very difficult to counteract by law and punishment.

We have conclusively argued the question, and have shown that man is governed by law the same as other things in nature; and that he is not strictly free to act, in any sense, is especially evident when we consider the circumstances and forces which act upon him from every direction, in every stage of life, —the time and manner of his advent on earth, and his exit from this mundane sphere of existence.

We will now consider what we understand by an accidental crime. This is an event without one's foresight or expectation; an event that proceeds from an unknown cause, or an unusual effect of a known cause, and therefore not expected; a crime committed without an efficient intelligent cause and without design. The inquiry may rise, can such a crime ever be perpetrated? It is quite possible that such crimes can be committed. They are occurring every day.

A crime committed during a temporary fit of insanity is an accidental one, and many persons are liable. A gentleman of first respectability, in New York, a few years ago, after the day's work in the office, while splitting some kindlings, that his wife might start a fire and cook him some supper, imagined that he saw a monstrous fiend approaching him, and to fight for his life, he thought, was the only alternative. It was his wife, who had come to the woodshed after the wood. She was killed outright by her husband, who ran to the house, to tell his wife of the terrible fight he had had, but could not find her. After a few minutes he recovered his sanity, and it almost made him permanently insane to learn that it was his own wife he had killed, instead of the horrible monster which he imagined he saw. It was proven that they lived happy together, and never had a quarrel, which fact cannot but lead one to believe his statement. He was also a man of fine intellect and culture, and religious in his every-day life. This murder was accidental.

A few days after the battle of Perryville, while dressing the wounded, in a field hospital, we were summoned immediately to call and see a man who, it was reported, had been killed by the cook in one of the mess tents, in the other end of the camp. When we arrived, the man was quite dead. The cook stated that the man kept "tormenting him" by disturbing the fire, and snatching little pieces of meat from the kettle,—all in sport, however. The cook commanded him to cease, or he should "slap his mouth for him," which he did, with the palm of his hand, on the side of the face. The man fell dead as though he had been shot. This statement was proven to be correct. The cook was a powerful man, and it was thought that he dislocated the man's neck; but a *post mortem* examination revealed no evidence of any internal derangement, and hence we decided that the man died from a nervous shock, produced accidentally on the part of the cook. This was purely an accidental murder. The railroad company at Dayton, Ohio, three years ago, were repeatedly informed by a competent engineer that their steam boiler was dangerous, and further use would jeopardize many lives; but they gave the matter no attention. The boiler exploded, and killed eight or ten men, and wounded some twenty others. This was an accidental crime, though brought about by neglect on the part of the officers of the company. Still we class it among the accidental crimes. They reasoned thus: "The boiler has lasted so long, and will, perhaps, last a few days longer, when it will be time enough to have the matter investigated." In the meantime, it exploded.

A train of cars is thrown from the track by reason of a broken rail, or a defective tie, and a number of lives are lost, which is all strictly accidental; yet, we hold it is criminal, for had the road been properly inspected and put in order, the accident would, in all probability, never have occurred. This is also mainly the result of a strong propensity on the part of the company to make money; hence they avoid all possible repairs of their road until it is too late. After a terrible accident has taken place, they repair their road, on the principle that after the thief has stolen your horse, you lock your stable. The crime consists in want of vigilance, and is attributable to men not doing their whole duty. A child is allowed to play near a stand on which is burning an oil lamp. By accident the child upsets the stand. The lamp explodes, and, ten chances to one, the child is burnt to death, and the house, and, perhaps, a whole block of buildings burned. The crime is accidental. The mother did not think her child would upset the stand. A thoughtless act, and hence a crime. A man in Adams County, Ohio, heard a number of boys in his peach orchard, stealing peaches. He thought he would only scare them a little by firing his gun through the bushes; but in so doing he killed one of the boys. He did not mean to kill the boy; yet, from want of forethought, he became guilty of a crime,—yes, a murder, the most horrible of crimes,—for which, though accidental, he should be held accountable, for we cannot allow an exchange of life for a peach.

This man, it was believed, had no intention to murder this boy, still he made use of very dangerous means to scare the boys. He might have caused a rushing noise through the bushes, called to John, "Go around on the right," and to James, "Go on the left; let us surround them," at the same time calling his dogs, etc., and the boys would have left in haste. Or, what was better, if he had called the boys to him and given them what peaches they could eat, he would have taught them a moral lesson and perhaps cured them of stealing peaches ever after.

We might cite hundreds of instances of accidental crime, murder, etc., occurring every day in all parts of the country. We believe in punishing, in a proper manner, all such crimes. The kind and degree of the crime to be ascertained by the actuating motives, and the means at hand by which such a crime might have been avoided; that is, such as forethought, and the means which science and experience have taught men by which to prevent calamities, accidents and crime.

The high premium which is paid by our nation for condensation of various sensational vibrations, high-wrought brain action, and velocity of motion, at whatever the risk or cost, destroying the very soul of our civilization, is a danger overshadowing the general mind and heart of the

PRESENT ERA.

The general interrogation is in a half-breathless way: What do you know? What can you do? How quick can you do it? How much money have you? How long did it take you to make it? etc.

The politician first responds: "I have been tried, as it were, in the fire! I have traveled hundreds of miles, and can bolt my meals at irregular hours; can travel further in fewer days than any of my acquaintance; write hundreds of letters; make scores of speeches; talk more hours in private; sleep less;

read a greater number of books, and still my health is in a good condition, my mind fresh and vigorous. It does not injure me. No, no, I know how much I can bear." So answers the moderate drinker, and before he is aware, he is a diseased man, having gradually acquired a mania for liquor, and he dies an accidental death. Was guilty of crime.

The general business man comes forward and must be heard, claiming that "he can do a little more" than any other—build more houses, get the most rent, loan the most money, get the best interest, work the greatest number of men in the shop, is up early and late, sleeps only a few hours out of twenty-four, bolts his meals as does the statesman, at irregular hours; but all this, he thinks, does not injure his mind, only his liver. I said to a gentleman of forty, a few days ago, you overtax your brain; you must sleep more, and forget your business, at least for the space of ten hours out of twenty-four. "No, Doctor," he said, "it is not my brain, it is—for fifteen per cent. I will let you have—" when I interrupted him. Recovering himself, he thought "it was his kidneys. Doctor," he continued, "can't you give me something that will straighten me up for a few days? then I will come and take a regular course and obey your prescription, but just now, Doctor, I have to meet my obligations and finish that block; you know I am not one that will allow any one to out-do me in business." "But, sir," we remarked, "your brain and mind is diseased, and it will require some considerable time to effect a cure; and suppose you should die to-morrow—" "Oh, well, Doctor," he interrupted, "you are trying to frighten me, and you may be right, but I have not time to give the subject much attention for a few weeks." Well, well, all right, take this medicine, and call again in three days; you will be better and perhaps be able to finish that block of buildings.

In November, 1872, one dreary night, we were aroused about two o'clock in the morning, by the ringing of the door-bell. The messenger requested us to visit a man at one of our fashionable hotels. On arriving, we were directed to room —, on the fourth floor. Being introduced by the landlord, as the Doctor sent for, our patient immediately sprang to his feet, and presenting a huge dirk knife, said: "Doctor, had it not been for this dirk, I should have been killed more than an hour ago." I asked him to let me examine the knife, which he did. I then handed it to the landlord, and he took it away. I then requested the patient to keep quiet while I felt his pulse. I found him feverish and mentally a wreck. He thought himself surrounded by demons who sought his life, and hence he fought desperately with them during about three hours of the night. I gave him a strong anodyne, and remained with him about an hour, when he fell asleep. The next morning we found our patient somewhat better, but still deranged. We now recognized in him the same person whom we had previously prescribed for at our office, and who had been for a month very much improved by our prescription, but at length disobeyed our advice, and continued overtaxing his mind for a few months, until we now find him almost a hopeless maniac. He was restored in about three months, but, honestly, we do not believe this man is yet cured, as he is liable at any time to meet with an accident and commit a terrible crime. Such persons require from one to three years of the very best treatment before we can safely say that they are thoroughly cured. Some never recover. He was a man of good habits, so far as his eating and drinking was concerned, but in regard to his mental labors, he was a debauchee, a slave to an unbalanced condition of the faculty of acquisitiveness. He had more of this world's goods than any one individual has a moral right to have.

The present period of "fast living" is wonderfully affecting all classes, and men and women in every station of life are nursing the monster that will impel the steel and pierce their own hearts. The almighty struggle of this epoch is for outward wealth. The maddening spirit of the age is "electricity." Man's principle of intrinsic goodness has been converted into the fiery prince of the "powers of the air." Men fancy they have scientifically caught and commercially harnessed their absolute master. And yet he cracks his whip of live lighting over our heads; he teaches and insists that we *shall do everything with lightning speed!*

The rebuilding of Chicago is a fair illustration of this age of "electricity." My friend, from Boston, writes: "Obediently, we race, and rush, and push, with wild, headlong energy into everything and over everything we undertake to do, or conceive a fancy for doing. We immediately begin to overwork, and overeat and overdrink, and overchew, and oversmoke, and overlive, and at last, when too late, we discover ourselves to be *overdead* in trespasses and sins."

The wickedest demon of our day is the "imp" of impatience. It attacks the nerves, the brain, and in a twinkling of an eye it is in a "murderous rage." The blood becomes feverish, the heart throbs with excitement, and if the victim does not thrust a dagger into his own bosom, he may into that of his neighbor, and down goes his subject, covered with the mantel of "sudden disease." The over-sensitive condition of the brain and nervous system sends the victim to an asylum for the insane. So wonderfully subtile is this force which gradually undermines human happiness, that before we are aware, we are guilty of an involuntary or accidental crime. Why is it that those who are drifting in the direction of the city of destruction will not heed the admonitions of those who from knowledge and experience can give proper advice, is a mystery for future generations to reveal. When science positively teaches a man how to avoid disease, and he still persists in his murderous course, we sometimes feel discouraged, but no one can tell what an amount of good is done every day by the many efforts that are put forth to reform mankind; for if not a school, church, or institution which has for its object the improvement of the condition of the human family, were in existence, then crime and murder, and human depravity would soon be indescribably great. As it now is, our daily papers are full of all sorts of crimes, suicides, and murders, committed every day, in all parts of the country. By the combined effort of good people, much can be accomplished, on the principle that "by the testimony of two or three a truth shall be established." The "erring ones," being admonished, and "hailed," as it were, by those on the right, one after another will be added to the testimony, until, by and by, those on the left will begin to heed the teaching of the good, and reform.

We will suppose a captain starts from Cincinnati upon the Ohio river, with an intention to go to Pittsburgh. If he allows his boat to drift down with the current, he would go further and further from his designed destination. Now, we will further suppose that heaven is at Pittsburgh, and the "city of destruction" at New Orleans. The flag upon the main-mast of the vessel has inscribed upon it the word "Heaven," by which all passers-by may know whither the ship is bound. My dear reader, every human being that enters upon the current of life has written upon his physiognomy, Heaven, by which all may know whither he is bound. The ship, however, drifts along easily for a time, until, by and by, it is observed by those watching its course that the captain is sailing in the wrong direction. He is hailed. "Heigh-ho, Captain, whither are you going?" "To Heaven, of course! don't you see by the flag of my ship whither I am going?" "But you are on the wrong road; you are on the way to destruction." "Don't believe it, for I am gliding along *so* easily." A little further down, and another "heigh-ho" comes from the shore. The captain is undisturbed, and he drifts a little further down the current toward the city of destruction. He is now more frequently hailed by the good people on the shore of safety, who are rapidly winning their way back;—they may have started further down than the Captain did, but are moving in the right direction.

The repeated "Heigh-ho," and warning of danger signals ahead, now arouses the captain to a conviction that perhaps he *is* on the wrong road, and he begins to throw out the lead, and feel about him; but behold he is already among the breakers, and in a mist of darkness. He is now in great trouble. His ship is momentarily in danger of being dashed to pieces; life-boats are manned and sent out for his rescue, and in case he should lose entire control of his ship, they are ready to take him in, and if possible, save not only his life, but the lives of all those that keep him company. The captain, however, is by this time fully convinced that unless something is done he and his ship will be destroyed. If he now makes use of the proper means which he has at hand, he can save himself from destruction. He has a compass, a pilot, a rudder, and fuel to fire up, all sufficient to create a counterforce, and "stem the tide;" he will by economy, and care in the use of the small store of supplies yet left him, be enabled to get back at least from whence he first started. In this, of course, he will be much encouraged by the good people that are going in the same direction. It is doubtless true—at least those who have gone in that direction tell us so— that as we approach the celestial city—a state of heaven, or happiness—the wind is more favorable, the climate more genial, and, by hoisting occasionally an extra sail, our progress is steady and sure. Had the captain heeded the first warning as to the "right road," he would not have spent half a life-time in experimenting in the opposite direction.

The majority of the present generation are down among breakers. First, those drifting down the current of "fast living," and merely enjoying the sensual, and neglecting the use of natural talents with which they were originally gifted, do not heed the admonitions of those on the shore, who are daily laboring to instruct the stray wanderers, and warn them of the danger ahead. Secondly, those who are on the shore of safety do not call out loud enough, and are not sufficiently united in supporting each other and in making a common effort to save their fellow man.

CHAPTER VIII.

ON THE PRINCIPLES WHICH GOVERN THE ACTIONS OF HUMAN BEINGS.

Action is requisite to a state of existence; where there is no action, there is no life. Life as a force is the result of a combination of other forces, and without a correlative action of all the forces, it is not generated, or at least is not manifested.

We have stated in another chapter that life operates through organization, and is a physical force; also that mind operates through organization the same as life, and is also a physical force. Mind is, therefore, created by a combination of various forces the same as life. Now, as a greater number of forces are requisite to produce life than to produce light, or any of the single forces that combine and create life, so a greater number of forces are requisite to create mind. The same is true of the moral nature of man. A combination of faculties, each performing a certain function, creating a moral force, and each faculty requiring also a greater number of forces upon which the exercise of its function depends.

To bring this subject more fully before the mind of our readers, we copy a brief sketch from the author's work on "The Human Five Senses," page 7-9.

"It is a fact that life is a force, sustained and created by other forces, and is, therefore, an activity which can not exist independent of other things. Our surroundings, the objective world, the elements, light, heat, atmosphere, electricity, magnetism, etc., focalize, stimulate and sustain, or even create this activity which we call life. If it were possible to place a man far off into space, where the objective world could not act upon his senses, he would not live one moment—that is, this life activity would become conserved, or rendered latent. The effect would be the same, if there were nothing for the eye to see, the ear to hear; nothing to taste or smell, or come in contact with, as if the senses of the body were destroyed by disease or accident. So we exist simply because other things exist. It is not by bread alone that we live: it is by contact.

"The same is true of the mind. No one has ever originated a thought, for it is impossible to think of anything that has not, or never had, an existence. The objective world acts upon the various faculties of the mind, through the medium of the five senses of the body, and thus starts us to thinking. The internal organs of the body are acted upon in like manner,—through the same channels,—which starts them to work and perform their functions. The eye gives rise to thought in connection with what we see. We think of sound, and study its nature, in proportion as we are capable of being impressed by the different waves of sound, and thus we gain ideas. We feel by coming in contact with things that surround us, and the mind is thus stimulated into a state of activity. Through taste and smell, the mind becomes conscious of odors and flavors, and we think of them.

> In this manner all nature combines,
> To form, to create the human mind.

"It is evident, then, that the more perfect these organs, the greater will be our means of communication; and the more we see, hear, feel, taste, and smell, the greater will be our knowledge of things that surround us, and the better are we fitted for reflection, to contemplate, to philosophize, to reason, and finally, to understand the many mysteries that are now hid from us in darkness. So long, then, as the five senses are in harmony with our relations, we are growing intellectually and morally, and in every way are capable of an extensive experience, which is God and nature's own method of unfolding and maturing the human mind. Like the acorn that germinates and grows into the stately oak, under the genial influence of light, heat, moisture, atmosphere, and other immediate life-sustaining forces, so the mind unfolds each day, each moment, during the wakeful time of the being, by being variously acted upon by things, circumstances, and conditions from without."

Each separate faculty or propensity of the mind is so intricate that it requires years of study to correctly understand it,—how to cultivate it; what its true relation to other faculties are, and the relative function in the mind, all of which together aid in producing a moral character in men and women. Take, for example, the faculty of reason, and thousands of circumstances, agencies, forces, and conditions are required to stimulate and exercise its function. So any of the social faculties, or those of a selfish nature. For example, acquisitiveness, the faculty that gives man a desire to accumulate property,—and what a field for study!—love, hatred, conscientiousness, veneration, caution, and other faculties which distinguish men from brutes. Then consider those which have a closer relation to animal life, such as destructiveness, combativeness, and others, each of which is dependent upon a combination of many forces and conditions to call it into action. Each separate force or agency which enters into the whole, in producing and actuating a single faculty, requires a careful study, in order to understand properly the faculty as a whole. When we take this course in studying the mind, there is some probability of learning something about it. Now, a correlative operation of all these forces is requisite in order to produce a heathy action of the constitution of the mind, for it is through a combined effort of these forces, acting through each faculty respectively that mind is created, also a moral, intellectual, and social character. The highest of all these forces is

KNOWLEDGE.

The universe thus focalizes and creates this most powerful force, which is the ultimatum of all human experience, cultivation, and development of both the physical and mental constitution. It is this that makes man happy or miserable. It brings happiness to know the wrong, the false, and the imperfect in ourselves, also in our surroundings, for by having such knowledge we are impelled toward the right, the good, the perfect. Having knowledge of the truth, the beautiful, the good, we are made doubly happy, positively to know that we are in the right. True, knowledge teaches men of their depravity, their short-comings, their violations of the laws of God and nature, the wrongs committed toward their fellows, and defines strictly criminal actions, which, when men see their fallen condition, are miserable and unhappy so long as they know that such is the case.

Mankind never are absolutely happy, and happy only momentarily. Neither are they ever absolutely miserable and are only so for a short space of time. The mind naturally argues itself into a greater state of happiness, or a lesser degree of unhappiness and suffering. Men naturally flee from pain and sorrow. It is an innate principle that all mankind desire to be happy. The line of demarcation between the right and the wrong, the beautiful, and the good, and the evil, and imperfection of nature or the actions of man, is difficult to establish for all mankind. Each individual draws this line of division as they understand, and are enabled from their knowledge previously acquired as to the real and the true. These, then, are only relative virtues, and conditions, and each moment of existence establishes its own condition, state, or being, which makes mankind happy or unhappy as the nature of the actuating principles may decide.

To acquire knowledge, and attain a state of happiness is the primary motive-power of all human actions. This being the "chief end of man," we may consider the human family on a grand march, some in the front, some in the rear, and all on the road in search after the promised prize.

Those who follow horse-racing understand full well that the horse of good stock, the one best groomed, best trained, and longest in practice, will win the prize. So in this grand human march, those of good parentage, proper education, and every-day practice in the right direction will take the advance, and win the prize. All along the line of march toward human happiness are innumerable by-ways, cross-roads, which have greater or less attractions, and entrap those unaware of the evil results. Many of these alluring channels, that lead in the wrong direction are so intimately blended with the right path at first, that often years of toil are spent before the deception is discovered. These roads leading so many to destruction, so gradually diverge from the high road of happiness, that even the wise sometimes lose themselves, and spend half a lifetime in the wrong direction.

How needful it is, then, that every individual of this generation, who has acquired knowledge of these places of danger, should erect a finger-board, or build a wall, as it were, closing up these places which make attacks upon and ensnare those who are unprotected and easily persuaded. Then the next generation passing along this line of march to happiness will have much less opposition to contend with, and thus we may bring about a total abolition of crime.

Human beings are so differently organized, and so many different conditions exist, that in this grand march through life, we are variously acted upon, and are susceptible to the influences of so many diverging by-ways that we have scarcely a reasonable hope of ever so reforming the world that all mankind shall be enabled to obey the injunction that comes from on high, namely, "do unto all men as you wish them to do unto you." Yet we have such faith in God and nature, and in the application of correct principles and strict obedience to natural laws, that such an event seems possible. The various allurements, and enticing means which are so profusely distributed along the

STRAIGHT ROAD

to happiness, and which lead men from the path of virtue and distinction, may be divided into the corporeal, moral, intellectual and social. Those of the corporeal are mainly those which act upon the bodily senses; something good to eat; something pleasing to the eye, ear, and the feelings, which, if not rightly understood, cause great bodily disturbances. Many labor simply to please the sense of taste; others, that of sight—to dress well, to be fashionable, etc.; and so the bodily constitution may become diseased, and years of time be spent in trying to correct the difficulty.

Through the same channels, the moral nature is acted upon by what is called *moral action*. The principal allurement which leads men astray in their moral nature is wealth, and a man will stretch his conscience as far as he thinks it is policy—even as far as his neighbor. The farmer will open the best bag of wheat first to sell his grain. The merchant will show the bright side of his goods, and hide all defects. The capitalist will use his best argument to prove that money is worth fifteen and twenty per cent. So it is in nearly every channel of commercial intercourse between man and man; and thus men deal with each other as though all were rogues. In this manner men are gradually entrapped into selfish practices, which, of course, will grow much faster on some than on others. Those who have by nature a strong inclination to steal, soon become dissatisfied with the lie only, and now begin thieving. Before they get back into the right path again many commit a murder. Thus man becomes morally depraved, and little by little, unconsciously, is led into wrong habits. By and by, the disease becomes chronic and the cure will be very slow. Intellectual allurements which cause perversion and misunderstandings, are mainly those which we may call wit, sharp trading, and using every intellectual acquirement in a selfish way, to learn how to make the most money, and be well spoken of among men of commercial standing. Some robbers are very shrewd men. Most people study human nature, the laws of their country, and even the sciences, only to brighten their intellect, to appear brilliant in society, and to be well qualified to explore every avenue, and manipulate those with whom they deal in such a manner as to make the most money, and, if possible, to attain wealth and fame. This is a fruitful source, which gradually leads men to ruin. The perversion of man's intellectual powers, will eventually react and bring sorrow upon the individual.

Social means of every shade are continually drawing men and women into the pathway of error. Thousands are persuaded by the many promises and plausible arguments brought to bear upon those who have been more or less disappointed in life. Those who do not consider consequences before they act, are gradually entrapped and carried with the tide down the stream of vice. Those who have the social organs relatively large are constantly on the look-out for some golden opportunity when their most sanguine anticipations may be fully realized. Disappointments often end in crime, and a greater number of murders are perpetrated by reason of a perverted social nature than from any other one cause. Men rob and murder for money mainly, some may hold, but in nearly every instance the mainspring is traceable to a social disappointment of some kind,—not enough money to appear well in society, to attend theaters, the gambling hall, to buy the social glass or otherwise sustain themselves in satisfying the social appetite. Hence they often rush headlong into the various channels of vice and evil, thinking sometime to be happy, if not in one direction, in another, and so keep trying until after the meridian of life is passed; and if they do not end their life by suicide, otherwise die disgraced and broken-hearted, succumbing to the destroying forces of an unhappy life.

To recapitulate, briefly, we end the first part of this work, by reminding the reader of two prominent facts which we have honestly labored to establish in the previous chapters. The first, we remark, is a hereditary predisposition to crime, and the second an acquired disposition which gradually lead persons into criminal action, and we are justified in stating a third condition which we denominate accidental. We have conclusively shown that parental transmission has much to do with the bodily health, the moral, intellectual, and social qualities of the rising generation. Even in infancy, early traits of depravity are often observed, as well as good traits of character. In either case, the actions in after life are governed, to a great degree, by the peculiar constitutional "make up," both of the physical and mental. One will be susceptible to culture more than the other; one will be easily impressed in the direction of right, and the other in the direction of wrong.

Acquired conditions are mainly those brought about by education, habits, surroundings, associations and necessity, gradually establishing a disposition and inclination which become finally the controlling power, and lead the being to a state of happiness, or sorrow and suffering, according as the various educational means of development are good or evil in their nature. Accidental crimes are seemingly unavoidable, yet when we come closely to reason on the subject we shall find that nearly all such occurrences are easily avoided. We are safe in stating that nearly every accidental crime is the result of neglect, want of forethought, and a lack of employment of proper means to prevent such accidents. This may be through malice, ignorance and indolence.

There are crimes that can scarcely be named or classified. We will state a case, and then allow the reader to judge as to what sort of a crime he considers the following: In the winter of 1864, we followed a lady, of the upper class, on Third street, Cincinnati, mainly to learn where she was going, where she lived, and who she was, all only to gain an idea of course, for we were almost moved to tears in beholding her little six-year-old, trotting along by her side, going to prayer-meeting, with its little legs almost entirely exposed; its panties did not reach quite over the knees—the cotton stockings too short, so that every step it took the knees and the greatest portion of the thighs became entirely exposed. The meantime the mother was muffled up in fur, and a large cloak covering her extremities, and in every way well protected from the cold. With the Bible and hymn book under her arm, she entered the house of prayer, and for one long hour and a half, she forced her dear little pet to sit on a bench, with its little legs hanging unsupported, until at length it was relieved of its suffering, only to freeze on its way home, with an occasional murmur of "Ma! I'm so cold," shivering in the storm. We thought it was high time that somebody should pray.

We have thus far in our work presented many important points for consideration and profound thought, on the part of our readers. We have given our idea of the origin and immediate stimulating cause of crime, and we believe if men would rise to the highest enjoyment of

HUMAN HAPPINESS,

an effort must be made to learn the sciences, and not only have this knowledge vested in the minds of a "favored few," but within the reach of the masses. Harmonious and correlative operation of all the faculties must be developed in every individual, in order to bring about harmony in society, harmony in the family, and in the government.

Modern science recognizes one fact, that the law of the globe, and of all things that dwell upon it, is the law of progress. Man a natural being, created, lives and moves in nature, so is he affected by the same law, hence we may expect to unfold and to go on unfolding. This great primal law is as true to-day as it was at the beginning of creation, and has been operating ever since, raising the world higher and higher, and doubtless will continue to carry the world onward and upward. As intelligent human beings, however, we may assist nature much in her effort to produce the perfect man and woman, by obeying the law of physiology. Wherever this law is strictly obeyed, the offspring invariably proves to be healthy and harmonious. It is admitted by our most scientific physiologists, that the child inherits the peculiar character and constitution of its parents, and if the education is to develop that peculiarity, it will continue and be the governing principle through life. Now, it would follow, that the wisest course on the part of those who intend to unite in marriage, would be to give this matter a thought, and endeavor to understand the law that governs perfect organization. If inclined to disease, consult and obey every principle of hygiene, give yourself a thorough overhauling, and if possible consult a scientific physiologist. These are vital principles, and if man will give this matter as much attention as he does in growing horses, sheep, cattle and pork, he will rise in the scale of human perfection, the same as the animal kingdom, for by proper selection steadily, from year to year, and from generation to generation, the beasts of the field rise and become more perfect. Rev. H. W. Beecher says, "the human race never will be carried up until man learns that there is a law, by obedience to which, generations shall transmit transmissible excellences."

This I believe to be true in a physical as well as a spiritual sense. Behold the children of the crude, undeveloped parent, and no wonder that rigid legislation is still necessary to govern men and nations, and from the present indications the next generation will be but slightly improved, hence, the most noble work that we can engage in is to teach and learn and try to understand nature's laws in this respect. From observation and scientific research we gather that nothing is surer than this: that a tendency in any given direction is transmissible by education. "A tendency to good or evil is transmitted and becomes a fixed quality if it be educated." So writes a modern scientist, and as facts are difficult to overcome, we had better at once yield the question, and go to work and better the condition of things in this respect. Upon the principle that a certain muscle may be developed by giving it the proper exercise, so may we develop any faculty of the brain, or inner man, by giving it proper exercise or rest. If a man has the organ of combativeness very large it may soon be subdued by giving it rest, and exercising the opposite principle, that of love and peace, and soon that individual will be a law unto himself, and the next generation will have less of combativeness. The same is true of every department of human life. Let the world practice the opposite to evil and man will soon become constitutionally redeemed and be a law unto himself. This if ever accomplished will have to be done on scientific principles. Nature is ever true to right action, and the more we are stimulated to act in harmony with nature the faster is our progress, hence, the necessity of teaching, preaching, lecturing, reading, writing, debating, thinking, reasoning, criticising and continuing our research until we understand more and more of the divine laws, and thereby grow more and more beautiful, more good, healthy and happy; and instead of the sins of the parents being "visited upon the children of the third and fourth generations," the good deeds and right actions are transmitted to future generations, that the coming man may have the pleasure of journeying along the path of life, decorated with flowers and evergreens, the noble and the beautiful.

PART II.

CAPITAL PUNISHMENT.

CHAPTER IX.

HISTORY AND PROGRESS OF CAPITAL PUNISHMENT.

Since the earliest record of human history, capital punishment has been considered by nearly all nations, as a just punishment for capital crime. The practice of punishing crime by death may be traced far back in human history, even to savage nations where it had its origin. According to Agassiz, Darwin, Hugh Miller, Humbolt, Spencer, and other scientists and naturalists, capital punishment is traceable only to heathen origin. It seems to be an established fact that this mode of punishment was not first suggested by any enlightened person or nation. It is a practice merely continued as a relic of the benighted ages, the same as some forms of worship. It cannot be successfully established that it was ever a command of God. The only command that was ever given on the subject, was, "Thou shalt not kill." We make this statement without fear of contradiction, from the fact that heathens punished by death before ever the Mosaic law was established. Heathens inflicted the death penalty in the most brutal manner, and for mere trivial offences. The Pagan nations also inflicted death in a very barbarous manner. The first mode was by stoning the criminals to death. The next was by burning them to death; first by tying their hands and feet, and then throwing them into a fire prepared for the occasion. At the time and reign of Nebuchadnezzar an oven was built and kept heated, to a proper heat, and constantly in readiness for the purpose of destroying the life of condemned criminals. We read that three young men Shadrach, Meshach, and Abednego, were condemned to death by this brutal king; and the oven was ordered to be heated seven times hotter than for ordinary executions. At another period wild beasts were kept in dens for the express purpose of devouring condemned criminals. At a later period criminals were nailed on a cross and tortured unto death. During this period of the history of capital punishment Christ was executed on a cross, as was then the mode of inflicting the death penalty. Afterward death was inflicted by beheading the criminal, John was the first who was beheaded by authority of the rulers. During the progress of the early ages of what are termed Pagan nations, or of the children of Israel, the death penalty was often inflicted in the most inhuman manner and for mere trivial offences. Adultery was then punishable by being stoned to death, and at other times the most noted criminals were dragged by the heels through the streets in order to inflict the greatest possible torture. This was often done in the belief that God had pleasure in criminals being punished in the most brutal manner. Gentile nations punished their criminals still more inhumanly than did the "children of God." Prisoners of war were also put to death in the most torturous manner, and the rulers and people often took great delight in torturing their criminals unto death.

Since the Christian era, various modes of inflicting the death penalty have been practiced. Different kings and rulers had different modes of inflicting death, according as they saw proper. Beheading has been the common mode and is now practiced in the old country. At different periods, however, criminals were put upon the rack and bones broken, one after another, until dead. Others were required to drink the poison hemlock, or confined in a dark dungeon and starved to death.

During the remote ages, and even down to the present day, men have made it a study how to put criminals to death in the most expeditious manner, rather than how to reform mankind and make them better. During the present era it has been the object to inflict the death penalty in the easiest and most painless manner, which is, no doubt, a premonitory sign of abolishing it entirely. In this country the death penalty is inflicted by hanging, and which no doubt is the most painless manner of killing men, except by chloroform, or by some subtle, narcotic poison. But a few years ago criminals were executed in public; now it is done almost everywhere in private, which is another sign of the incoming reform. The one great truth which we derive from the history and progress of capital punishment is, that the manner of inflicting the death penalty has been, from time to time, greatly modified. The death penalty is now inflicted by civilized nations for murder and treason only, and in a less shocking manner than even a century ago. Less than fifty years ago, men were lashed for crime,—sometimes until the flesh was cleft from their backs. Men were caused to run the gauntlet, were placed in stocks, and suffered many other most inhuman punishments, which often were worse than death itself; as, for instance, having the eyes put out, or the body mained in some other manner, disabling the criminal for life. This was often done to maintain national power or pride, and when no real crime was committed. The man who constructed that great wonder, the clock at Strasburg, had his eyes put out by order of the rulers, lest he should go into other countries and construct a similar clock, or, perhaps, a greatly improved one, and thus wound the national pride. Notwithstanding the severity of the punishment inflicted for crime, during the earlier periods of human history, crime was then more prevalent than now; for as nations became more enlightened, crime grew proportionately less as well as the severe modes of punishment. It is an admitted truth by those who have given the matter any thought, that it is not the severity of punishment that prevents crime, but the *absolute certainty*. The proper education of the moral, intellectual, and social nature of man is the surest means of mitigating vice. The more intelligent a nation, the less the number of crimes committed, and the greater the happiness of the nation, as compared with those possessing a lesser degree of intellectual attainments.

As we review the scale of human history, and note the progressive development of man's capabilities, we find a decrease of intelligence and a greater discord of the moral and social nature, until we at last reach the heathen, where those virtues which distinguish man from the brute are yet in a state of chaos. Crime and the mode of inflicting penalties therefor run parallel with the progressive or retrograding epoch of human intelligence. Crime in our day is gradually diminishing, and the inhuman modes of inflicting punishment are greatly modified. Reasoning from the past, the time is not far in the future when capital punishment will take its place among the things that were.

If we are thus progressing, it may further be argued that the time will come when crime will no more be known among men, and, consequently, *no kind of punishment* necessary. What a glorious habitation this earth will then be!—when men and women will live, as it were, "a law unto themselves." This, it may be affirmed, is an impossibility, from the very nature of man, who is naturally inclined to evil. It will be admitted that individuals have attained to such a degree of perfection that they are enabled to live lives of beauty and goodness. Now, if it is possible for individuals to attain the ultimate design of human life, which is happiness, then it is possible for all nations and races of men on earth to attain that state. Though this may require thousands of ages, yet we believe the ultimatum of human life originally designed by our Creator, is a state of happiness. If this reasoning is not correct, every effort to harmonize and reform men is a failure, God himself would be a failure; creation would be a failure. But this is not possible, for the tendency evidently is, and has been since the advent of man on earth, to rise out of chaos. Everything in nature is more perfect; the atmosphere is more pure; the flowers are more beautiful; vegetation is more healthful; animals are more refined in their nature, and more easily domesticated; birds are more happy in their songs,—than six thousand years ago. Of course, man is keeping pace in the development of his powers; in his ability to obey natural laws; in his comprehension of the mysteries of nature,—even in understanding the wonderful operations of his own mind.

But it may be again affirmed that, so long as men exist, crime will exist, and all the difference there will be, is that he will be more capable of discerning criminal action, and the line between virtue and wrong-doing will be more marked, so that this work of choosing between right and wrong, which is now infinite, will be simplified; that the two principles of right and wrong are only relative conditions, which have existed from all time, and will continue to exist throughout all eternity; that the grosser mind is only capable of discerning crimes of the crudest and lowest forms, while the enlightened mind is capable of discerning crimes which to the unenlightened mind seem no crime at all, and so on *ad infinitum*. However this may be decided by our readers, we do not believe that there is a constant strife between

CHAOS AND ORDER.

Order, having once taken the place of chaos, is absolute in its power. Since the planetary system began to move in regular order it has never deviated from its natural course. Everything in nature moves in accordance with the law, governing, in the very nature of things, the universe and all within it, by absolute power.

Actions of men are absolute in themselves, though they may only have a relative existence. We can not recall an act, a word spoken, a criminal or good deed, restore life, or change the natural order of things, any sooner than we can

> "Call back the wind,
> Or undo what time has done;
> Beckon music from a broken lute;
> Renew the redness of a last year's rose;
> Or dig the sunken sunset from the deep."

Actions, then, are absolute, and we cannot recall them. All that lies in our power is to prevent the recurrence of similar deeds or actions. God and nature have planted in and around us means by which we may overcome evil tendencies, and avoid a repetition of wrong-doing. The very fact that a man can outgrow evil inclinations, and make reparation to injured persons, proves our position—that any person may control discord, and become organically and constitutionally harmonious within himself, and at length be naturally inclined to live in harmony with " Law and Order." The history of capital punishment, as before remarked, favors our views, as to its gradually becoming extinct. A more rational and efficient mode of punishing criminals will soon take its place in this country, as well as in other of the more enlightened nations. As soon as the masses can be made to believe that an " ounce of prevention is better than a pound of cure," and that the only sure means of averting evil is a well-balanced and universal education of the rising generation, we predict that it will not be necessary to put human beings to death as a punishment for crime.

CHAPTER X.

ON PUNISHMENT OF CRIME IN GENERAL.

It is evident, from experience and daily observation, "that the way of the transgressor is hard." The laws of nature hold a firm grasp on those who oppose her teachings. From these laws men have learned to establish certain rules or laws, by which to govern their own actions. As everything in the universe is governed by law, man has a right to rule and govern even to hold accountable those who transgress the laws of right in their dealings and intercourse with each other. The object of man, then, is to enact laws which agree in spirit with the laws of God and nature, to which they will approximate, in proportion as he understands the latter.

The laws of man, as well as the laws of God and nature, have for their primary object the correction and reformation of those who are transgressing the laws of right, and also to keep those in the right who are right. Laws exist from necessity, and nothing in the grand universe can exist without law and order. As man progressed in intelligence, he learned more and more, of the governing princlple of things and men; and since man first began his career on this globe, the line between right and wrong has been drawn closer and finer. Hence the laws of necessity have changed from time to time, and even now men enact laws according as they understand the right and the wrong. Governments have progressed from anarchy to monarchy, and from monarchy to republic,—in this country,—and may, in time, become democratic. This enables men now to enact laws by a majority vote, by which means an average expression of the intelligence of the people of any community or state may be ascertained. In this manner we can also obtain an average expression of the conscience of men, and the most rational course to be pursued in punishing crime. In this manner also laws are established by men to govern their own actions in general intercourse one with another.

We have stated that there is nothing that is not under law, from the little atom of dust under our feet up to man. Without law and order, the universe would become a chaos, time would cease, and a wreck of worlds, and mingling of the human soul with the general mass, would be the end. Law is simply a rule of action. Now, if action according to rule is law, then any action contrary to rule is a violation of law, and is, therefore, approximating to chaos, discord, and will, like the "crash of worlds," become a wreck. Therefore, there can be no law without a penalty. There can not be a transgression of law without a corresponding penalty following such transgression as a natural consequence.

Withhold one of the life-giving elements—as light, for instance—from the plant, by placing it in a dungeon, and it will wither and die. Place a man in a dungeon, and *he* will wither and die; he will be of no consequence to himself, to man, nor to heaven. The consequences of any violation of law we denominate, in accordance with a popular idea, "penalty," which every general or special law defines, prescribes, and deals out, according as the nature of the crime may indicate. If the law says, Thou shalt not steal, then the law must also define to what extent you shall not commit such a crime; or, when found guilty, prescribe the punishment, in order that justice, which is the end of the law, is not defeated. We see, then, that all human beings are subject to punishment, either when acting in violation of nature's laws or the laws of man.

Whether it can be said that nature punishes or only causes suffering, is a question. To punish, implies to deal out a certain amount of torture. This is not what we wish to have understood when we use the word punishment. (See Part Third of this book.)

Nature is always true to herself, sure in her workings, and never fails to correct her own wrongs; hence, no one who violates any of her laws can ever escape the penalty—suffering. "Though a man flee to the ends of the earth, *nature* will be there to require obedience, until the last farthing is paid." So long as men are, by creation and education, inclined to do wrong, and so long as men are guilty of crime so long will it be necessary to govern men's actions by legal enactment, the object of which is plainly to point out the right and define the wrong. It is evident, from the knowledge we have of nature's laws, that man is required to live in harmony with, first for his own happiness, and secondly for the happiness of others. For the same reason, men have established law and order,—first to restrain one's unnatural inclinations, and to bring happiness to the individual; secondly, to the whole human family.

The end of law is justice,—justice to the individual—justice to the whole human family. Nature guards her children against further violence by producing pain. Bodily violation of law produces bodily pain. Moral transgression produces moral pain; and were it not so, the destroying forces would continue their destructive process, until the body or the soul is destroyed. Hence, pain is an affliction just and right. This, however, nature does not inflict from any malice or revenge; it is an act of mercy, the object being mainly to reform and make better those who are so unfortunate as to come in contact with, or act in opposition to, the harmony of God and nature.

The primary object, then, of all law and punishment is and should be, first, reformation of the criminal; second, compensation to the injured; and, thirdly, prevention of further crime.

We remark here briefly, that as nature restrains men in their criminal course, by setting up an opposite force,—pain,—so are men justifiable in restraining those who are infringing on others' rights, by apprehending, trying by a court of justice, and, if found guilty, punishing them according as the nature of the crime may indicate. On this point we all agree, and even favor a strict enforcement of law in every instance of criminal action. But we proceed now to consider the

DIFFERENT MODES

of punishment or means of correction. As we have stated, the first object of law and order, and the subjection of persons to penal service, is to reform, if possible, those guilty of trangression. We differ widely from those who incline to the present mode of reforming our criminals. This, we hold, can not be done by inflicting a greater injury, on the principle of *contraria contraribus curantur;* that, by producing an artificial disease, we can cure the natural one. Neither can this be done on the homeopathic principle of *similia similibus curantur:* that treatment similar to that which produces a disease will cure it. In surgical practice, if we would heal a wound, we must not produce greater irritation, by applying friction, on the principle of "an eye for an eye, or a tooth for a tooth." In all those conditions, sanitive and restorative means are indicated. We therefore, can not admit that to cure the criminal of his malady, it is best to apply the lash, or in any manner to inflict corporal torture; but only to restrain and subdue the evil—disease—and stimulate the healing powers, by which means we accomplish the primary object, namely, curing our patient of his criminal inclinations. By this we mean to be understood that a person convicted of crime, sentenced to imprisonment for a given number of years, condemned to hard labor, and sparingly fed, can not so be reformed. Some provision must be made by which the various faculties of the mind can also be cultivated. We would have a prison where the convict is subjected to eight hours' hard labor, eight hours for intellectual, moral, and social instruction, thus improving his mental condition, and eight hours for rest and sleep. (See Chapter VI).

Simply to condemn a person to penal servitude for a given length of time and make no effort to reform him, is an outrage, not only to the criminal, but society in general. The criminal, after serving his time in prison, is allowed again to mingle in society, and if there is any difference in his nature he is less capable of self government than before, and is liable at any time to commit a greater crime than before. But recently a murder is reported as having taken place in the state of New York perpetrated by a returned convict, who served seven years for stealing a small sum of money. On his return home, he killed the man who had caused him to be convicted. Now, if this convict had been properly treated, in those seven years, such a high tone of moral duty might have been acquired that he would have forgiven rather than murdered this man.

In this city hundreds of criminals are sent to the work house called the "Bridewell,"—some for a few weeks and some for a few months,—then liberated again, only to commit a greater crime. The maltreatment they receive in these prisons feeds the faculty of revenge, and the punishment, in our judgement, is not reformatory. Hundreds of vagabonds, thieves, gamblers, and "black-legs," are convicted, and those who cannot pay a fine are sent to the prisons, which, in turn, send out the poor victims again to mingle in society, without having been taught a single lesson to aid them in overcoming their evil natures, and be better men and women. They have nothing to show that they are reformed, hence they are discarded from society; and though they may have formed resolutions never to do a wrong deed again, nevertheless, by and by, when they find no one to sympathize with them or assist them in avoiding the seducing influence of their surroundings, and find that the "spirit is willing, but the flesh is weak," in a short time they are entrapped again in crime. We hold that this is an outrage practiced both upon the criminal and society. All persons who are convicted of crime, where imprisonment is deemed necessary, should be sent to a

REFORMATORY PRISON,

where they should be required to remain until they can be sufficiently reformed to enable them to live at least an average moral life.

To acquire such abilities, time is necessary, also the best known means, to so regenerate both body and mind that it will be safe to give the criminal his liberty. For our idea of the kind and form of prison we recommend, we refer our readers to Chapter XI. Here the convict should be required to labor in the pursuit of some trade or vocation, where his labor will produce enough to pay all expenses, and whatever amount he earns more than will be necessary to defray expenses, should be applied, at least, partially, to

COMPENSATE the party whom the criminal injured at the time of committing the crime. Eight hours of well-regulated labor will produce enough profit to pay all expense of conducting the business of the prison, and of the educational department, and reap a daily profit which should go to the injured party until full restoration is made; after which, the amount due should be at the prisoner's disposal, to be paid to his wife, children, brother, sister, parents, or friends, as he may direct.

There is no moral right why a state should appropriate the earnings of a convict further than to pay all expenses. I am not aware that all states give a lease to some one for a stipulated time and sum of money, but I know that the state of Indiana, some years since, leased the Jeffersonville prison for a number of thousand dollars to a gentleman who, of course, would make all he could out of it, and send home, in as good a condition as possible, those who survived his treatment; and we can imagine the kind of reformation they would receive.

Compensation is our second claim, which should be one of the prominent features in punishing criminals. This should be required in all instances, and under all circumstances. If a man sells his little home, receives his pay for it, and in the night he is robbed of this money, he has lost all he has in the world. Is it not right that this money be refunded to the man by the robber? If the robber is not speedily arrested, he will, most probably, have spent nearly all of the money, and the injured man will be required to wait until the robber can earn it in prison. But if the state appropriates all the profits, or makes no effort to accumulate profits, by good business regulations of the states' prison, then, of course, it will be difficult for the prisoner to earn enough to pay back the injured party,—unless he has property, when it should be held in the same manner as for debt.

I think many will see as I do on another point. An injured party who has lost money by theft should be compensated. If it is impossible for the prisoner to make restitution; an appropriation from the general county funds should be made. We cannot see why this is not good reasoning, for the injured party may have been a good citizen for a lifetime, and paid taxes, and expected the protection which every citizen has a right to claim at the hands of the law. Even if the prisoner is not competent to make full restoration, the injured party should not be entirely defrauded.

It is plain to all that punishment should be reformatory, and compensatory; and this brings us to our third question, namely:

PREVENTION OF CRIME

How to prevent crime has been a study for ages, and is even now a subject of serious thought. Notwithstanding the many aspiring church-steeples, schools, benevolent associations, and reformatory institutions, which ornament our comparatively civilized nation, still our newspapers chronicle each day so many murders, robberies, mobs, insurrections, and crimes of all shades and character that men become almost discouraged, and often feel like abandoning the work.

Thus far laws have been severe enough, and, in many instances, too severe, and hence cannot be enforced by any jury. The most prominent reason that we give as to why law and the punishment are incompetent to counteract the criminal inclinations of men, is first, the uncertainty of enforcement of the punishment, and second, the idea of bodily torture simply as a means of reformation and reparation of the injury done by the criminal. The uncertainty of punishment of our criminals at the present age is so prevalent, that it is almost useless to have any one arrested. The prosecuting attorney is sworn to enforce the law, and vindicate justice in every instance of violations of law. The criminal hires the best talent to defend his case in law, which he has the money to pay for. This attorney is also sworn, only, however, to do his duty by his client. These two antagonistic powers meet in courts of justice, and each endeavors to defeat the other, and the one that can present the finest argument wins the trial. Each lawyer uses his best powers to appear "sharp," and thereby hopes to gain reputation. We will illustrate how criminals are tried and punished,—how the public is protected, and justice vindicated. It is like two gamblers at a game of chance. The one who has had the longest practice and is also naturally "sharp," knows best how to manipulate the game, and he comes out ahead. Right or wrong, he is ahead, and wins a name among gamblers as a "good fellow"; so our courts of justice are but little else than a game of chance, and the sharpest lawyer comes out ahead. Here men are taught to lie and those who are not very sharp naturally are "brightened up," and go out having learned, as they say, "a thing or two," and the next time, they know better how to "pull the wires." This is called justice. This is called prevention of crime. The uncertainty of punishment is one reason, then, why "law and order" is not better observed. And punishment, being mainly of a corporeal nature, does not reform the criminal, and hence is not preventive. Punishment, in many instances, is too severe, and hence many are allowed to go "scott free." It is an established fact that Stokes killed Fisk, and can justly, according to law, be found guilty of murder in the first degree, the only punishment of which, is *death*. Men hesitate to vote to kill their fellow man, and the law is not enforced. This is neither reformatory, compensatory, or preventive; neither justice to the criminal nor to the public. According to our idea of punishment, this case would have long since been disposed of; the criminal would now be doing something for himself and others, and thousands of dollars would have been saved to the public. (See Chapters XI and XII.)

To prevent crime, the following suggestion, if strictly observed, will, we think, accomplish more in one year than has hitherto been done in twenty years; and if persevered in for a century or two, will almost entirely eradicate crime from among us:

First, *Compulsatory Education*, which is sufficiently elucidated under that head, and the reader is therefore referred to that chapter. Second, *rigid legislation*, and the absolute certainty of punishment; the establishment of reformatory prisons; compensatory measures to be required of every criminal; and, thirdly, the abolition of all extreme, unnatural punishment, which includes all corporeal means of correction, the setting aside of which will enable our courts of justice to enforce the law, and thus make punishment certain without violating their own conscience.

CHAPTER XI.

STATE'S PRISONS AS A MEANS OF REFORMATION. WHAT WE UNDERSTAND BY A REFORMATORY PRISON. HOW IT SHOULD BE CONSTRUCTED, AND HOW CONDUCTED.

We believe in rigid legislation for all crimes and vices. There should be no possible escape from justice; justice to the individual as well as to the public.

As soon as a person is convicted of crime, all right to liberty on the part of the criminal should be considered as forfeited, and should not be regained by a mere money fine or by any executive pardoning power.

To punish merely by a money fine—only so far as compensatory means are necessary to repair injuries done by the criminal, etc.,—makes the perpetrator only more angry and revengeful. It does not subdue the evil nature. We can hear every day such persons declare by everything great and good that they will see the day when they shall be even, etc., seeking how to revenge themselves on those, who, perhaps, have honestly testified in the case.

We claim that any crime committed as the result of depravity is too serious a matter for any one to be permitted to buy their liberty by simply paying a certain sum of money into the county treasury, and at the same time make no restoration to the injured party, such as is due every good citizen who has suffered at the hands of a debased criminal. It is not reasonable that a mere forfeiture of property should cure the criminal of his moral, intellectual, social, or bodily depravity. It would seem equivalent to buying salvation for a certain sum of money, and thus gaining a seat in Heaven.

Liberty, therefore, can only be restored to a criminal after he has made full reparation, to the best of his ability, and shown visible evidence of thorough regeneration.

Nature never pardons offenders against her laws. The moral statute book which is accepted as a guide by Christians, also teaches, beyond a doubt, that all who would be saved must make use of the means which God and nature have implanted in and around man. Science teaches that a man must grow to be good or bad. If he is to become pure and holy, he must strive for it daily, and " usure with his talents," and thus gradually overcome evil inclinations.

From this standpoint of reasoning we claim that any county, state, or government, has a right to enforce by legal action compulsatory reformation, especially in those who have proven an incompetency to self-government.

If a man persistently commits a crime, by reason of a depraved nature, we cannot see how he can receive consistently a pardon and be allowed his liberty. We are safe in saying that this would only stimulate his evil propensities, and he would be liable at any time to perpetrate a greater crime than before. For one resting under the ban of the law to regain liberty visible and indisputable evidence should be required, to show that he or she has been thoroughly restored to a better condition—has acquired the moral and social qualities common to those who mingle in good society.

To accomplish this end,—a general reformation among our criminals,—which is the primary object of law and penal service, as well as to prevent crime, we ask permission to here introduce our idea of what we call a

REFORMATORY PRISON.

In the first place, a prison should have various departments, where every convict can be furnished with daily employment.

Employment is necessary for healthy reformation in prison, as well as out of it. To labor for a subsistence is one of the first laws of nature.

In this respect, our prisons are sufficiently arranged, even now, but we can not admit that a violation of the first law of physiology, by imposing too much labor and utterly neglecting the cultivation of the mind, can be termed reformatory.

Convicts are now required to labor for the state ten to twelve hours daily, which is too much—in prison, as well as out of it. Those who are competent workmen are permitted to make extra time, which is credited on the prison books, and either paid for in money, or by an abreviation of their term of imprisonment. Not long ago, we met a convict who had served six years in prison, at Michigan City,

Indiana, whose crime was committed strictly under force of necessity. His family was greatly in need of subsistence, and two men of short acquaintance with him persuaded him to assist them in robbing a man whom they knew to have money about his person, agreeing to divide with him the proceeds of the transaction. He consented, and in a dark place, on his way home these three men robbed their victim of one hundred and thirty dollars. The other two, who had the money, escaped, and this man was arrested and served six years in the State's Prison, at hard labor, simply for being accessory to the crime. This, of course, made matters worse, and his family suffered greatly for want of support. He was a cooper by trade, and a good workman; so he requested a daily task, with a view that, if he worked well, he could make extra wages, and be enabled to send money to his family for their support. This was granted, but it required all of ten hours to complete his task, although he was an extra good workman. After completing his daily task, he worked three and four hours each day, the proceeds of which he sent home to his family. He said that he repeatedly begged the officer to lessen his task, so that he could do better by his family, but was not granted his request.

After three years, his health failed, and he was no longer enabled to make extra time, and how his family fared after that time he said, "God only knows." This man's soul was overflowing with revenge. He felt bitter, and swore that before he died he should have revenge of those who injured him.

This case is a fair specimen of the unregenerated condition of returned convicts generally; not very well qualified to take their place in good society.

The following is the statement of a New York correspondent, copied from the Chicago *Tribune*. It shows how little sympathy criminals get, and how little attention is given to reform them, or to do justice to the public:

> "The investigation into the condition of the Tombs Prison and Blackwell's Island, by one of the morning papers, shows that criminal justice here is administered in the most reckless and unjust manner. The prison discipline and management at Blackwell's Island are wanting in influences calculated to inspire any encouragement for the reform in the inmates. Police justices are constantly committing prisoners in disregard of facts. It is a common thing at the Tombs to have cases disposed of at the rate of one a minute."

Eight hours of hard labor is enough for health, in prison or elsewhere, and if more is exacted, as a rule, the body suffers and becomes diseased. We have shown elsewhere in this volume that bodily perfection is a requisite condition of mental improvement.

After the day's work, in nearly all prisons, the rule practiced is to lock the convict up in his cell until the next morning, when he is required to repeat his daily task. No conversation is allowed in prison among the convicts. Nearly all state's prisons have a library; but none are required to read or study. They can do so if they choose. This should be made compulsatory. Occasionally they have preaching on the Sabbath, but not often. Now, we hold it to be a scientific truth that a prisoner condemned for crime has as much moral right to the exercise of all of his mental faculties as those who are not prisoners.

There should be departments in every prison where all convicts should be required to receive mental training daily. After setting apart eight hours for labor; eight hours for rest and mental recreation, out of which three hours will be necessary for mealtimes, and one hour, on the whole, in taking a bath and giving attention to the toilet,—which is necessary to keep healthy,—there yet remain four hours, during which each convict should attend school. A place could be arranged like one of our school halls, where they may be taught, at least in all of the common branches of education, dividing them up into classes according to the different degree of intellectual attainments; each convict to learn and recite his lesson the same as our children in schools, so as to make education practical.

It is not necessary to introduce the Bible here as a lawful text-book; but the exercises should be opened and closed by music, singing, and prayer, in which each convict be required to join. This, we hold, is necessary, from a scientific point of view,

PROF. TYNDAL

notwithstanding; for we know that music and singing have a charming effect on not only men but animals. Without music the lion and tiger could not be controlled at all by man. It operates on ideality, and sublimity. In a word, it causes men to forget the "ups and downs" of life, and relaxes the grosser nature. If things heavenly are allowed to assert their claims, though only for the time being, they have a harmonizing effect. So with prayer; it has a harmonizing effect, and though it acts on a different set of faculties, still it is a potent means to subdue the gross and conflicting nature of man. The simple act of bowing in humiliation is prayer, and a good process, by which convicts may be much benefited. to change from an audible prayer, by the sound of the "gavel," call every one on their knees, requesting ten minutes silent prayer by all, while at the same time a bell or large triangle is tolled silently, as it were, at "low twelve," so that the bell seems at a far distance; at the same time darken the room to near twilight. At the end of ten minutes a single sound of the "gavel," and all be required to say "Amen," aloud.

This, we believe, has a greater harmonizing effect than an audible prayer by some one presiding. Some such exercises should be had at the beginning and closing of every evening's instruction of the poor criminal.

We ask permission here to give our views on the subject of prayer, which we believe to be scientifically true. Prayer, like music, has a harmonizing effect on the one who prays, and on no one else. Harmony is healthful, and the first object of nature; therefore, any process which produces harmony, where discord previously existed, is good and useful. We do not believe that prayer to God will ever change his general course, or induce him to act by special decree, even to pardon the criminal of his sins,—without strict obedience to "His laws fixt fast in Fate." How, then, is prayer answered? Simply by the process of humiliation; it has a harmonizing effect, subduing the grosser feelings, and in this respect those who are in need of prayer are blessed, and made happier and better. You will observe that the man in business who prays much, is always the most successful, other things being equal; for the greater the harmony in one's disposition, the better qualified is he for the duties of life. On this principle, Prof. Tyndal would find himself defeated in his proposed "prayer test;" for any thing that has a harmonizing effect, indulged in at proper intervals and proper times, is good even for the sick. This every well informed physician must admit to be correct reasoning. Music and prayer, then, should constitute part of the mental exercise, not only on the Sabbath, but every day, during the four hours of school exercise, which we propose. All persons, including convicts, will be much more refreshed bodily, after the eight hours' hard labor, than if no such exercise is had. For each evening in the week have different exercises. At least one night in the week some one should be invited, free of charge, to lecture on some subject relating to human science. If these lecturers come from abroad, the traveling expenses should be paid. No creed, sect, or religion in particular should be required as a qualification of any who give instruction to convicts.

Woman should particularly be allowed to exercise her power in these places, as teacher, lecturer, etc. The reason why woman should be invited and hired for these places, and to bring her influence to bear on the prisoners, requires no explanation.

Different lyceums should be organized, to meet in

different halls, according to the the degree of depravity or intellectuality of the prisoners, where subjects of importance should be allowed to be debated by the convicts, thus drawing their attention away from their fallen condition, that they may, by and by, arise from their groveling nature and aspire to sublime contemplation. One evening, at least, in the week should be set apart for some innocent amusement,—amusement, however, which always has a moral underlying it.

Here we must make a greater effort to moral culture than with the child. The child requires a greater variety of education; but here everything should have a moral to it. The faculties of reason and conscience should by all means be well instructed, and all unruly faculties subdued, and induced to rest, and by this means bring into a greater activity a higher order of faculties. An extra suit of clothing should be provided for Sunday, and all underclothing be changed twice a week, and, if possible, a clean night-shirt be worn, as all workingmen should do for health.

Hygienic rules should be as strictly enforced in prison as they are in our insane asylums. Water is cheap, and every state's prison should be well supplied with bath rooms, and daily bathing be required. Bath rooms should be supplied with hot and cold water. Hot water can be furnished by the same fire that supplies steam-power to the shops, etc.

The cells, or sleeping apartments, should all front south, so that the sun can shine into them, and a large yard or grounds be provided, where, at a given hour, prisoners should be allowed to exercise in the open air and sun-light.

Do this, and men will work better during the eight hours, be much easier reformed and controlled, and instead of coming home vagabonds, they will return respectable men and women, having truly been benefited by the punishment of the law.

Wherever we have failed in our suggestions, or failed to mention all necessary departments belonging to a truly reformatory prison, we hope others better qualified than we may complete the plan. We would, however, suggest a separate prison for

MURDERERS.

This, of course, our readers will say, " is not necessary,—inasmuch as we hang most of our murderers." But we find that only one out of fifty murderers is ever hanged. Why this is so will be the subject of another chapter. While we shall argue that capital punishment is wrong and inhuman, we shall also show that solitary confinement in a dungeon is also wrong, and worse than hanging. Hence, we shall require a prison for the safe keeping of such as are so far depraved as to kill one of their fellow beings. This kind of a prison should be built doubly strong, and arranged so as to give each a separate apartment, and provide employment daily by which expenses can be defrayed. It should be conducted about the same as the prison for minor offences, although a more rigid government should be had, from the fact that a murderer is evidently more depraved than one who simply has stolen. Again, the educational department may be made optional. We believe in the imprisonment for life, where a man takes the life of another; and no pardoning power, save that of the jury and community who have found him guilty of murder, may, when circumstances demand it, reprieve him. The culprit should labor in the reformatory prison, where he can acquire better and more easily such qualifications as society demands for its protection. We think, however, that all murderers had best be sent to penal servitude for life, and caused to earn enough, if possible, to compensate those whom they have injured permanently. This prison may closely approximate to the reformatory prison, where the same machinery can be made to supply power, water, etc. The educators, lecturers, clergymen, and scientists, who visit the reformatory prison, may easily visit the murderers, and speak a word of encouragement, to render a heavy heart lighter, and to prepare them for another life. These prisons may be conducted like clock-work; for we certainly have enough knowledge of science and human nature to construct rules and systems that will work well and profitably, if people only can agree, and see alike.

One thing is true, and that is, but little attention is given to a criminal by society. He is sent off to state's prison, and that is the last of him. This certainly does not speak very well for a Christian people. It augments crime instead of decreasing it. When a murder is committed in a county, there should be a day of prayer and humiliation, each person examining their own condition; and, instead of, as now crying out, hang him, they should visit the poor wretch, and pity rather than despise; for we can not imagine a greater sorrow, or a more deplorable condition, than to be a murderer.

> "The ugliest fiend of hell! a deadly venom
> Preys on his vitals, turns the healthful hue
> Of his fresh cheeks to haggard sallowness;
> And dries his spirit up.
>
> "Good stars, that were his former guides,
> Have empty left their orbs, and shot their fires
> Into the abyss of hell.
>
> Curs't is the wretch enslaved to such a vice,
> Who ventures life and soul upon the dice."

CHAPTER XII.

REFUTATION OF THE DEATH PENALTY. HAVE WE A RIGHT TO INFLICT PUNISHMENT BY DEATH? REASONS IRREFUTABLE; NOT A SINGLE RATIONAL ARGUMENT LEFT WHY WE SHOULD KILL TO PUNISH.

Capital punishment is doubtless a relic of the dark ages, and is one of the evils afflicting enlightened and civilized nations of the present era. The same human ingenuity that applies science, in the use of electricity, of steam, and other inventions, in rendering general good to mankind, is, we think, sufficiently advanced at this age to devise some substitute as a means of punishing capital crime aside from the death penalty. It is a serious question whether death is a penalty at all, and when we come to argue the point, our readers will see the force of this assertion. In previous chapters of this volume we have canvassed, to some degree, the causes of crime, also advanced a few ideas as to how to prevent it. We are now persuaded that our readers are sufficiently prepared to receive, and consider

OUR ARGUMENTS

and reasons why the death penalty should not be inflicted. In the first place we remark that, as we have already stated, the primary object of law and punishment is reformation of the criminal, and we hold should be compensatory as well as preventive of future crime. As to the first proposition, all will agree that it is right and good to render happier all those that are in sorrow, and that it is a glorious work.

Punishment, it is believed, should be reformatory in its character; if possible, to restore the criminal to a normal condition, not only for his own good here and hereafter, but also for the general good of mankind.

This, then, it is evident, cannot be accomplished by inflicting the death penalty. For when a man is dead, all earthly means of reformation is to him lost; it is corporal punishment; it is like striking a man in the face to reform him, or kill him to make him better. The heathen mother throws her infant into the river Ganges to appease the wrath of her god. The Christian hangs his fellowman to appease the wrath of his God; and believes it a command of God "that he who sheds man's blood by man shall his blood be shed."

In the second place, we cannot see how punishment can be compensatory after a criminal is dead. We can not benefit those who are dead; who were murdered, by murdering also in turn. It can not benefit the injured party, who are living, to inflict the death penalty.

There can no possible benefit be derived by hanging a man, either to the dead, to the living, to the culprit, or to society, except, perhaps, the carpenter who is fortunate enough to get the job to build the gallows.

The popular belief is that one who has been instrumental in taking the life of another, should be required to forfeit his life also?

It can be no satisfaction to the dead to know that, as he was ushered out of life prematurely at the hand of the assassin, the assassin will also have to render up his life prematurely for having done such a deed. It reminds us of the time during our late war, when retaliation was talked of, viz., to hang one of the southern prisoners north, for every one of our men hanged by the southern army. That this would deter the south from hanging our men, it was believed; but what satisfaction could it have been to one of our men to know that while he was being hanged south, some one was meeting the same fate north. We apprehend none. The dead, we think, cannot be affected in any manner whether we hang or do not hang the perpetrator of their murder. To simply say that a murderer deserves to die, is no argument why he should die. This is almost the only argument put forward deliberately in defense of capital punishment at the present day. Many, without taking a second thought, often, on hearing, or reading, of a terrible crime being committed, exclaim, "swing up the scoundrel," "he deserves to be cut to pieces," "he ought to be hanged by the heels." Similar expressions we hear every day, which expressions we conceive to be utterly wrong if made a reason for continuing the death penalty. It is neither more or less than the sentiment of gratified vengeance; it is a vindictive emanation, unworthy of any enlightened soul. It is no part of our province to deal out the deserts of iniquity, as such. The rights of society do not include this power of rewarding or punishing the individual on purely moral grounds. Another says, "with the abstract rights or wrongs of human actions society has nothing to do; it must regard them solely as beneficial or injurious to social order, and scrupulously forbear from assigning to them either reward or punishment on the score of their moral character." A murderer may, or may not, deserve to be hanged, still we should be willing to trust to God for the proper adjustment of man's irreparable wrongs.

To murder is an irreparable crime; we cannot restore life. Can society repair the injury by legally taking the life of the guilty criminal? or by a second wrong act, right the first? If it is wrong to murder in an illegal manner, we can not see that it is right to murder in a legal form any more than that it is wrong to steal illegally, but right to steal by legal action. Reparation is the second object of law. The punishment, therefore, should be in accordance with the spirit of the law, which, it is plain, the enforcement of the death penalty is not.

We deem it right and necessary that all persons found guilty of murder in the first degree should be put in prison for life, without the prospect of being pardoned out. We agree with the sentiment expressed in an editorial in the Chicago *Evening Mail*:

"We do not see any better reason for permitting the executive to pardon a man when convicted and sentenced than there would be to permit the same power to waive both trial and sentence. With the aid of counsel, a prisoner usually has all the mitigating circumstances in his case presented with amplitude and power to the jury. Each point of law is acutely analyzed and settled before the presiding judge; the right of appeal remains, and it surely seems that when all the guards which the law throws around criminals upon trial are exhausted and a final verdict and sentence are secured, the matter should go on to its consummation."

Those found guilty of murder in the second degree should be returned to imprisonment for life, with a pardoning power vested in the jury or community which finds them guilty. This we believe to be just, for two reasons. First, it will give the murderer some opportunity during his natural life to reform, and prepare for a higher life; and, secondly, it will give him a chance to make at least partial reparation for the great wrongs he has inflicted upon those injured by the death of their relative—father, husband, wife, sister, or brother.

The murderer's prison, as well as the reformatory prison, can be so conducted that a considerable profit will be made, which should go to repair the injuries done by the prisoner's crime. Where no relatives exist to receive such compensation, the profits of a murderer should go to sustain some benevolent institution. The profits of the convicts in the reformatory prison, should, after full reparation is made, be at the disposal of the prisoner, to be paid to his family, or other needy friends, if he so wills it; or it may be allowed to accumulate, and be paid to the prisoner when he has satisfied the law, and is entirely cured of his malady. This would give him something to start with in life again, and would be an impetus without which he might feel very much discouraged.

If the death penalty, then, is neither compensatory nor reformatory,—and so far all will agree with our mode of reasoning,—there are still

OTHER REASONS

why we should banish this barbarous practice from the land.

We notice, in this connection, the difficulty in the enforcement of the terrible penalty of death, from the fact that every effort is put forth to evade the law, and save the life of the criminal. Thousands of dollars are spent in trying our murderers, both by the culprit as well as the public, and a new trial is often granted on the most trivial mistakes in the pleadings on either side.

It generally requires from one to two years to decide whether a murderer is guilty, and whether he shall be hung, or be imprisoned,—all owing to the penalty being unnatural and most severe. It is hard to get a jury to agree on a verdict of death, unless the criminal is very unpopular, and the party murdered of some standing in society. Take, for example, the Stokes, Rafferty, and a great number of other cases which we might mention, where the law yet remains uninforced against men proven guilty of murder in the first degree. Some technical flaw is discovered by some good judge, and a *supersedeas* is granted, only to prolong the life of a fellow being for a few months, or perhaps a year. It is due to the fact of the penalty being too severe, that men hesitate, equivocate, and falter in their power to inflict it until the murderer either escapes, or the farce becomes so tedious that it is finally decided to execute. Previous to the enforcement of the penalty, every exertion is made to obtain a reprieve from the governor. Of course, a man's life being suspended on a single thread, it becomes a matter of some importance how the approach shall be made, and what arguments shall be put forward. With the governor, it is a matter wholly technical. He considers the popularity or unpopularity of the case. He decides in accordance with the power vested in him. He does not inquire upon the moral right or wrong in regard to killing the murderer or sending him to prison for life, but only on some sharp points of law. The best lawyer comes out ahead. All are actuated by the amount of money to be made out of the case, on the one hand, and on the other, by the dread of enforcing the extreme penalty of the law; and under these circumstances justice is "shorn threadbare," and the law is almost entirely defeated. Only one murder out of fifty in the United States is ever executed according to the law. This great uncertainty of punishment increases crime, and is a good reason why capital punishment should be entirely abolished.

Another point which we wish to consider is this: Life we can not give; hence we should not take it from another. In case of fraudulent or circumstantial evidence, upon which many persons have been convicted and executed, who were afterwards found to be innocent, the mistake is so irreparable that if one innocent person is put to death once in a hundred years, it is sufficient reason why the death penalty should be entirely dispensed with.

In the state of Ohio, a few years ago, it was positively asserted that, some twenty years since, they executed a man for murder, who, it seems, was innocent. The facts came out by the dying testimony of an old man who died in the neighborhood, and who, of course, would not criminate himself, and therefore saw his neighbor die innocent.

F. E. Abbot remarks, in speaking of capital punishment, that "it is a punishment which, if inflicted upon the innocent through mistake or perjury, admits of no redress; and there are overwhelming proofs that it has often been inflicted on the innocent."

Victor De Tracy said, in the French Chamber of Deputies, in 1828, that within six months eleven sentences of death were reversed by the higher courts of France, for *errors of facts*. In the British Parliament Fitzroy Kelly said that fourteen innocent persons were hanged in England during the first half of the present century. Another eminent jurist adds his testimony. Daniel O'Connell makes the following statement: "I myself defended three brothers who were accused of murder. I saw the mother clasp her eldest son, who was but twenty-two years of age. I saw her hang on her second, who was not twenty. I saw her faint when she clung to the neck of her youngest boy, who was but eighteen. They were executed, and *they were innocent.*" A single instance of this kind is sufficient reason for abolishing capital punishment for all time to come. It is sufficient to arouse every human heart and to inspire confidence and hope in a new system of punishment. We must not wonder, when such awful mistakes continually occur, that the immortal Lafayette exclaimed, in 1830, in the French Chamber of Deputies: "I shall demand the abolition of the death penalty until I have the infallibility of human judgement proven to me." Or that King Louis Phillippi exclaimed, "I have detested it all my life long." Charles Hugo was fined one hundred dollars and imprisoned six months for publishing the following in his paper, after the execution of Montcharmont, although defended most eloquently by his father, Victor Hugo: "Whatever be the hand that commits it, homicide is never moral teaching. However honest and conscientious may be your tribunals and your judges, it will never be by killing that you will prove 'thou must not kill.'"

The celebrated scholar and clergyman of Toledo, Ohio, F. E. Abbot, said in a lecture as follows: "The growing uneasiness with which civilized communities regard the death penalty, is clearly, in my opinion, occasioned by the expanding conscience of the race, which begins to realize the truth that no man is wholly a brute; that criminals are men, and that something better can be done with them than to stamp their life out under the heels of the multitude. The great faith in man, which lies at the root of American civilization, and is the grand inspiration of free religion, begins already to teach the individuality of human life, and to throw a sacred protection even over those who have themselves dared to violate it. Yes, society is slowly learning that hardest of lessons, how to overcome evil with good,—how to take the desperate outcast out of his desperation, and, while restraining him from further evil, to melt his hardened heart with kindness and love."

We now introduce a strange question which perhaps the reader has not investigated, and which is another good reason against inflicting the death penalty. In the first place, we assert that it is a question whether this penalty is not an outrage, as the premature time of death is in violation of the laws of nature. The absolute process of dying is not painful; it is a natural law, and nature should, therefore, be allowed to assert her rights. To take nature's work in our own hands and inflict death upon one of our fellow beings, whom God and nature sees proper to let live and continue to supply him with the necessary elements of life, until he has run his course, is like a mob taking the work of the law in their own hands, in an unlawful manner, inflicting the death penalty by "lynching."

It is as natural to die as it is to be born; and hence, when death absolutely takes hold of us, we are unconscious of the process of change that is going on. One who dies a natural death in a "green old age," brought on by the natural course of things, is happy in death. Were it not so, nature would outrage her children. Those who bring about such an event prematurely, by living in disobedience to natural laws, often suffer severely, bodily and mentally, during the process of inducing death previous to the actual death, at which time all is at peace. Those who are executed suffer severely for a time after the death sentence is pronounced upon them; but the closer the time draws near, the less are they affected by the idea of death, and hence we have an obvious reason why criminals walk with a steady step on the gallows, and face death. The common expression is, "they were of good pluck." Our people who delight in tragedies are those who read the *Police Gazette*, and similar papers,—gamblers and "jockey fellows," who all speak of such coolness in meeting this death as a mark of heroism.

When death is the only alternative, the culprit assumes an air of indifference, unless he is innocent, or his spiritual adviser can arouse him on the subject of religion. The seven notorious horse-thieves, who were hung in public, some years ago, near Cincinnati, Ohio, requested as their last and dying privilege, to smoke a cigar. They were granted their last request, and, in their own language, "were having a jolly time together." While they were yet smoking, the trap fell, and each swung into eternity. In nearly every instance of those who are executed, we learn that they all sleep well the night previous, eat heartily at breakfast, and are in every way much less concerned at this stage of their fate, than those who are required to enforce the penalty of death. Many meet their fate with malice and revenge in their heart, as did the murderer at Peoria, Ill., a few weeks ago, who declared his innocence to the last moment of his life.

If the object of the death penalty is to torture the

criminal, it should be inflicted within the space of twice twenty-four hours after the sentence is pronounced. Then the suffering would be truly great. If it is argued that such a course would be inhuman, and that it is much easier for a person to meet death after having a month's time for preparation,—which is a truth,—we ask, would it not be better to give him his natural lifetime for preparation for the hereafter, and leave him to meet his death when God and nature decrees it to be so. Further, we ask whence the authority for a judge, jury, or a community to say to a condemned man, " Make your peace with God, for in so many days thou wilt be hanged." By what method has it been ascertained how long it takes one to prepare for eternity? Nature and God both say plainly that man needs a natural lifetime for reformation; for regeneration is a growth, and can not be the work of a moment.

The notorious highwayman and murderer, John A. Murrel, once met a poor wood-chopper in the woods, whom he requested to " hand over his money;" but the poor man declared he had none, and that he had a wife and eight children to maintain. The robber thinking that a man so poor as that had better be dead, pulled out his watch and pistol, and gave the poor man five minutes to make his peace with God. The man fell upon his knees, and prayed aloud for himself and for the robber; but the robber kept his word, and shot the man at the end of five minutes.*

---

* See the Confession of Murrel.

Now there was as much propriety in giving the wood-chopper five minutes to "make sure his salvation," as it was for the judge afterward to grant Murrel thirty days in which to prepare himself for Heaven; and it strikes us very forcibly that the poor wood-chopper accomplished more in five minutes than the notorious murderer could in a lifetime. The very fact, then, that it seems to be humane to give a criminal time to prepare himself for eternity, and qualify himself to meet death, is evidence to show that the death penalty is unnatural and barbarous.

It may be further held that imprisonment for life is also unnatural and barbarous. We answer, it is the only means we have for self-protection, which is a law of nature. It is an evil, we admit, but one existing from necessity. So long as society neglects the child crime will be committed, and so long as crime and murder are committed, so long will we require prisons, to govern those who are incapable of self-government.

Thus far, we believe our reasoning to be good, and now, before we close this chapter, we will consider briefly a few thoughts more, and inquire whether capital punishment is an act

OF CHRISTIAN DUTY.

The primary object of religious teachings are mainly to reform those who are in a degenerated condition. All education which teaches the way to happiness is reformatory, and this is the work of religious organizations and Christian educators. The object is to bring sinners to repentance,—if possible, to lead them to glory, and make sure their salvation.

This can not be done by enforcing the death penalty, which, we have already shown, is also a direct violation of the laws of nature, and consequently not a Christian duty. The command is, "Thou shalt not kill." Nowhere in the New Testament is capital punishment recommended or commanded. Under the new law we are taught to obey the laws of the government,—to love our criminals rather than despise them, and "do good to those that hate us." Under the old law, it was taught "an eye for an eye and a tooth for a tooth, but a new command I give unto you, love one another."

"Those who take the sword shall perish by the sword." So it has always been. The best swimmer will sometimes drown; the best pugilist is sometimes whipped, and those that fight with the sword are in danger of being killed by the sword. So we see that this is not a command to punish by hanging. If so, why is it not strictly obeyed, and our murderers put to death in the same manner in which they murder their victims? If a man takes the sword, he should be killed by the sword, and not hanged by the neck. Under the old law, the death penalty was enforced by stoning the culprit to death. If this is taken as a guide, why, then, do we not stone our murderers to death instead of hanging? If capital punishment was right under the old law, why was it repealed under the new law?—" A new command I give unto you, love one another." If it were right and pleasing in the sight of God to punish capital crime by hanging, why was not an explicit command given which all men could read and understand? The truth is, we are commanded to obey the law; but it was not decreed that law shall not be so changed and amended as to meet the necessary demands of every age, nation, or country. We are also taught that "a murderer can not enter the kingdom of Heaven."

This we believe to be scientifically true, whether a murderer in heart or in deed. So long as we have murder in our heart we are in a terrible state of discord, and can not attain to a state of harmony so long as this discord exists. In those who have carried out the desire of their hearts, and actually murdered in deed, the discord is still greater, and they are also further from a state of harmony, or, in other words, Heaven. Now, if "a murderer cannot enter into the kingdom of Heaven," then, of course, he is doomed to share the sufferings and sorrows of the opposite condition, termed hell, which is a condition the poor victim may outgrow in this life, by making use of proper means; and after he is regenerated even a murderer may enter into a heavenly state, but he can never get there having murder in his heart.

Now, if it is necessary for murderers to outgrow these conditions before they can enter into a state of happiness, and if it is also true that there can be no repentance hereafter, then we ask, is it a Christian duty, or an act of charity to send a man to hell by inflicting the death penalty? This deprives him of life, time, earthly means, and the grace of God operating through these means in the conversion of his soul. It may be, however, affirmed that it is possible for this conversion to take place during the probationary time between the sentence of the felon and the time of his execution. If this were possible, however, we still more strongly than ever persist in abolishing capital punishment; for as soon as a man is regenerated, and a converted sinner, he is quite good enough to live, and even to have his liberty. It is evident that it is not a Christian duty to enforce the death penalty as a punishment for capital crime. It is not reformatory; it is not compensatory; it is very uncertain, thus encouraging crime. Lastly, it is not in keeping with the spirit of the Christian religion, the teachings of science, of God and nature, and is an outrage, disgraceful and unworthy of an enlightened civilized Christian nation.

CHAPTER XIII.

ON THE DEATH PENALTY AS A PREVENTIVE MEASURE OF FUTURE CRIME. IS SOCIETY THEREBY PROTECTED, AND SHALL WE CONTINUE TO KILL?

In the previous chapter, we presented a number of important questions for the consideration of our readers, and we believe that what has been said is conclusive and convincing. So far, we have not discovered the slightest reason which might be brought in defence of punishing crime by death. The justifiable objects, as we have already stated in previous chapters, for the infliction of penalties are three,—reformation of the criminal, reparation of the injured party, and the prevention of future crime. The death penalty can neither reform the criminal nor repair injuries done to those who are murdered; its only possible justification must, therefore, be the prevention of future crime. The whole question of defense of capital punishment must turn on this one point. It is to this part of the subject we propose to devote the present chapter, and discuss the merits and demerits of capital punishment as a preventive measure. We admit that "dead men tell no tales," and that the dead can never commit crime. But we can not admit that, with the present knowledge we have of mechanics and architectural science, we are not competent to construct a suitable prison for the safe keeping of murderers as well as other criminals. Then, if it is argued further that under nearly all circumstances they are liable to escape and flee from justice, we reply that we are about as willing to risk the liberty of a man guilty of murder in the first degree as one convicted of murder in the second degree, or a base, low, unregenerated, ignorant vagabond, who is liberated after a few months' penal service, unreformed, and, in many instances, better qualified to commit crime than before—thanks to the manner in which our prisons are conducted at the present time. Then there can be no reasonable argument offered on the score that, the prisoner being liable to escape from prison, society is left unprotected. A mere possibility in the course of a lifetime of such an occurrence taking place, ought not to cause us to act in a recklessly inhuman manner at the present, by inflicting the death penalty.

We think that imprisonment for life is a sure preventive of further crime, and a sufficient protection to society, at least so far as the condemned is concerned; for it certainly restrains him in his murderous course,

In the next place, we will consider whether the death penalty is a protection and means of prevention of further crime, by creating a terror or fear, as it is held. We often hear it remarked, "Were it not for the death penalty, more people would be murdered."

If this is correct reasoning, we would suggest that the means by which such fear is created be made available to all persons, and of every age, by hanging being made as public as possible. On the day of execution let all places of business be closed, and the community *en masse* attend, and look on the felon as he swings into eternity. Let the gallows be erected in the most public place, and on an elevated platform, so that thousands may be permitted to behold and drink in the elixir of terror, that they may fear the law, and be deterred from committing such a terrible deed as to take the life of a human being. This mode of teaching and reforming would, we think, like all other teaching, need to be repeated frequently that people might bear it in mind. For one to acquire any of the branches of education, most studious habits and daily application is necessary; so perhaps it would be well to hang pretty often, in order that this means of prevention of crime be successful. If no criminals are on hand, pick up any one who has no means of support, or one who is of little use to society, and make a sacrifice of him for the "good of the people," that it may be now as it was eighteen hundred years ago when it was considered necessary that some one "should die for the people."

" Death with torture is now universally disused; and the punishment inflicted is simply the extinction of life ignominiously. Little importance attaches to the ignominy as a deterring influence: First, because the mind that will brave death itself, will not be much influenced by the attendant circumstances; secondly, because, by destroying life, the consciousness of ignominy and of every other emotion is extinguished; and, thirdly, because the same amount of ignominy, if it were necessay, might easily be inflicted without the accompaniment of death. Simple death, therefore, remains as the staple of the punishment. Now, by the ordination of God, we are all under the sentence of death. The clergy admonish us to bear it habitually in mind, and to prepare for it; the warrior is praised for disregarding it; and the philosopher glories in resigning himself to it with cheerfulness and equanimity; and I ask, on what principle, consistently with these views, can its infliction be justified as a punishment—as the most terrible of calamities—as that which is to restrain the reckless, excited, daring villain, after he has become insensible to all other earthly motives? He may tell the jury which convicts him, and the judge who condemns him, that they also are under sentence of death, and that the brief space of time which will elapse between the execution of the sentence on him and them, is no very formidable consideration to his disadvantage. Such a remark would be justified by religion, supported by philosophy, and sympathized with by men of courage who were neither religious nor philosophical. How, then, I again ask, can we reconcile such heterogeneous modes of viewing the most important event of our mortal existence? If all who should not be put to death for crime were naturally immortal in this world, I could understand the consistency of depriving a criminal of life, as the acme of human infliction; but in our actual condition, it appears to be not only barbarous, but immoral and irreligious to do so. If we value moral consistency as of any importance in criminal legislation, we shall be led to abandon the notion that death is the most awful of punishments, and regard it simply as an institution of a great and merciful God, to be encountered with courage and constancy at the call of duty, to be prepared for by the aid of religion, and to be submitted to with calmness and resignation, when it comes to us in the course of Providence."*

As the author is penning the present paragraph,—one o'clock P. M., Friday, March 14th, 1873,—George Driver, in this city, and Osborne, at Knoxville, Ill., are being executed for murder. This very moment the trap falls; and as we look out on the street, we see the usual busy throng. No one seems to know or think for a moment that two souls are being swung into eternity for the good of humanity—for the prevention of crime. We ask why this indifference on the part of the people? If capital punishment is to be a lesson, why not by law cause the bells to be tolled during the dreadful hour of death, business to be suspended, and worship ordered in all public halls and churches,—and let all "enter into their closets" and humiliate in silence. After the hour of humiliation and prayer, let the community gather together and march in procession, the band playing some funeral dirge, and thus follow the felon to a suitable place of execution, and cause him there to expiate his crime. If capital punishment is to deter and thus to prevent future murder, why not give the community the full benefit of it?

If the death penalty was inflicted in the manner we suggest, then there might be some hope of deriv-

---

* George Combe, on Capital Punishment.

ing some good to mankind from an execution. History shows that when criminals were publicly executed, murders were often committed before the crowd was dispersed. Near Covington, Ky., a few years ago, two murders were committed inside of an hour after a public execution. The Rev. I. Roberts ascertained that out of 168 condemned criminals, all but three had witnessed executions. Observations made by Buxton go to prove that it is notorious that executions very rarely take place without being the occasion of new crimes. Dr. Forden, who was largely acquainted with criminals, makes the same report. He says: "An execution makes no more impression than a fly." We have overwhelming facts which show how little power there is in these sickening spectacles to deter from crime. Executions, whether public or private, are of no use either for punishing criminals or deterring others. We would almost be willing to wager though an execution takes place to-day in our city, that before the morrow's sun a murder—or at least an attempt—will take place. Each day our newspapers report murders and tragedies in all parts of the country, averaging about ten to twelve a day, making in the aggregate about four thousand each year in this comparatively Christianized United States. "Every execution," said Dr. Lushington, in the House of Lords, "brings an additional candidate for the hangman." Those who are sufficiently depraved to commit murder are also prepared to hold death in perfect contempt. This, with the hope of escaping the uncertain penalty, takes away almost entirely the force of the penalty. A notorious pirate said to his comrade, while they were undergoing the torture of the wheel, "Why do you make all this noise? Did you not know that in our profession we were subject to one more malady than the rest of the world?" It is reported as a matter of history that in 1822, John Lechler was hung at Lancaster, Pa., for murder. The very same evening one Wilson, who had been present, met a weaver named Burns, with whom he had some misunderstandings, and murdered him on their way home from witnessing the execution of Lechler. He was arrested and handcuffed with the irons hardly yet cold from the wrist of John Lechler, who had that same day been executed. An Irishman, executed for forgery, was given back to his family, and while his wife was lamenting over him, a young man came to her to purchase some forged notes. Forgetting her grief, she was selling him some, when, being surprised by the officers, she thrust the notes, in her alarm, into the mouth of the corpse, where the officers found them. So much for the example of her husband's fate. The influence of the last speeches of criminals go directly to show that there exists a morbid appetite which leads to crime. Our daily papers, the day after an execution, meet with far better sales than before. An English paper states that from one and a half to two and a half millions of copies were sold of each of the penny narratives of the executions of Rush, the Mannings, Courvosier, Good, Conder and Grenacre. This class of literature, doubtless stimulates and feeds the tendency to crime by exciting appeals to the imagination.

The evils of public executions become so great

and disgusting, and their pernicious effects so apparent, that private executions have now nearly everywhere taken their place. Yet this change does not improve the moral lesson, as it was thought it would, by doing away with that very publicity and disgraceful spectacle always attending public executions. The change, however, proves clearly that society is secretly ashamed of its own proceedings, and makes a gradual approach to total abolition of the death penalty.

It can not be successfully shown that capital punishment deters people from committing crime or murder. Punishing by inflicting the death penalty has been practiced since the world's history, and it would seem by this time, if it is such a potent means of prevention, murder should be almost unknown. The fact is, nearly all murders are perpetrated under the influence of a terrible force—an

OVER-STIMULATED

condition. Under the influence of whisky, anger and revenge are variously superinduced; and often men murder and are unconscious of the fact until some time afterward, when sanity is restored. This is one reason why so few murderers make their escape. Under these influences men are not afraid to die. Driver, the wife murderer, said, "God knows, I never had any intention of killing her; I did not get the pistol for that purpose; it was all the impulse of a moment." Again, he said, "It was whisky that brought me upon the gallows." His dying advice to all was, "Let whisky alone." The Peoria murderer declared his innocence to the last. Doubtless he was under the influence of liquor at the time he injured his wife. As a rule, we are safe in stating that nine out of every ten murders are committed under some uncontrollable and irresistible force at the time which knows no reason. Under the influence of excitement,—the thoughts of patriotism, fame, victory, the stimulus of an encouraging speech from the general, and the music of fife and drum,—men are lead to the cannon's mouth in time of battle. Under these influences men fear not death.

Those who, by education, and the influence of unfavorable surroundings, acquire a constitutional predisposition to murder, are only stimulated in their evil propensities by seeing a man hung. Two years ago, while a young man was arraigned in the court at Cincinnati for murder, his brother attempted to murder one of the important witnesses on the stairway that led to the court-room, while the court was in session. Notwithstanding the death penalty, and the policeman standing at the head of the stairway, who was at hand to arrest him, and whom he saw, still the terrible feeling of revenge against this prosecuting witness was greater than all. Having no capacity to control his feelings, he began the work of murder.

It is not the dread of law and the punishment attending crime that will prevent murder. It is the placing of a high estimate on human life. The greater elevation attained by any people in the scale of civilization, the more value will be put on life. The Empress Elizabeth abolished it in Russia, declaring,

"Experience demonstrates that capital punishment never yet made men better." Her successor, the great Catharine, adopted this reform in her code of laws and remarked to Count de Sigur, "We must punish crime without imitating it. The punishment by death is rarely anything but a useless barbarity." We labor for the abolition of this great evil, the barbarous practice of putting criminals to death; and in this the author does not

STAND ALONE.

Thousands of the best minds are with us, on this subject. The eminent jurist, John Bright, writes as follows:

ROCHDALE, January 5, 1868.
H. M. BOVER, Esq.,

"*Dear Sir*,—I do not think the punishment of death is necessary to the security and well-being of society; and I believe its total abolition would not tend to increase those crimes which it is now supposed by many to prevent. The security and well-being of society do not depend on the severity of punishments. Barbarism in the law promotes barbarism among those subject to the law; and acts of cruelty under the law become examples of similar acts contrary to the law. The real security for human life is to be found in a reverence for it. If the law regarded it as inviolable, then the people would begin also so to regard it. A deep reverence for human life is worth more than a thousand executions in the prevention of murder, and is, in fact, the great security for human life. The law of capital punishment, whilst pretending to support this reverence, does, in fact, tend to destroy it. If the death penalty is of any force in any case to deter from crime, it is of much more force in lessening our chief security against it, for it proclaims the fact that kings, parliaments, judges, and juries may determine when and how men may be put to death by violence, and familiarity with this idea cannot strengthen the reverence for human life. To put men to death for crimes, civil or political, is to give proof of weakness rather than strength, and of barbarism rather than Christian civilization. If the United States could get rid of the gallows, it would not stand long here. One by one, we "Americanize" our institutions; and, I hope, in all that is good, we may not be unwilling to follow you. I am very truly yours," JOHN BRIGHT.

The eminent lawyer and jurist, Edward Livingston, in his arguments against capital punishment, published in the introduction to the criminal code of Louisiana, in 1820 and 1824, remarks:

"It (the necessity of taking life) exists between nations during war,—or a nation and one of its component parts in a rebellion or insurrection,—or between individuals during the moment of an attempt against life which cannot otherwise be repelled; but between society and individuals, organized as the former now is, with all the means of repression and self-defence at its command, *never*. I come, then, to the conclusion in which I desire most explicitly to be understood, that, although the right to punish with death might be abstractedly conceded to exist in certain societies and under certain circumstances which might make it necessary, yet, composed as society now is, these circumstances can not reasonably be even supposed to occur; that, therefore, no necessity, and of course no right, to inflict death as a punishment, exists."

F. E. Abbot, a celebrated clergyman and author, whom we have already referred to, comes in strong support of what we have aimed to impress upon the minds of our readers:

"Highly as I value human life, it is not, in my estimation, above all price: freedom is worth more, honor is worth more, virtue is worth more, country is worth more, the welfare of the race is worth more, great ideas are worth more. For such as these, a man will cheerfully sacrifice his life; and to preserve them, nations and communities are summoned to sacrifice the lives of their children. But nevertheless, life is worth more in proportion as the race becomes civilized; and, in fact, the value set on human life is one of the chief criteria of the elevation attained by any people in the scale of civilization. Savages fling it away in mere pastime; but the wise man would not die as the fool dies. A high-reverence for human life is so priceless in its influence on social well-being, that every means may well be taken to enhance it in the community. It is precisely because the death penalty cheapens human life, breaks down the guards of its sancity in popular estimation, that capital punishment, the moment it ceases to be absolutely necessary, immediately becomes an enormous outrage. At the very best, it is a necessary evil in certain disorganized states of society; but in every organized community, it is a demoralizing agency of fearful power. The people that permits legalized murder when other penalties would better accomplish the same end, educates its children to bloodshed, and wilfully fosters crime in its own borders.

"For proof of this statement, one need but consider the effect of public executions. The sight of bloodshedding exercises a terrible influence on the imagination. I saw, a year or two ago, in the daily papers an account of a little boy of nine years, who, having seen his father kill and dress several hogs, afterward induced his younger brother to play at killing hogs, and murdered him in the horrid sport. The school-master at Newgate, England, says that 'he has seen his pupils, before the bodies of criminals were taken down from the scaffold, play the scene over again, one acting the convict and the other the hangman.' The famous Volney, just after the French revolution, relates that he was deeply affected at seeing crowds of children amuse themselves with chopping off the heads of cats and chickens, in imitation of the dreadful scenes of the guillotine which had then grown infrequent: —'Even childhood had become inured to scenes of blood, and imitated the most frightful tragedies for sport.'"

"Jas. Montgomery, aged 11 years, while playing at hanging Foster, yesterday, at the residence of his parents, in Brooklyn, strangled himself."—*Tribune.*

The good Rev. W. H. Thomas, of the City of Chicago, in a sermon on the subject of "Hanging," preached the Sabbath after Driver's execution, speaks in clear and pointed terms, and comes in strong support of our position. We give his own words:

'The occasion could not pass without bringing up in many minds the old question whether hanging is the best thing society can do with a convicted murderer. All are agreed that whilst the law makes death by hanging the penalty for murder, it should be executed; but all are not agreed that this is the best law in such cases. It will hardly be claimed that it rests upon any command of the scriptures, although they may be quoted as authorizing the death penalty, for they make death the penalty for some fourteen other and minor offenses, such as blasphemy, man-stealing, adultery, witchcraft, etc. Surely no one would claim that we are under that law. Nor will it be justified on the ground that hanging is the only punishment that will satisfy the claims of justice. This kind of administration belongs to God. The idea of punishment in human laws is not retributive, but administrative, or for the protection of society. And the one question is, can this be secured as well, or better, by some other means. We think it can. It is found in experience that it is almost impossible to secure the conviction and execution of a murderer. Every possible technicality of the law is exhausted, involving long delays, and keeping the subject painfully before the public, and then, if conviction is secured and sentence passed, the pardoning power is importuned in every conceivable way for extension of time or commutation of sentence. Now it seems to me that there is something sadly wrong, either in the law itself, or in its administration. The very element most essential for the prevention of crime, that is, certainty of speedy punishment, is to a very great extent lost. The penalty of hanging is so great that it defeats itself by the difficulty of its execution. A murderer runs about as many risks of being killed by accident as he does of being hung. And when at long intervals some wretch is executed, it is not at all certain that the effect upon the hardened portions of the community is either deep or lasting. What was the result last Friday? When was there seen such a crowd of the very worst characters? And as they hung around the jail, from morning till nearly night, feeding their coarse, fiendish natures on the thoughts of human suffering, the day seemed to them more as a holiday than the solemn administration of justice. Who can say they were either bettered in their natures, or deterred from crime by the experiences of that day? Then the effect upon the public at large is, to say the least, not pleasant. Was there a thoughtful man or woman in this vast city that spent the hour from 1 to 2 o'clock without painful feelings? To those who witnessed the execution, the scene was trying to the last degree. If such things occur, we can not blame the press for publishing them, but it is certainly not good for the public morals to be so constantly occupied with the details of crime and trials and punishment. It has come to be the larger part of our daily reading. Were the penalty different, so much attention could not be called to these cases.

"The public good demands speedy, straightforward trials on the merits of the case, and then where found guilty I would substitute certain imprisonment for life in place of hanging. This imprisonment should be in a separate department of the penitentiary, constructed especially for murderers, and the pardoning power should be taken from the executive, and placed in nothing less than the unanimous vote of both branches of the legislature, and with these only in cases where the absolute innocence of the convict is proven. This right to pardon, in any case, is a constant source of perplexity and annoyance to governors, and in all cases holds out the hope of pardon to offenders of all grades, greatly weakens the dread of punishment, and thereby encourages crime. This certain imprisonment for life at hard work would protect society from any fear of danger from the murderer, and would, I think, have a greater influence in preventing murder than the present uncertainty of hanging, and the usually long term of such convicts would make their labor profitable to the state, and the profits might go to support those left dependant by their crime."

If it were further necessary to convince our readers of the *rationale* of our position, by giving the opinion of others, we might fill ten volumes with the names of good men and women throughout the United States, who are in favor of abolishing capital punishment. We proceed, however, to notice further the effects which the excessive penalty of death has on the criminal, on the friends of the criminal, and the community in general. We have shown that it does not prevent crime. George Driver was hanged yesterday in this city; Osborn at Knoxville, Ill., the same day. This morning, March the 15th, 1873, our papers report a number of murders,—one shooting affray, in this city, at one o'clock, A. M., in a saloon, by a young man; and we may expect a number more during the next twenty-four hours. Thus far, we have not been able to see any good whatever resulting from the death penalty; but, on the other hand, much harm is done, and crime thereby increased instead of lessened. In consequence of the severe punishment awaiting the murderer, every effort is made to defeat the law.

Lawyers wrangle and quarrel over weak points in law. The one for the benefit of the culprit, tries to weaken the facts in the case; the prosecuting attorney on the other side, through pride, strives with energy not to be defeated, though life may be involved; thus giving practical lessons in lying. The last dollar is spent by friends to save the life of the murderer, and thousands of dollars of the public treasure trying to take his life. The uncertainty of punishment gives the criminal a hope of escaping, and stimulates the friends to plead for a *supersedeas*, new trial, commutation, stay of proceedings, etc., all involving thousands of dollars, and neither doing justice to the criminal nor to the public. Let murderers, as well as other criminals, when found guilty, be immediately disposed of, and sent to a suitable prison, where they can be of some use, and begin the work of reparation and reformation. No commutation, no *supersedeas*, no reprieving power; let the punishment be certain; and we affirm that this will truly prevent crime. Instead of keeping a murderer in jail, one or two years, trying to convict him and enforce the death penalty, which does no good whatever, would it not be far better to assign a place for safe keeping, where he can work and earn something, and do good to some one in need. For example, George Driver left a family of five or six children, uneducated and unsupported. Society will not educate and support those children as they should be, though accessory to the crime of the murder; still, by the death penalty, the last support of those children is taken from them, while, by imprisonment, the criminal could have done something for their benefit. Again: if the penalty were lighter and less uncertain, Driver would not have spent his last dollar in trying to save his life, and this money could have been saved to his family, and in a few weeks he could have been doing something more for them; besides saving thousands of dollars to the public.

It is estimated that from three to four hundred thousand dollars is expended in the United States each year in trying murderers alone. Now if this money were expended in supporting institutions which have for their object the proper training of the rising generation, who receive not the proper attention from parents, we apprehend that this would do more to prevent future crime than to spend this amount in simply trying to save the lives of our murderers. The severity of the penalty, and the uncertainty of enforcing it, has rendered our courts of justice ludicrous, and people are dissatisfied. All the public asks is strict enforcement of the law. If the law is unnaturally severe, they are willing even now to have it amended, so that it can be enforced. This defect has given rise to all manner of opinions, and newspaper comments, censuring our officers of the law. One of our evening papers states as follows:

"Stokes has received an extension of life for an indefinite number of months, if indeed he does not entirely escape punishment. Judge Boardman examined the flimsy pleas of the murderer's lawyers for a stay of proceedings, and refused them, whereupon Judge Davis, a man of less backbone, was called upon, and he promptly granted a stay of proceedings. How utterly the execution of the laws depends on the judgment, temper or preference of the judge, is shown in this case where, with precisely the same facts before them, one man decides that Stokes must hang and another grants him indefinite reprieve. If anything were needed to utterly remove public confidence in our legal tribunals, such farces as those in the cases of Stokes, Perteet, Rafferty, *et id omne genus*, would suffice. Hereafter, let murder trials be decided by flipping up coppers."

New trials are asked for. Everything is done to save life, and this is quite unnecessary. When it is plain that one is guilty of murder, why have trial after trial? If the death penalty can not be enforced, abolish it, and stop this wrangling and expenditure of money. Rigidly enforce the law and such editorials as the following would not appear:

"Rafferty, our policeman-murderer, after two trials and convictions, was sentenced on Saturday, to be hung on March 7th, and it seemed as if the last obstacle to the execution of justice was removed. But, behold, the villain's counsel straightway went to work to prepare a "bill of exceptions," and will besiege the Supreme Court for another trial! This is outrageously purile and utterly disgusting."—*Evening Mail.*

Some time previous to the execution of Driver, the newspapers were full of opinions like the above; and this preys on the wild imagintions of the people, arousing simply the emotions; and all sorts of expressions can be heard, such as, "The officers should be hung as well as the murderer;" "The lawyers ought to be made to take the place of the prisoner;" etc., coming merely through the organ of revenge. We can not expect any mitigation of crime. One can judge where the editor stands who gives his readers the following:

"George Driver, one of the crew of cold-blooded wife-murderers who have done their deeds in this city within the past few months, was yesterday found guilty of murder in the first degree, and sentenced to be hung. This, of course, is to be considered the commencement of a pleasant little farce, the end of which is far off. First will come a new trial, then an appeal to the Supreme Court, then a reversal and remanding, then a change of venue, then a *supersedeas*, then an appeal for executive clemency, if by any chance the first verdict is sustained; and finally after months of time and thousands of dollars of the people's money have been wasted on a wretch whose life is a curse to the world, he will probably be required to board a while at the expense of the State, or get free altogether."

People are yet uneducated on this subject. They know of no other means of punishment, and no other means of prevention of crime than the death penalty; hence, under these circumstances, the uncertainty of enforcing the law, we need not wonder when a New York reporter makes the following statement:

"New York is becoming agitated at the alarming frequency of murder in that city, and the people are demanding that somebody shall be punished. The past few weeks have been a harvest of crime."

The editor of the *Herald of Health* has an opinion differing some in tone and sentiment:

"HANGING A MAN.—In Brooklyn yesterday a man was hung. He had killed a policeman in attempting to escape from his grasp. To-day the papers are full of graphic and disgusting accounts of it. These accounts, we believe, have a very bad effect on morals, and upon the health of delicate invalids, and upon the susceptible brains of children. They do no good whatever. Now if men are to lose their lives for murder, we say let it be done as decently as possible. If society decides that the murderer can not be safely kept alive on the globe, for fear he will do more injury, let it take him out of the way without shocking sensitive wives and delicate invalids, and tender-hearted children with a brutal exhibition. How can this be done. We would not even have the prisoner know it himself. Within a few years a method of butchering animals has been invented, in which they suffer no pain. Their brains are deliriously intoxicated by a peculiar anæsthetic, and nothing can hurt them. Such an anæsthetic might be silently passed into the prisoner's cell while he slept, and the work would be done. Would not the ends of justice be quite as well met? Would not the public be saved from a most disgusting spectacle, and the papers that deal in such news betake themselves to some other means of gratifying the public ear more in accordance with public sentiment?"

To evade the law all manner of questions and excuses are brought forward with the hope of saving one's life. This dodging of the law, we think, would cease as soon as the death penalty is abolished.

The most common expedient to evade the law is the

INSANITY DODGE.

This subject we notice more at length in another chapter, on the subject of insanity. We will state, however, that insanity can not be made an excuse for crime, or a reason why punishment should not be inflicted. If a man must be in his rational mind before he is fit to be hanged, then we argue, when he is so, he is also quite good enough to live. All persons are insane, in a degree, who commit murder, for one of a sound mind would not do so, hence insanity can not be made a reason why punishment should not be enforced in individual cases. In a very few instances, perhaps one in a hundred, or perhaps in two hundred, murderers may be considered wholly insane and fit subjects only for an insane asylum. Yet a terrible effort is made to clear murderers on this plea. In nearly every murder trial insanity is made a plea upon which to base a hope of saving the life of the accused felon. The following we clip from the New York correspondence of the Chicago *Tribune:*

"Scannell, the New York murderer, now on trial, has already found direct evidence that he is insane. The family physician has come forward to swear to it. In connection with this evidence, it is interesting to inquire into the responsibility of the Scannell family, the family physician, and the authorities who permitted this insane man to roam about with murder the special object of his insane malignits. It will be remembered that Scannell made several attempts upon the life of the man whom he finally killed, and once injured him so severely that he barely escaped death. Why did not these evidences of Scannell's insanity induce the authorities to inquire into his mental condition at the time, and put him beyond the possibility of carrying ou t his murderous purpose? If insanity is to be recognized as an excuse for the crime of murder, it should also be recognized in cases of attempted murder, and the demented creatures should be consigned to the asylum or prison. This is a case in point, showing the failure of the police system that does not attempt to prevent crime as well as bring criminals to punishment."

If it is right, a Christian duty, and a benefit to the public, to execute men for murder, why then so many different opinions, and why make an effort to commute the sentence of one guilty of murder. It strikes us there must be something wrong about this law or no one would even try to oppose it, or pray that it might be either amended or wholly abolished. If all were right no one would ever think of praying for a reprieve, save the criminal or his family. Mrs. Putman appeals to Governor Dix, of New York, to have the sentence of Foster, the car-hook murderer of her husband, commuted to lesser punishment. The New York *Times* also urges a commutation of Foster's sentence.

"The case," the *Times* remarks, "excites much public attention." A letter from the Hon. Wm. Orten, President of the Western Union Telegraph Company, is published in the *Times*, in favor of commutation, based on the application of the jurors, stating that they never regarded the condemned guilty of murder in the first degree. If capital punishment is right,—if it is preventive of crime,—if it is a Christian duty,—why make such an effort to save life; or why need we be afraid of the people? If it is a moral lesson, and does "so much good," as it is claimed; why need we an army of police to enforce it? The following is a dispatch from New York, on the morning of the execution of Foster:

"Superintendent Kelso, with two hundred policemen, was on hand this morning at 9 o'clock to preserve order. Foster, after passing a restless and almost sleepless night, arose from his bed about 8 o'clock and dressed himself for the execution. He then partook of a little food, not seeming to have any appetite. Dr. Tyng called and administered spiritual consolation, praying and reading the scriptures to him. His father and brothers called between 8 and 9 o'clock, and took their final leave of the unfortunate murderer. The scene was affecting in the extreme. Foster bore up bravely, while his father and brothers were convulsed with the burden of their grief. They had done all that mortal men could do to save him, and now they must part with him forever."

The sole question is, is capital punishment necessary to prevent crime? Thus far we can see no reasonable argument why it should be continued, or that it has prevented a single murder.

So long ago as the time of Nero, it was perceived by the philosopher Seneca, that retribution was a just punishment. " No wise man," he says, " punishes because crime has been committed, but only in order that crime may not be committed." Unless essential to the prevention of crime, capital punishment can not be for a moment justified to an enlightened conscience. Finally the reader may say, " you theorize very well, but

WILL IT DO

when put into practice?" Wherever it has been tried it has worked well. Michigan, since she abolished capital punishment, has had comparatively few murders committed within her borders. Wherever the experiment has been made, it has always been with the best success. In Tuscany, where the death penalty was abolished for twenty years, the Grand Duke officially announced that "all crimes had diminished," and Franklin stated that in Tuscany only five murders occurred in twenty years, while in Rome and its vicinity, where the death penalty was inflicted, sixty murders occurred within three months. It is reported by Sir James Mackintosh, in his farewell address to the grand jury, that after capital punishment was abolished, in Bombay, the commission of murder was reduced in the ratio of one to four. During the reign of Henry VIII. 72,000 criminals were executed—about 2,000 a year; yet crime, it is reported, continually increased. "It is not the severity," says Seymour, "but the certainty of punishment which deters." Make the punishment too severe, and it will not be inflicted. When a theft of forty shillings was punishable by death in England, within a space of two years, 553 perjured verdicts were rendered for thefts of thirty-nine shillings and eleven pence. It is everywhere admitted that juries will not convict honestly, if the penalty is excessive. Statistics carefully compiled in Michigan since the abolition of the death penalty, show only twenty murders, while in the city of Chicago alone one hundred have taken place during the same period of time. It is well to quote the words of the great Roman orator: "Away with this cruelty from the state. Allow it not, O judges, to prevail any longer in the commonwealth. It has not only the fatal effect of cutting off so many of your fellowmen in so cruel a manner, but it has even banished from men of the mildest temper, by the familiar practice of slaughter, the sentiment of mercy."

The eminent Bishop Simpson says, "Not only is capital punishment demoralizing to the public mind —not only are there frequent and fatal mistakes in putting the innocent to death—but also it is as useless as it is barbarous and unjust."

We believe now that the question of capital punishment is settled, and will be no longer questioned as its doing any good whatever. It cannot reform the criminal or compensate those who were injured. It is not a Christian duty for it has been proven that it does not deter others from committing murder, hence is not a preventive measure. It violates the laws of nature, and is contrary to the spirit and the teachings of the New Testament. It is a relic of heathen nations, and is a disgraceful tolerance of enlightened Christian communities, where science and reason are said to be in the zenith of glory.

CHAPTER XIV.

ON COMPULSORY EDUCATION. SUGGESTIONS HOW TO PREVENT CRIME. PUBLIC EDUCATIONAL INSTITUTIONS FOR THE FRIENDLESS, ETC., ETC.

"When ideas enter a barren brain, they lay inactive and dead, like seed cast into sterile ground. But when they fall on genial soil, they are almost sure to germinate and spring forth in some new and beautiful form."—*Horace Mann.*

"The 'Coming Child.'—At the risk of being thought fanatical, we assert that the 'Coming State' must take all the children who are abused and kept in ignorance by brutal, drunken, vicious parents, and educate and train them up to be useful and happy citizens. It is a disgrace to the nation that tens of thousands of children are growing up in the filth and slime of our cities and villages in the grossest and the most shameless moral degradation."—*Truth.*

"The next progressive move among advanced nations will be, first in considering, and next in executing a plan for transforming swindlers, petty thieves, and beggars into steady and useful laborers."—*N. C. Meeker.*

The problem, how to prevent crime, requires great wisdom to solve the mystery. A mere *a priori* conclusion is unsafe, and hence a thorough knowledge of the entire constitution of man is requisite to form a correct opinion. To arrive at the truth, a majority of the people of the United States must possess scientific knowledge of the human constitution—the physical, the moral, the intellectual, and the social natures—in order to be enabled to adjust man's laws in harmony with the laws of nature. Until this is accomplished we need not expect to be very successful in our legislative enactments, with a view of preventing crime. From the standpoint which we occupy in viewing the subject, we can not other than recognize in the criminal actions of men simply the symptoms of a diseased condition. This diseased condition has become chronic, we think, and, having been treated for many thousand years unsuccessfully, a general consultation of all the best minds of the nation may be of great benefit. Sufficient scientific knowledge has been acquired by the medical profession to know that, to cure a diseased condition the cause must be removed; then the effect will cease. Those, however, who are not capable of recognizing the real cause, treat simply effects, and thereby only palliate the difficulty which is liable at any time to break out in the most malignant form. To radically heal an old sore on a man's leg, we will suppose, the constitution must be restored to perfect health, and while this is being done local treatment is also necessary. To treat only the sore by local applications, thereby subduing the active symptoms, is running great risks, and jeopardizing the life of the patient. This kind of treatment is much as if the "life guards" on the sea shore, on beholding at a distance a flag of distress waving from the mast of a vessel in great danger, were to man the life-boat, and make every effort to reach the scene of threatened disaster, but, instead of rescuing the passengers aboard, they were simply to cut down the flag of distress, and console themselves with the idea that they have done their whole duty. This is a fair example of the present mode of treating the diseased conditions which pervade the body politic of the nation. Men indulge in the belief that they have done their whole duty, when they have poulticed the sore by exacting money fines for crime, or by sentencing a criminal to hard labor for a few months or years; and think when the sore is healed the cause is also removed. By enforcing the death penalty, they simply cut down the flag of distress. They argue that the danger has ceased because the flag announcing such condition has disappeared.

This palliative and insufficient treatment of crime is the main reason why it continues to be manifest. The active symptoms may be suspended for a time, but soon make their appearance again, often in a different form and more malignant in character. If the sore is healed on the man's leg without radically curing the constitution, the next manifestation of the disease is very liable to be in the form of consumption and to kill the patient. So in punishing crime simply by healing the apparent symptoms, the same disease is very liable in its next appearance to be in a form of greater severity, perhaps of thrusting the dagger into some one's heart. The only rational treatment would be a removal of the cause, whereupon the effect will cease. To treat simply the effect is dangerous; but to ascertain and treat the cause alone is uncertain. While we are engaged in removing the cause, the effect has a certain influence, and we make slow headway. While the constitution is being treated, the sore requires cleansing and various local treatment, in order to prevent re-absorption of the poisonous virus. This statement of the case is comprehensive; and all agree as to the correctness of the diagnosis. The only point on which we can differ is in regard to the means to be employed in the treatment of the difficulty. We cheerfully give our mode of treatment, and the remedies which we would prescribe, and trust to the nurse,—society,—to administer them promptly. We are aware that our prescriptions are suggested at a very prolonged period of the patient's disease; and we are also conscious of the fact that a great amount of treatment has already been given,— much, no doubt, with a good effect, and perhaps some having a very bad effect; yet, as the saying is, "so long as there's life there's hope," and we are willing to make an effort in common with many others to counteract, if possible, the diseased tendencies. The ultimate object is perfect restoration. To accomplish this, it is necessary, to understand correctly the nature, character and cause of the disease we are treating, and also the constitution, and idiosyncrasy of our patient. These conditions have been sufficiently canvassed in the first part of this volume, to which the reader is referred. All that now remains to be done is to indicate the treatment, and whether the *healing potion* can be successfully administered.

We have intimated that in the treatment the grand object is to bring about revolution,—restoration,— and, to accomplish this, the cause must be removed, or the effect will not cease. This may be done in two ways: in the treatment of the constitution by constitutional means, or by local application in correcting the effect. The constitutional measures are moral suasion, and the local measures legal suasion. The two should operate corelatively until the effect requires no further treatment. We wish it to be understood by our reader that we figuratively compare society, or the entire human family, to a body variously organized. Let us now consider first the

CONSTITUTIONAL MEASURES

by which we propose to remove the cause of crime. In the first part of this volume, we have shown that men are mainly actuated by the force of circumstances;—surroundings, habits, associations, and education affect men in all stations of life. We have also stated that crime—which is only a symptom—is the result of a depraved condition, which may have been hereditary or acquired.

This depravity exists generally physically as well as mentally. Physical depravity is the result of disobedience to physiological laws, and mental depravity is the result of ignorance or disobedience of the natural laws governing mentality. It is scarcely necessary to refer the reader to one universal fact, which is that nearly all of our criminals are depraved and ignorant whose early training was woefully neglected. Read the history of any of our most noted criminals, and it will be conceded that the crime may be traced back to a depraved ancestry, neglected early education, and improper culture of the moral and intellectual capabilities. The Buffalo murderer, who was recently executed, was raised and educated among harlots, gamblers, and thieves. His whole life was devoted to crime, and hence was well calculated to culminate in the most terrible of crimes. The Galesburg murderer, Osborne, was a man of no education and lived a wicked life from childhood. He had no one to lead him in the path in which he should go in after life. With the Peoria murderer it was the same. The notorious Probst, the murderer of the Deering family, was more like a beast than a human being. His history shows that he never was taught by a mother; that none interested themselves in his moral training while a child. Driver of Chicago was a man of no moral training; ignorant of physiology, and the most common branches of natural philosophy. The Boston murderer who is doomed to die in a few days, is ignorant of even the most common branches of education,—an orphan child, allowed to grow up like a weed. Foster, the car-hook murderer, is reported as of a depraved, uncouth organization, of intemperate habits, and no moral education. So we might go on and fill volume after volume to show that crime and ignorance, neglected early culture, and bodily and mental depravity, go hand in hand. We make not an exaggerated statement when we affirm that not one in a hundred of our murderers is an enlightened person. These conditions, of course, exist in different degrees of activity, from a murderer down to a common liar. The disease assumes so many different forms, that it is difficult to discern it, until very positive symptoms have been developed. It is hard to find the line where virtue ends and crime begins; it is hard to find in the body politic one who says," I have enough; I will loan you money at six per cent. per annum."

Having examined this subject in all its bearings, we are satisfied that the best constitutional treatment, as indicated, is a universal education of the rising generation,—a general diffusion of knowledge in all its branches, and so educating every faculty of the mind that where discord now exists harmony may take the place.

In addition to the institutions of learning that now exist, we recommend others. The vehicle through which we propose to accomplish the general diffusion of knowledge, is

COMPULSORY EDUCATION.

Let the state enforce by law the education of every child in, at least, all the common branches, and, where it is practicable, even in the higher ones.

Aside from obliging parents to send their children to school, until the boy is eighteen and the girl sixteen, the state should educate and support all the paupers, orphans, and vagabond children. It will be much cheaper than to support prisons, jails, and criminal courts, and the effect will be far more preventive of crime than the infliction of an excessive and unnatural punishment.

The *Tribune* in an editorial, March 19, 1873, which we give below, verifies our statement:*

---

* "Governor Dix, who has always been peculiarly happy in his aphoristic sentiments, says in his letter declining to interfere in the Foster case: 'Every man who strikes a murderous blow at the life of his fellow, must be made to feel that his own is in certain peril.' There is a need that this should be a guiding principle at this time, and at all times, in dealing with the dangerous classes. The present importance of Governor Dix's advice has just been illustrated almost simultaneously in New York and Chicago. On Monday evening, in New York, a party of three roughs, without

The execution of Driver in this city, executions in other places, and Gov. Dix's letter, at about the same time, it seems, had not the desired effect. The editor of the *Tribune* thinks that it is "only necessary that Driver's murderous companions should be tried according to law to have them go the same way he went last Friday. It is only by ridding the community of these outlaws that the class to which they belong may be brought under the terror that alone can restrain their murderous propensities." In our mode of treating this class of people, we would have them placed in a reformatory institute or prison, long

---

provocation, began their murderous work in a saloon, and, evidently maddened at the sight of the blood they caused to flow, kept it up after going into the street, cutting and slashing with their knives at every one they chanced to meet. Early yesterday morning, a somewhat similar slaughter occurred in the disreputable neighborhood of Halsted street and Canalport avenue,—where Rafferty killed Officer O'Meara, and where the two police officers were forced to kill the two McVeighs to save their own lives. In yesterday's *melee*, one man had his throat cut from ear to ear, others were badly damaged, and it was only the singular chance which is noticed in rows of this kind that prevented a more general destruction of human life. The neighborhood in which this latest murder occurred is crowded with dangerous characters of the Rafferty and McVeigh stamp, who seem to be entirely uncontrolled by law. There is but one way in which an impression can be made upon such a community, and that is the way which Gov. Dix suggests. The rapid and certain execution of the law, death to actual murderers, and the severest punishment possible to would-be murderers, is the only effectual remedy that can be applied. Nothing short of this will appeal to the brutal instincts of the classes who defy the laws, and permit their passions to run wild. The man who deals a murderous blow ' must be made to feel that his own life is in certain peril.' "

before they commit such horrible deeds as murder. We do not believe it to be a good practice to continue to treat the effect alone, which is only the active sympton of a poisonous virus infecting the entire body of society.

It is said to make a deep impression on the mind to touch people's pockets; and they will at least hearken to what you have to say. In this connection we beg permission to give a few figures. In the year 1870, Chicago had over 25,000 arrests and trials for crime. St. Louis had, during the same year, 26,500. To this number add New York, Philadelphia, Buffalo, Cincinnati, New Orleans, Nashville, and other cities of like reputation in crime, and we have, in the aggregate, in the United States, during the year 1870, over 500,000 crimes which were tried and disposed of according to law. It is further estimated that it cost the people of the United States annually about thirty-six million dollars to punish this great army of criminals. Chicago alone supports five hundred police, St. Louis over six hundred, New York sixteen hundred, Philadelphia eight hundred, and at a rough estimate the United States supports constantly an army of police and officers of justice of nearly thirty thousand, costing Chicago alone over half a million of dollars,—enough money when properly invested to educate and support all of its paupers, orphans, and children of neglectful parents, and have enough money besides to defray all expenses of a free public lecturing hall, in each ward. All this money may be saved to the public, after ten years; for if we educate our children in earnest, and strictly according to the laws of their nature, we can so bend and train them that in ten years we shall have no need of five hundred ablebodied men parading our streets, "armed with an implement of death," to keep the people in the path of virtue. It is doubtless, much cheaper for the state to feed, educate, and train up its paupers, orphans, and children of criminals and neglectful parents, than afterwards to keep them as outlaws and criminals. It is far better and easier to train the young heart than to frighten the adult into right doing. Let society do its whole duty by the child, and it will not need to strangle the adult. For the education of this class of children we recommend a

STATE INSTITUTION.

Let the state make an appropriation and, if necessary, levy a special tax to build a house of correction or a reformatory educational institute, where all children, six years of age and upwards, and even adults of doubtful moral habits, may be sent and made to work and be schooled so as to train them to a useful life. This institution can be made self-sustaining by the proper cultivation of about five hundred to one thousand acres of land, which may be bought very cheap, and by this means give all the inmates practical lessons in farming. Here the child may learn something about nature which it can never learn in a city prison, or the so-called house of correction. Eight hours for educational exercises in school, part of which time may be devoted to the toilet, bathing, etc.; and eight hours for labor, during which time the teacher, at the signal of the bell, marches with her class to a place assigned to her, where she can give practical instruction in cultivating vegetables and small fruits for the table, beautiful flowers, and young fruit trees for the market. Little girls, as well as boys, should learn something about tilling the soil of mother earth. This is healthful to the body and gives the mind variety of thought. During the winter season these children should, instead of farm exercises, be required to take practical lessons in housekeeping, sewing, or learning some trade, all of which will fit them—aside from the intellectual and moral education which they receive in school—to take their place in society when they are grown.

The farm should be divided up, so as to suit the ages and different classes—from the child to the adult; the girls being only required to cultivate flowers, vegetables, and small fruits. All manner of industry may be taught here, also every branch of education. No one should be allowed to leave this institution, without they are sufficiently well qualified to enable them to enter good society, and make an honorable living. This institution should be so arranged as to provide every means of development. All the different natures of man,—all the faculties,—should receive attention. It should contain lecture-rooms, lyceums, gymnasiums, and bath-rooms. It should be provided with amusement, and music, worship, social training, lessons in conversation and concerts would lend zest to more practical occupations.

Attached to the institute should be play-grounds, parks, and a few small lakes. It should also be provided with a museum, containing varieties of wild as well as domestic animals, that practical instruction may be given in natural history. The schools should be conducted about the same as our public schools. An institution of this kind can be sustained at much less expense than our present system of treating criminals. Aside from the state institutions, which we have suggested, the compulsory education of the masses is absolutely necessary.* Parents should be

---

* ON COMPULSORY EDUCATION.—" A peculiar feature of the legislation of the past winter has been the unprecedented number of measures designed to secure more general and more regular attendance of children at school.

"Not only in the National Legislature, but in several of the State Legislatures, bills have been introduced for the promotion of public education by devices ranging from penalties for non-attendance at school, as proposed in the state of New York, to rewards for regular attendance (by remission of taxes), as proposed in Illinois. Though these schemes have been, for the most part, unsuccessful,—the time not being ripe for them, as their friends allege,—they have shown very clearly the drift of public opinion. The nation has been aroused to a sense of its educational poverty, and is earnestly casting about for a cure. It has learned that some millions of its population are illiterate; that millions of children are growing up unschooled; that ignorance is everywhere associated with, if not related to, poverty and crime ; and that the productive force of the country is seriously weakened by lack of intelligence. The natural inference is, that a wider diffusion of elementary instruction would go far to inaugurate a happier state of things. And the inference is just. But when people assume, as the advocates of compulsory schooling do, that the instruction now given in the schools is a certain cure-all for the evils noticed, and that the one thing needful is some means of

compelled by law to send their children to school
from eight years of age until the boy is eighteen and
the girl is sixteen. In the little province of Wittenberg, Germany, this has been a law for over a century,
and now, with a population of seven million souls,
murder is a rare occurrence

---

bringing all the children into the schools and keeping them there, then their position may be reasonably questioned. It is by no means evident that such an extension of the scope and power of the public schools would be an advantage. Indeed there are reasons for suspecting that it might prove a national calamity unless a radical change were first made in the matter and methods of popular teaching. Let us not be charged with hostility to public schools. We believe in them firmly. It is not only the wisest policy but the highest duty of the community to make education a public concern, and to see to it that no poverty, indifference, or greed shall be suffered to deprive the young of suitable opportunities for instruction and culture. We believe, further, that a well devised and properly conducted system of public schools is the directest, cheapest, surest, and best means for securing the instruction of all classes. Nevertheless, we seriously question whether the existing system is anywhere near that state of perfection which would warrant us in stereotyping it, and enforcing it on all children. We are by no means sure that the instruction given in the schools is, in the main, such as the children need. We doubt whether the mental habits fostered by the schools are really beneficial to inhabitants of a working world like ours. We doubt whether instruction is offered at the most suitable times and for the most suitable periods. In short, there is not a feature of the popular school system that we should not wish to have carefully reconsidered before extending its sphere and power. The perfection of the system is to be found in Boston. It is the professed desire of the advocates of compulsory education to secure, as far as possible, to all the children of the land, the school advantages provided by that city. In view of the testimony of the hundred and fifty physicians who have joined

No child should be allowed to be employed in factories or elsewhere, when the employment positively prevents it from acquiring a proper education, during its school days.

If it is not in the power of parents to educate their children without receiving some income from their earnings, then it is the duty of society to educate

---

with the parents of the pupils in the Boston Latin school in protesting against the system of long hours and cramming enforced in that school in particular, and in the public schools in general, we may be pardoned for accounting those 'advantages' something fearful. 'I cannot doubt that the modern system of forcing the tender brain of youth lays the foundation for the brain and nervous disorders of after years—the cases of melancholia, paralysis, softening of the brain, and kindred diseases becoming so fearfully prevalent.' So writes Dr. Clement A. Walker, Superintendent of the City Hospital for the Insane. Dr. George A. Stuart adds: 'Of late years the majority of diseases seem to have assumed a nervous type, which in most cases may be traced to over-taxation of the mental powers of the young, both male and female.' And Dr. J. B. Treadwell: 'Hundreds of pupils of our public schools are ruined in health every year; this I know from personal observation.' And Dr. H. F. Damon: 'The amount of vital power has its limits, and these limits, in my judgment, are far exceeded by the present system of overtasking the pupils in our public schools.' Dr. E. B. Moore writes that he has a son now in the insane asylum, 'the result of excessive study and disappointed ambition.'

"We do not infer that such would everywhere be the inevitable results of the proposed extension of public schooling, but such results would be possible, indeed probable, unless the system were materially modified; and we ought to be very cautious in erecting a national god so likely to turn out a Moloch. If the choice lies between healthy ignorance and ' an overtaxed brain, a dwarfed body, a weakened intellect, a variety of diseases, and a premature grave,'—which Dr. P. D. Walsh says is the natural, or unnatural,

them. This being done, we believe that the constitutional disease, which now prevades society, will be largely mitigated. How many parents who have sufficient means to support and educate their children, force them to labor daily in shops or the field, only to have them earn a few dollars so that the parent

result of the current system of schooling,—commend us to an abundance of healthy ignorance.

"Even if much study were never a weariness to the flesh,—if the requirements of the schools could be complied with without any risk of broken health, the present cost of schooling would be needlessly great. The complaint that our schools are spoiling our more promising youth for work,—that they foster foolish ambitions and aversions to material pursuits, is not wholly without foundation. Ten or fifteen years of exclusive devotion to books is very apt to develop tastes and habits unfriendly to productive labor. The youth leaves school a young man (in his own estimation at least), and very likely with exaggerated notions of his own importance. He is too old, and too proud, and 'too much of a gentleman' to begin at the bottom of any craft, and, by doing a boy's work, acquire that familiarity with details on which the mastery of any business depends. Besides, in most cases, he can not afford the time for such an apprenticeship. He must begin to earn wages at once. The consequence is, the country is full of unprofitably 'educated' men, who, having neither rude strength nor skilled hands, are glad to get employment at lower rates than are paid to common laborers. The loss to the country from this needless diverting of youth from productive labor is beyond estimation. It is due very largely to the unwise requirements of the schools in the matter of time. They suffer no rivals. Their pupils must give the best part of the day, regularly, to school work, or withdraw. It may ruin their health, and deprive them of opportunity to acquire the practical business training on which their future happiness and usefulness will chiefly depend. No matter; the character of the school is at stake, and the school, not the student, is the primary consideration. The Boston Board

may be enabled to accumulate money. Such persons are proper subjects for legislation.

Again, no person should be allowed to marry without they can show visible means to support and educate a family. A young man should have a legitimate vocation, aside from a given amount of money,

---

admit this inversion of the proper order of things with unconscious frankness, in their refusal to lessen the amount of study required of the Latin school boys. 'It would be impossible,' they plead, 'to point out any eminent school of this grade in which a less number of hours is found sufficient.'

"At the lower end of the social scale is another class of victims to the unwisdom of our school conductors. The records of our Board of Education show that half the children who enter the schools never pass beyond the primary grades; that is, they leave school before they can read a newspaper, or work a simple sum in fractions. Mrs. Holmes's 'Children who Work,' in our last number, tells what becomes of the most of them. Their sad condition justifies legislative interference; but it would be going to as injurious an extreme to compel them to stop work entirely, and go to school all day. They must live; and they must earn their living soon, if not now. The school of letters is to them a need, the school of labor is an absolute necessity; and, as things are, they cannot take both. Nevertheless, they could have, and should have, both; and we believe that the public schools ought to take the first step toward making this consummation possible, by offering instruction at such times, and for such periods, as shall least conflict with the primary requirements of the children. The current six-hour system is destructive at both ends, and in the middle. It is ruinous to health, it prevents the practical education of the well-to-do, and it shuts out from school privileges that large class which cannot command the whole day for book-learning. A system so doubtfully adapted to the circumstances of the case needs very careful looking to before it is made absolute in power and dominion. Indeed, our Boards of Education are in urgent need of some scores of Huxleys to insist, as Professor

on which to begin life. The young woman should also be required to own a reasonable outfit. This is a law in some states, in the old country, and it is said to work admirably. Such a law would inspire a spirit of economy and industry, make young men and women more steady in their habits, and instead of producing paupers would very soon render even the term obsolete.

Public halls should be erected in every township, and in every ward, for free lecturing purposes, lyceums, and amusements, each night in the week. The hall to be under the control of a janitor, who may be appointed or elected, and who should be required to light and keep it in order for some exercises each night, whose salary should be fixed by the county commissioners and paid out of the county funds. It should be generally understood that on every Monday evening a lecture will be given by some one who may volunteer or officiate by special request. In this home talent should be encouraged as much as possible. On Tuesday evening we would suggest a debating lyceum; on Wednesday, a concert; on Thursday, dancing; on Friday, children's temperance lyceum;

Huxley did at a late meeting of the London School Board, on a reconsideration, not only of the subjects and methods of elementary instruction, but of the hours given to schooling. Our public schools may never become perpetual fountains at which all may draw as they have opportunity; but they will cease, we hope, to hedge themselves about with needless exactions and impassable barriers. They will not insist on six hours' attendance a day, when three hours are the limit of profitable study; nor will they insist on three hours' study or none when any number of children can command but one hour."—*Journal of Education.*

and on Saturday, political debating meeting, where all, either men or women would have a right to speak, speaking being limited to ten minutes, and no ill-natured discussions being allowed, or dogmatic decisions by the house; simply a statement of opinion. Persons may be called on to speak, but those who prefer to read short paragraphs from papers or books, may be permitted to do so. These exercises should never be allowed to be prolonged after half-past nine o'clock, the time of beginning being about half-past seven o'clock. These exercises may be made attractive, interesting, and useful, where the working man and woman can spend their evenings to a good advantage. Compulsory education, we believe, then, to be the only hope of regenerating society, so that, in time, wrong-doing will cease.

We come now to consider briefly in addition to what has already been suggested in other chapters, as to how to co-operate with moral suasion in the treatment

OF THE EFFECT

by legal persuasion. We believe it to be necessary and right to suppress all business of an illegitimate character: such as drinking-shops, gambling houses, lectures and places of amusement where the moral welfare of mankind is not the chief object. Business, of every kind, should, by law, be suspended each evening at half-past 6 o'clock, (see Chapter V., Part First), then people will finish the day's work in a day, and not take part of the night to do it. Then people will strive to administer to the spiritual and moral nature as well as to provide for the body. All persons moving into a neighborhood, should have their names registered, stating their vocation, in order to ascertain whether they have an honorable means of support.

This will put a stop to loafing, effectually. Any one found intoxicated should be arrested, and his liberty restrained. He should be sent to a house of correction, of the kind heretofore indicated. If he is a married man, his property should pass into the entire control of his wife, or a guardian appointed by the court, to control the business affairs of a drunkard, until he can show sufficient evidence from the reformatory institute that he is cured, and capable of conducting his own affairs again.

There should be no money fine as a punishment. Drunkenness should be made a penal offense and punished the same as other crimes, which are considered violations of law. This would be death to inebriation which now goes unpunished; then we shall not be required to hang men for murder, perpetrated while under the influence of whisky. Some one asks, "Will this then be a free country?" Yes; free to do and act just as you please, only you will not be free to do wrong. We are opposed to punishing the criminal by exacting a certain sum of money; it is no punishment whatever; it is no more punishment than to pay an honest debt.

This will not reform the criminal, either physically or mentally. If crime is the result of depravity, which we think will be admitted, then the punishment should be to cure that depravity, and not to foster it. Nearly all of our minor crimes are punished by fines, and those who can not pay are sent to a work-house until they can pay to the city or county the amount required as a fine. This is what we call corporal punishment, and has never reformed a single criminal. (See chapter on that subject.) As to the bail system, we have for a number of years been opposed to accepting a bail bond to insure the criminal's appearance at some time in the future, to answer to the charges against him. The *Tribune*, this morning, March 17th, 1873, gives an official report where thirty-five criminals have escaped justice, the bail bonds proving worthless, defrauding the county out of $20,000. We are in favor of abolishing this uncertain mode of administering justice. Bring the accused to a speedy trial, and inflict punishment promptly, and thus dispose of a criminal in a few days, and put him to work where he can be reformed. So long as we accept money as a payment for crime, we are allowing the virus of the sore to be reabsorbed, and this is a constant source of constitutional poisoning.

A word in regard to religious teachings or sectarian ideas. We would have

IT REMEMBERED

that we are not in favor of mixing things up too much. The Sabbath is set apart legitimately for worship and religious instruction. Let the evenings during the week, then, be devoted to scientific education, which is the handmaid of religion. The clergy may here use their powers and talents in giving lectures on philosophical subjects. It is as well for a mechanic to know the composition of water, as for a physician, a lawyer, or clergyman; or to understand the use of the air we breathe, the influence of light, heat, etc., on life; or to acquire knowledge on any of the branches pertaining to physiology, hygiene, mental and moral philosophy. Here is a work for physicians that is unlimited. We do not think it proper to teach people medicine, but too much knowledge on physiology can not be diffused among the people. It teaches how to eat, how to exercise, how to sleep, how to train the physical organism as well as the mental. If we would prevent crime and overcome evil, we must labor to diffuse knowledge among the masses on all subjects which teach men how to live rather than how to die. It is the sentiment of the profession, expressed by that great and good man, the immortal Horace Greeley, when he said that "children need training just as much as colts. Like them, they are animals, though something more—having physical organizations, and souls inside of them. But these latter, however grand in themselves, are dependent for their mode, method and power of expression upon the physical organizations in which they dwell, and with which they are so intimately connected. To bring the soul out, the body must be trained. Herein is the relation of parents to children in this country, most lamentably defective. I do not overlook the fact that much of the success in training depends upon the quality of the physical organization."

In a lecture on the "Coming Man," delivered in Philadelphia, and published at the time in one of the city papers, we said that "the only hope of the 'coming man,' occupying a higher station in life, capable of perpetuating a republican form of government, and continuing his march toward perfection is in a general diffusion of physiological knowledge in addition to the moral teachings of the church. Man must first be organically and constitutionally regenerated, before he can enjoy a spiritual and moral harmony. So long as man is physically depraved he is incapable of imbibing higher truth, hence physicians have a work which is as important in the great work of man's reformation as that of the clergy."

Now we believe, and it seems quite rational, too, that if the suggestions advanced in this chapter alone were carried into effect and properly systematized, crime—which is the effect of the great disease pervading society—could soon be controlled and "checkmated," that but few symptoms would be manifested, and the cause removed by universal education through moral suasion, administered by the strong arm of legal persuasion. Thus by purifying the constitution, and at the same time suppressing the effect, we may reasonably hope that the day is not far distant when crime and human depravity will be superseded by virtue, and enable every member of the human family to enter into a glorious state of happiness.

CHAPTER XV.

WHAT WE KNOW ABOUT INSANITY. WHO ARE THE INSANE? AND SHALL WE MAKE INSANITY AN EXCUSE FOR CRIME?

"If man exercise only his spiritual powers on earth, and confine their activity alone to the spiritual portion of the brain, disease will follow, and there is danger of a dethronement of reason. A healthful activity is the regulator of the whole man."—*Huxley*.

"As reason exalts man above, so the lack of it degrades him beneath, the animal consciousness."—*Davis*.

This world may be looked upon as one grand asylum for the insane. The difference between those within the walls of a house for the safe-keeping of those which the law considers absolutely insane and those on the outside is not so great as one might suppose. Insanity assumes as many different forms as crime.

Insanity is the result of a diseased condition of the physical organism as well as of the mind. Crime is a manifestation of a depraved condition of the mental as well as of the physical organism. Right actions of men are the manifestation of a healthy mental and physical condition of the being. Those whom we consider insane are persons whose actions are discordant, and not in harmony with the common actions of men. Insanity, like crime, has its origin in hereditary transmission; also in an acquired condition, which demands a simultaneous attention and study. We have stated in the first part of this volume that consumption, scrofula, and other diseases are transmissible from parent to child, and are, therefore, often peculiar to families. The same conditions may be acquired by even the most healthy and robust persons who have no preceptible hereditary taint in their system. The same we have stated to be true of crime, virtue, and mental power. Sanity in the human mental constitution, like health in the material body, rewards its possessor by lifting his sensations and thoughts superior to self; while the insane mind is punished with an unconquerable and obtrusive egotism—is supremely rapt in self importance, even as a diseased body gives its proprietor no rest neither day nor night. An insane man incessantly thinks of himself. A sane mind, on the contrary, thinks for the benefit of others. Society, with its intense antagonisms, and organized hatreds, develops insanity in individuals, by compelling each to be practically tyrannical and unceasingly selfish. Obedience to the sanitary laws of the mental constitution would remove the individual from the vortex of conflicting interests. He would choose the good and reject the evil; and thus he would become "insane," in the opinion of all narrow and selfish minds, because he could no longer respect their assumed rights, nor harmonize with their diabolical methods.

Sanity in the human mind is celestial and harmonial health; in exchange for which, earthly riches are poverty.

The sane mind is instructed by the past, thankful for the present, hopeful for the future; but the insane man turns his back to the future, quarrels with the present, and sees the past as a universal grave of hopes and longings. It is important to note, that not only the mind and body are governed by laws, but that they are, to a great extent, governed by the same laws. Whatever improves the physical qualities of the brain, improves also the mind; whatever deteriorates the brain impairs the mind. They have a common development, are equally increased in vigor, capacity, and power by systematic and judicious exercise, and are alike injured by deficient or excessive effort.

The brain is exhausted by thinking, as the muscles by acting; and, like the exhausted muscles, it requires time for the restoration of vigor through nutritive repair. As thus the mind is dependent upon the conditions of the brain, while the brain is controlled by the bodily system, we see how impossible it is to deal with the mental powers in a practical way without taking the material organization into account. Diseases of the brain are, above all others, complex and obscure. Those of subordinate parts affect only the organic function; but when the higher nervous centers become disordered, thought, feeling, will, conduct, and character are implicated, and the whole circle of individual relations and actions becomes a study of symptoms—a field of diagnosis. So great is the difficulty and responsibility of the task, that only the educated and capable physician, who devotes his life to this specialty, is competent to deal with these cases. And yet all members of the community have a vital interest in the subject, because, first, health and vigor of mind are of the highest importance, and these interests each person has in his own immediate care; second, the causes that undermine them are numerous and insidious; third, society has a duty to perform toward the defective minded, which should be performed not ignorantly, but intelligently; and, finally, a real knowledge of the characteristics and causes of mental deterioration is the key to a true understanding of the constitution of human nature.

We will now speak briefly of the different forms of

MENTAL IMPAIRMENT.

We have stated that, owing to certain conditions of the body, false appearances and various disturbances of the senses are liable to arise. These errors are of several kinds. We are here largely indebted to Huxley, Youman, and others, for our statements. One of the simplest forms of mental aberration is

HALLUCINATION.

All the senses are subject to this deception. Sights, sounds, tastes, smells, and contacts are experienced when there are no realities to cause them. These mistakes are very common, and the greatest minds are often subject to them. Byron fancied he was visited by a spectre, which he confessed, was but the effect of an over-worked brain. Dr. Johnson said that he heard distinctly the voice of his mother calling, "Sam," although she, at the time, was residing a long way off. Goethe positively asserts that he one day saw the exact counterpart of himself coming toward him. Descartes, after long confinement, was followed by an invisible person calling upon him to pursue the search of truth. Luther imagined he saw the devil, and threw his ink-stand at him. Hallucinations may thus exist in a sound state of the reason, which recognizes their true character. In the insane, they assume a thousand singular and fantastic forms. The first form that presents itself is what are called

ILLUSIONS.

In this case an object may be seen, but misunderstood, or mistaken for something else. These are very common. When the imagination becomes morbidly excited through the influence of fear, superstition, or otherwise, there is great liability to illusion. The folds of drapery, or pieces of furniture, seen by a pale, uncertain light, are taken for apparitions; the clouds are transformed into fighting armies; or the heavens appear filled with blood. When the mind becomes more deeply perverted, one person is mistaken for another; animals are mistaken for men, and conversely; an old hat for a royal crown, and a handful of pebbles for heaps of gold. Another deviation is what is termed

DELUSION.

In these cases, the seat of error is not in the senses themselves, but the judgment, in relation to objects of sense. The mind is liable to deceptions, and to accept as facts various false notions, which have no immediate reference to sense,—perceptions, —as where a person believes he is a prophet, or a king, or is the victim of a conspiracy to take his life, or has lost his soul.

From the illustrations given, it will be seen that hallucination and illusion may co-exist with a sound state of the reason, which comprehends their real nature; and it is maintained that, in some cases, the mind can rectify its own delusions. But if in any of these circumstances the individual is incapable of recognizing or correcting them when an appeal is made to his reason, the case is one of delusional insanity. These delusions are, of course, liable to involve the feelings, and the character of the insanity may depend upon the emotions excited. A person under the delusion of pride, who fancies himself an emperor or an angel, may be harmless; but if, under the delusion of fear, he imagines those around him to be enemies, seeking to take his life, or if he hears voices commanding him to kill them, his insanity is dangerous, and necessitates restraint.

EMOTIONAL INSANITY.

By this is understood a derangement of the affections, an abnormal deficiency of moral sense, or morbid activity of the propensities which give rise to extravagance of conduct. These diseases of feeling do not necessarily involve insanity of the intellect. A person may have a good degree of intelligence with a very low and defective moral nature; or he may be driven by insane impulses to the commission of acts which his judgment condemns. In the healthy balance of the faculties, reason guards the passions; but these may be so morbidly exalted that reason loses its empire; it can counsel, but no longer control. Moral perversities of character may be hereditary, or exist from birth, when the whole life of the individual is morally unhealthy; or they may be due to various causes, the effects of which are seen in a profound change in the conduct. Examples of the former kind are numerous, where inertness or obtuseness of the moral nature, and a controlling activity of the lower propensities, have been witnessed from childhood, and over which threats, rewards, and punishments were without influence. In some cases, persons in whom mental derangement has never appeared become the subjects of a gradual change of feeling and conduct. They are noticed to be unusually absorbed, reserved, and irritable upon the slightest provocation. As the cloud gathers, there is increasing suspicion and moroseness, and, without perhaps knowing the reason, the patient's friends regard him as an altered man. At last the storm bursts, and some outrageous act is committed. If it is not a breach of law, he is declared insane, and sent to the asylum; if the law has been violated, he is probably declared a criminal, and sent to prison or execution. Or the case may terminate in suicide, under a blind impulse to self-destruction. Doctor Maudsley gives a good illustration of emotional insanity. " A married lady, aged thirty-one, who had only one child, a few months old, was for months afflicted with a strong and persistent suicidal impulse without any delusion or disorder of the intellect. After some weeks of anxious care from her relatives, she was sent to an asylum, so frequent were her suicidal attempts. She was quite rational, even in her great horror and reprobation of the morbid propensity, and bitterly deplored the grief and trouble she caused her friends. Nevertheless, her attempts at suicide were unceasing, at one time trying to strangle herself, and again refusing to take food. After she had been in the asylum for four months, she appeared to be undergoing a slow and steady improvement, and watchfulness was somewhat relaxed; but one night she suddenly slipped out of a door, climbed a high garden-wall with surprising agility, and threw herself headlong into a reservoir of water. She was got out before life was extinct, and after this attempt gradually regained her cheerfulness and love of life." Doctor Maudsley exclaims: "In the face of such an example of uncontrollable impulse, what a cruel mockery to measure the lunatic's responsibility by his knowledge of right and wrong!" implying that there are those who would limit insanity to derangement of the intellect—a derangement so profound as to obliterate the capability of even discriminating between right and wrong. There has been a reluctance to admit the existence of what is termed moral insanity on the part of many, who confine their attention to the practical difficulties it involves as regards society. They are in the habit of believing that, for all practical purposes, the moral endowments of men are equal. Not exactly that they are equally benevolent, equally honest, equally true to the right and good; but that they have an equal chance so to be, if they choose. In the moral sense or faculty, it is easy to recognize two different elements, the power to discern the distinction between right and wrong, virtue and vice, the honest and the base, and the disposition to pursue the one and avoid the other. These elements, like those of the intellect, are unequally developed in different men, which inequality may be either congenital or produced in after life by moral or physical causes. And thus, though a person may appear to act with perfect freedom of will, unconscious of any irresistible bias, yet it is obvious that his conduct is actually governed more by these variable conditions of his moral nature than by any abstract notions formed by the intellect.

It does not answer the essential question to say that a person is good or bad because he chooses to be one or the other. In the considerations here presented, and in these only, are to be found a satisfactory answer to this question. The first of these we will call

MANIA.

This is applied to a large class of cerebral disorders, in which the balance of the mental forces is lost, and the mind is in a state of preternatural excitement, which exhibits itself in a thousand different ways. It may be either chronic or acute. In the former, it is somewhat modified and lessoned, approaching imbecility as the mind becomes more and more disorganized through the insidious and debilitating effects of the disease.

The acute form, as its name indicates, is an exalted violent action of strong unexhausted mental faculties whose action is perverted and uncontrolled by the will of the patient or of his friends. To say that these conditions are made, is absurd, to say the least.

The next form we have to deal with, is

MONOMANIA.

This is similar to mania, except in this particular, that it is limited to a single faculty, or a single idea. In all other things, and upon all other subjects, the patient may be perfectly *compos*, but on one particular subject he is, as they say, "wild as a hawk." It may be an intense desire to kill—*homicidal* mania; or a *suicidal* mania—an irresistible impulse to self-destruction. A case of this kind has already been described. A diseased propensity to steal is called *kleptomania;* and in *pyromania* there is the desire to burn buildings. There are monomanias of pride, vanity, etc. Dr. Bucknill describes the following case:

"An industrious, well-informed artisan had a fever that ended in an attack of maniacal excitement. From this he recovered, but grew irritable, morose, and quarrelsome. After the lapse of more than a year, he declared himself the Son of God. After this, his temper became more docile, with the exception of an occasional outburst of violence toward those whom he thinks ought to obey him. He is reasonable and rational, and works industriously at his trade." Another form of cerebral disorder, and one marked by depression, sadness and gloom, is the opposite of mania. The one is an exalted, furious condition; the other a lowered and depressed state of the mind, and is termed

MELANCHOLIA.

Melancholia takes a variety of forms. It may be an exaggeration of the patient's natural character, and have a long period of development. It is often a consequence of other forms of insanity, and may spring from the grief that follows sudden calamity. The diseased depression of the feelings characteristic of melancholia may exist without impairing the intellectual operations; but it is generally accompanied by delusions and hallucinations, although these generally derive their tone from the character of the disorder. They are insane explanations of the patient's wretchedness, or gloomy forebodings of what is to happen to him in the future. There is another form of insanity, characterized by a diminution of mental power, and by an incapacity, which gradually increases, and invades the whole muscular system. This is called

GENERAL PARALYSIS.

This disease is one peculiar to manhood. It is scarcely ever met with before thirty. Women are seldom sufferers from general paralysis.

The earliest symptoms of motor derangement affect the tongue, and are evinced in thickness of speech, and imperfect articulation of words, especially those abounding in consonants. It is a curious fact that the mental derangement accompanying this striking and fatal decay of bodily energy takes the form of an exaggerated feeling of personal power and importance. One man imagines he is the possessor of ship-loads of gold and silver; another, that he is the Son of God; another, that he is as heavy as the world; and so on through the list of kings, emperors, etc., each person having his own peculiar phantasy. We have three other forms of mental derangement. One, which consists of extreme debility, and results from loss, obliteration, or decay of the faculties, is called

DEMENTIA.

Another form, the result of profound infirmity of the cerebro-spinal system, caused by arrested development before birth or in early infancy, and which perverts or destroys the reflex, instinctive, and intellectual function, is known as

IDIOCY.

The third and last form denotes a degree of mental deficiency not so low as idiocy—a development rather retarded than arrested. The memory and understanding are in a state of feebleness, but they are capable of some education. This is termed

IMBECILITY.

We have here briefly described the leading forms

of mental disease, which in their ultimate stages dissolve the responsible relation of their victim to society. What to do with these cases is a question for the physician and the judge; but from the point of view of mental hygiene, which aims at their prevention, our attention is drawn to the definite causes of mental improvement, which are seen in many other effects beside those of overt insanity. There is much perverted mental action that never passes into mania; much mental weakness that never reaches dementia; much morbidity of feeling that never ripens into moral insanity. The classes in which mental defects are so prominent that the state must assume their charge are deplorably numerous; yet they form but a fraction of the total amount of mental weakness and incapacity which exists in the community. Massachusetts reports three thousand insane, twelve hundred idiots, about five hundred blind, and four hundred deaf-mutes. But, beside these, she has ten thousand paupers —persons incapable of taking care of themselves—and a large criminal class, who, from moral perversity, in which low and deficient organization plays a leading part, become the scourge of society.

All of the forms of mental impairment, and degrees of immorality and lawlessness, are the result of concurring influences, both internal and external. The causes are predisposing and exciting. The predisposing cause to insanity is most generally a transmitted condition, which the patient may have had from birth, only requiring some exciting cause to develop it into acute mania, which will manifest itself in the perpetration of some outrageous crime against society. Again, we may have mania from some external exciting cause, and have no former predisposition. A mind overworked, or overburdened with care and anxiety, from the slightest exciting cause may suddenly break down, and the manifest symptoms are those of acute mania, in most cases that of a suicidal form—an intense desire to end one's life. Defective nutrition of the cerebral structure is another cause of insanity. This may be due to an arrest of nutritive action in the organ, or a deficiency of proper nutrition of the body, which becoming weakened, of a necessity involves the cerebral functions. Without a sound body we cannot have a sound mind, and *vice versa*. That debilitated stock is a source of criminality and insanity, no one can doubt. How the running down of stock, through the loss of vital power, by hereditary influences, should swell the ranks of the dependent classes, or those incapable of self-support, is obvious. But this cause is equally powerful in reinforcing the dangerous classes who fill our jails and prisons. Immoral training and vicious associations are undoubtedly among the potent agencies by which these are educated for the career of crime and vice; but a co-operating cause, of far greater power, is low organization or defective cerebral endowment. They begin life with a nervous system, incapable of the higher controlling functions.

OVERTASKING THE EMOTIONS

is undoubtedly one great cause of insanity, and a

concomitant of advancing civilization. The savage state is marked by simple unchangeable social institutions, uniformity of manners and habits. The savage rarely laughs or sheds tears; he is educated to stoicism. On the contrary, our education, instead of being a training to self-control, and a systematic discipline of the emotions, through cultivation of the sciences of nature, is too generally conducted in the spirit of excitement; studies are pursued under the spur of sharp competition for the prizes and applause of public examinations, and, in place of sober and solid attainment, our culture degenerates into a mere preparation for trade and politics.

OVERTASKING THE INTELLECT

is an extensive cause of mental derangement, though less so than those just considered. The baneful effects of cerebral exhaustion have already been noticed to some extent. That study is carried often to injurious lengths, is notorious. Moderate use, undoubtedly develops the brain, and it is equally certain that if the amount of work is carried much beyond this point, the organ is endangered. It has been objected to this view that the lunatic asylums are chiefly peopled with inferior rather than highly cultivated minds; but inferior minds are just those most likely to be injured by excessive study. Any one can reason from the physical to the mental powers and see that this is so. The educated, trained muscles of the blacksmith will endure more continued hard labor than the uneducated, soft, flaccid muscles of the clerk, and just so in proportion the educated brain will endure more constant laborious study than the one that is not educated. It is not to be forgotten that there are evils of mental underaction as well as of overaction. While there is no evidence that, in the case of uncultured savages, the brain is liable to become diseased from lack of exercise, the same thing can not be affirmed of the cultivated races. The progress of civilization in these races is accompanied by a higher development and increasing complexity of cerebral organization; and this higher condition can only be maintained by a correspondingly higher degree of functional exercise. Without that activity which its greater perfection implies and requires, the brain of the civilized man degenerates. To end this chapter without giving a few hints and precautions would leave it unfinished. It is a serious error to suppose that, because there may be a predisposition to insanity in a family, therefore the members are to regard their danger in the light of a fatality from which there is no escape; on the contrary, these are pre-eminently the cases in which, to a wise discretion, forewarning is forearming. Where such a tendency exists, the education, occupation, and habits should be ordered with the strictest reference to it. The establishment of strong bodily health should be a paramount consideration. The physical education should be specially directed to strengthen the nervous system and diminish its excitability. Much study, bodily inaction, confinement to warm rooms, sleeping on feathers, are all favorable to undue nervous susceptibility. In the education of children thus circumstanced, in brain exercises, it is of the first importance to remember that whatever tends in any degree to impair the mental health, acts with redoubled power when co-operating with morbid tendencies.* While the brain is yet plastic and pliable, a little mismanagement, the humoring of precocity, the repression of physical and nervous activity, or overstimulation of thought, may awaken the germs of mental disorder, and lead to the most injurious consequences. To persons thus predisposed, steady and agreeable occupation, which does not try the patience or temper, or involve much responsibility, excitement, or exhaustion, is in the highest degree desirable. Religious, political, and reformatory gatherings, where the passions are aroused and the sympathies excited, should be carefully avoided, together with all excitements which tend to disturb the sleep.

Persons predisposed to mental disease should carefully avoid a partial, one-sided cultivation of their mental powers,—a fault to which their mental constitution renders them peculiarly liable. Let them bear in mind that every prominent trait of character, intellectual or moral, every favorite form of mental exercise, is liable to be fostered at the expense of other exercises and attributes, until it becomes an indication of actual disease. Here lies the peculiar danger that the very thing most agreeable to their tastes and feelings is that which they have most to fear.

There is another disposition of mind to be carefully shunned by this class of persons—that of allowing the attention to be engrossed by some par-

---

* See Part III, on Mental Training.

ticular interest to the neglect of every other, even of those most nearly connected with the welfare of the individual. The caution is especially necessary in an age where intellectual character is marked by strife and conflict, rather than calm contemplation of philosophical inquiry; and even in which the good and true is pursued with an ardor more indicative of nervous excitement than of pure unadulterated emotion. Where the mind of a person revolves in a very narrow circle of thought, it lacks entirely that recuperative and invigorating power which springs from a wider comprehension of things, and more numerous objects of interest. The habit of brooding over a single idea is calculated to dwarf the soundest mind; but, to those unfortunately constituted, it is positively dangerous, because they are easily led to this kind of partial mental activity, and are kept from running into fatal extremes by none of these conservative agencies which a broader discipline and a more generous culture naturally furnish. The result of this continual dwelling on a favorite idea is, that it comes up unbidden, and cannot be dismissed at pleasure. Reason, fancy, passion, emotion—every power of the mind, in short—are pressed into its service, until it is magnified into gigantic proportions, and endowed with wonderful attributes. The conceptions become unnaturally vivid, the general views narrow and distorted, the proprieties of time and place are disregarded, the guiding, controlling power of the mind is disturbed, and, as the last stage of this melancholy process, reason is completely dethroned.

Hence for the moral and intellectual elevation we

are not to look exclusively to education, but to whatever tends to improve the bodily constitution, and especially the qualities of the brain. In our schemes of philanthropy we are apt to deal with men as if they could be moulded to any desirable purpose, provided only the right instrumentalities are used; ignoring altogether the fact that there is a physical organ in the case, where original endowments must limit very strictly our range of moral appliances. But while we are bringing to bear upon them all the kindly influences of learning and religion, let us not overlook these physical agencies which determine the efficacy of the brain as the material instrument of the mind.

It is to one only of these pretended benevolences that we designed to draw attention, when we wrote the heading of this chapter, the plea of insanity, which is now so rife,—which is to become the scapegoat of every infraction of law, and justice, and right. Already has it come to the pass, that if a man eats himself to death, or guzzles bad liquor until he can guzzle no more, or studies himself to a skeleton and then jumps into the river, or puts a bullet through his heart, the merciful verdict is, "*He is insane.*" If he forgets his friend's name, or fires his neighbor's dwelling or his own store to secure the insurance ; or if a young lady allows herself to be abducted by another woman's husband, or a hysterical daughter of a millionaire marries her father's coachman, the convenient cloak of "insanity" is benevolently thrown around the delinquencies and aberrations ; and the next day the weak and the unprincipled alike show themselves in the streets, the "observed of all observers," the lions of the hour.

Is heaven-born charity and her sister, true benevolence, thus to mantle over all that is dishonorable and murderous, and to cover lechery from our sight? These things ought not so to be. The true philanthropist of our day and generation should wake up to the discovery of an effectual remedy for these evils.

But not to make our chapter too long, we propose, in short, that all persons be tried for the crimes fairly charged against them. Let the majority of the jury decide on the verdict as to the fact of the act; then let the plea of insanity come in. If not sustained, let the law take its course. If sustained, let the person be committed to an insane asylum for life, if the crime was a capital one, or, if cured of their insanity, to be transferred to the penitentiary for the remainder of their days.

If the act be only a penitentiary offense, let them be sent to the asylum, to remain for life, or until cured; and when cured let them serve the same time in the penitentiary which they would have done had they not been declared insane. For, beyond question, if insane, the asylum is the proper place for them; if not insane, the penitentiary should not be cheated of its workmen. In other words, either have no laws or enforce those we have enacted.

CHAPTER XVI.

ON CORPORAL PUNISHMENT IN SCHOOLS.—IN FAMILIES AND BY THE STATE.

"Spoil the rod and spare the child."

Stay thy hand and think ere you strike the innocent one.

Parent do not chasten your child by inflicting bodily pain : it can do no good.

Parent, teacher, ponder and be wise.
Help your child to grow and rise
To the land of angel skies.

The correction of wrong actions in the child by inflicting bodily pain is of ancient date, and had its origin in the belief that goodness can be "put into" the child by the free use of the rod. Like all modes of corporal punishment for crime inflicted by the state, it has an evil effect on the sufferer, and, instead of instilling virtue, veracity, intelligence, social and moral goodness, it arouses combative and revengeful feelings—in the child as well as in the adult. It was believed, and is now, to some extent, that when a child is disobedient, it can be made to feel sorry for its wrong deeds by inflicting pain upon the corporal system. This mode of punishment impresses the child, as well as the adult, with the idea that parents, teachers, and officers of the law are absolute rulers, —monarchs,—rather than teachers and protectors. It further impresses the child with the idea that it is "desperately wicked," and that it is necessary to be punished about so much daily to make it good. I have known children—those who are unnecessarily punished by their parents or teachers—to wonder why they have not had their usual whipping, if it has been somewhat prolonged by reason of the mother feeling more harmonious than usual. We were once at a neighbor's house, and while in conversation with the mother, the little three-year-old suddenly left its busy play, and, running up, said, "Ma, I haven't had my whipping to-day." It is also a doctrine with those who punish in a corporal manner that by the "free use of the rod" the child can be made to love its parents, its teachers, or its governess. Some of the nations of earth, evidently, however, of doubtful civilization, have a rule for the husband to whip his wife each day to make her love him. Where the husband neglects this duty, the wife, knowing no other mode by which her love for him can be made stronger, often finds fault with him for not whipping more. We have not tried this means of making women love their husbands in this enlightened country; but where it has been tried, in individual instances, the result, it is said, is not very satisfactory.

It is irrational and contrary to the laws of nature to entertain the thought for one moment, that by inflicting bodily torture the child's grosser nature may be thereby subdued, its inclinations to do wrong, cured, or its unruly disposition conquered. From the light we have on the subject, we think we can show that it has diametrically the

OPPOSITE EFFECT.

The child reasons as well as the adult, only the child reasons as a child, and not as a man or woman would reason. The child has feelings as well as the adult, differing only in degree and power. To make a child understand, one must come down to a child's comprehension; and to enforce obedience to rule or law, the child requires knowledge of the nature or character of such rule or law. Without proper instruction and acquired constitutional ability, the child will not be competent to comply with the laws laid down for its government. Parents and teachers have, then, two important questions to solve, first, that of the child's ability to obey certain restrictions, and secondly, if they are not requiring more of a child than it is able to perform. The first study will be how to increase the capabilities of the child, physically as well as mentally, and secondly, how to prescribe for its government, and how to exercise the acquired capabilities by giving practical lessons in every-day life. To require more of a child than it is capable of performing, from its very organization, age, amount of education, etc., can only irritate and perplex it. We ask, then, is it just to punish in a corporal manner a child who is incapable of obeying your requirements; or can you by so doing increase its natural power to perform? Here we have an explanation of the cause of so much correction, scolding, and whipping in the family and the school. The truth is, too much is required of the child; besides which, it is reproved, and many times punished, for the most trivial offenses. At length the child will no longer try to do right, finding it so unsuccessful, and it will come to the conclusion that a certain amount of punishment is part of life, as food or sleep. Before pursuing this subject farther, we will notice the effect which corporal punishment has, and inquire whether it is

THE BEST METHOD

of punishing children. The only lesson that a child can be taught by the infliction of bodily pain is that it is organized by nature to suffer pain. The first impulse which pain produces on the system is resistance. No one will submit to pain unless positively overpowered. Whatever comes in contact with our bodies, and by such contact produces pain, our first effort is to get away from or resist, and thus relieve ourselves from suffering as soon as possible. This is one of the first laws of nature, which is self-protection. The same feeling is produced in the child when corporal punishment is inflicted for wrong doing. Resistance is not only a nervous or physical force, but is also mental. When you strike your child so as to inflict pain, it is a law of the system to protect itself, and for this purpose the physical forces refer the matter to the brain for instruction. The brain and nervous system receives instruction from the mind, and the first faculty which is aroused is combativeness. The first impulse of this faculty is to strike back, to evade the blows, and protect its own organism. The faculties of hatred and revenge are also brought into requisition. Destructiveness is always close at hand and ready to be employed.

This is the reason why a child, when it is punished so as to produce pain, will stamp, kick, strike, bite, shed tears, and plead for mercy, and promise everything to avoid this unnatural mode of punishment. Reluctantly we must make a statement, which is scarcely credible, nevertheless it is true. We have seen parents, and many pretending to be religious too, who punish their children as long as they would resist the blows of the rod, often until they became exhausted, requiring them to promise to be good.

Inflicting any sort of corporal punishment, however light it may be, outrages the dignity and feeling of the child, calls into activity the animal nature, and instead of restraining their evil tendencies, it gives practical lessons how to carry them out. Children, like men and women, have certain rights. Strike a man or woman, with a view to make them obedient, humble, and submissive, and you will find the first effort they make is to resent the insult. So with the child; the first thought that is aroused is a desire to deal back the blow, and to defend and protect its body. It is difficult to know where the evil of this inhuman practice of punishing may end. It may bring the child to the gallows, for by it, it is taught practical lessons in crime.

Nearly all persons, who resort to the use of the rod, while punishing a child, are angry, often speak roughly, and sometimes use profane language. Thus the child is taught how to be angry, how to speak rough, how to swear, how to be inhuman and brutal. Not more than one in a hundred ever punish without requiring the child to promise to be good,—" never to do so again,"—and by this means force the child to lie, for while it is undergoing punishment, it will promise anything, whether it can keep it or not. Many parents do not delight in punishing, so they keep promising all day long, "to whip" and "to whip," and yet do not do it. This is giving the child practical lessons in lying. Others again are constantly scolding, finding fault with everything the child does, and it soon learns that whatever its parent or teacher says is very doubtful, and it grows up without any real culture or training. To tempt a child into wrong-doing, then, punish it. Such act is worse than barbarous; yet we have known intelligent persons to be guilty of it. We might fill a volume simply in enumerating how criminals are made through the barbarous practice of inflicting pain as a punishment for disobedience in the child. But a word in regard to a successful

SUBSTITUTE.

While lecturing on this subject, in the state of Indiana, a few years ago, we gave permission at the close of the lecture for any one to ask us questions of general interest bearing on the subject of entirely abolishing corporal punishment. A lady of middle age, of the mental motive temperament, and of more than ordinary intelligence, arose in the audience and said, "Doctor, I have a patient for you, and if you can prescribe successfully, in accordance with the theory you advance, I will give up the question. I have a boy," she continued, "three years old, who gets angry at everything that don't go to please him, and when he takes those fits of anger, he throws himself on the floor, kicks, and stamps, and strikes the floor with his hands and head, cries, and keeps this up until I comply with his wishes, or I must whip him until he is conquered." This, she said, "would take place, on the average, three or four times a day; and, Doctor, I have done everything in my power to overcome this terrible disposition. Now what can be done except to whip this ill nature right out of him?" We paused a moment, and gave a glance over our audience, which by their actions seemed to say, "There, Doctor, is a case which you can't control without whipping." We could hear it whispered, "That's a stumper," and many were expecting an admission on our part of failure; but we were not lost for an answer, or fearful to make an attempt to prescribe for the case, and which afterwards proved a perfect cure. It was a difficult case, and the first of the kind ever brought under our notice. "This child is too young to reason," one observed; and another said, "Doctor, you will have to give it up; it is necessary to punish by inflicting bodily pain to conquer some children." We turned to the lady, and said, "Will you, in the presence of this audience, agree to follow our directions so far as lies in your power?" To which she agreed.

We then gave the following direction. "In the first place," we remarked, "it will be necessary to remove all possible causes which have a tendency to cross your child. His surroundings must be as harmonious as possible, and, to accomplish this, it will require some study. Whatever crosses your child, avoid the occurrence of. And, in the second place, do not try to force him into submission. It is dangerous to attempt to force such children into absolute submission without giving time for them to outgrow their ill nature. The danger is in the liability of superinducing diseases of the body, while mentally they are liable to become imbecile. Do not cross your child too much, but gradually divert his attention, and, instead of finding fault with him for every trivial offense, praise him much; and after you have excited his faculty of approbativeness, then bring to bear your ideas as to his wrong deeds. This can be done without deceiving him, for every child has some virtue. If you are constantly harping on your neighbor's defective points, you will drive him from you, and bring ridicule upon yourself."

We further remarked to this lady: "When your child takes one of those terrible angry fits, then go away from him, rather abruptly, and simply remark, 'Mamma don't like to see Willie do so!' Go out of the room, close the door and say no more to him about his conduct. But do not stand at the door, asking him if 'Willie is good,' 'Shall mamma come back?' as you will only make bad worse. You may look through the key-hole, and you will find him in a few moments composed, and looking around and viewing his situation. Finding he is alone, he will now feel truly sorry, and will call for his mamma. You now may enter the room, cheerful, smiling. Take him up in your arms and kiss him, and never refer to his conduct until you are sure he is perfectly calm. For a change of treatment, you may turn him out a few times, or give no attention to him whatever, not even to speak to him. Do not try to persuade him or scold him, or promise him anything while he is in anger,—do not try to coax him or to force him,—but when he is good, treat him kindly. Be positive in all your treatment of him, but kind and loving as well, and, my word for it, your boy will soon be all you desire him to be."

About six months after we gave this advice, we received a letter from this lady, stating that her boy was almost entirely free from his malady. If this kind of punishment will effectually cure one of the worst dispositions, then, we ask, will it not answer in milder forms of obstinate organization; and if it can be done in the family, we claim it can be made a success in the school.

In 1867, we visited quite a number of schools in different cities in Ohio, for the purpose of informing ourselves how the new system of school government succeeded; and we found those that had totally abolished corporal punishment the most happy. The best schools are in Dayton, Ohio. They are constructed and conducted as nearly correct as any we have ever visited;. especially the new school, in the sixth district. Every room is well furnished with portraits, landscape paintings, house plants, and flowers of every kind. This variety of scenery is untiring to the eye, and pleasing to the child. Each pupil is seated separately, with a desk before him. The house is heated by steam-pipes running through every room; good facilities for ventilation. The classes are drilled in a large music-hall each day, in gymnastic exercises, vocal music, etc. This gives the mind rest and the body exercise, thus developing both. Scarcely any corporal punishment is resorted to. Several of the superintendents of the schools inform us, however, that those children who are whipped and knocked about at home require to be punished in that way at school. This is a disgraceful report for those parents who are continually whipping their children, as many unwisely do.

In speaking of certain injurious influences of schools upon the health and welfare of children, Prof. Rud. Virchow closes an interesting paper by enumerating the following agencies as of importance:

" 1. *The air in the school-room*, the quality of which is determined by the size of the room, the number of pupils, the mode of heating, the ventilation, moisture of the floor and walls, dust (cleanliness.)

" 2. *The light*, as determined by the situation of the building and room, the size of the windows and their relation to the desks, the color of the walls and surroundings, artificial light (gas, oil.)

" 3. *The sitting* in the school-room, especially the relations of desk and seat, size of the seats, their arrangement, and duration of sitting.

" 4. *Bodily exercise*, especially playing, gymnastics, swimming, their relations to sitting and to the purely mental labor, their arrangements and superintendence.

" 5. *Mental exertion*, its duration and variety, the individual amount, the arrangement and duration of recesses and vacations, the extent of home and school exercises, the date of the commencement of obligatory attendance, etc.

" 6. The *punishments*, especially corporal.

" 7. The *water for drinking*.

" 8. The *privies*.

" 9. The *means* (implements) *of instruction*, especially the choice of school books (size of type), and objects of illustration."—*St. Louis Med. and Surg. Journal*, from *Virchow's Archiv. and Boston Medical and Surgical Journal*.

The subject of corporal punishment of children is now being rapidly abolished in schools, and the most intelligent have long since wholly discarded it in their families. The day is not far distant when parents will learn that kind words will do more than the rod. The eminent Prof. G. T. Wise, of Ohio, said in a closing address on this subject:

"Oh pause! ye heartless and unthinking parent or teacher, ere the cruel rod in thy uplifted hand descends upon the back of thy wayward child.

"We do not believe in the torturing of children; the practice belongs only to the heathen mothers of the Ganges, and to the barbarous nations and ages of the past. It must not be in this enlightened day; it is revolting to God and conscientious humanity. Science, experience, and the finer sensitive nature declaim against it. The sayings of the wise man, Solomon, would have been indeed more properly rendered: "Spoil the rod and spare the child." Talk about breaking their stubborn spirits! Nonsense! It is nothing more or less than stifling their innocent prattle, their merry laughter, and their pure and guileless emotions, which only annoy prudish, nervous, old-maid school-marms and crusty, disappointed old bachelors.

"'I love it, I love it, so merry and wild,
The artless and innocent laugh of the child.'

"Better indeed have them grow up perverse and wayward than be reduced to an idiotic servility by blows from the rod upon the body, head, and face, which seems to be indulged in by many parents and teachers as though it were a pleasant pastime.

"There is a proper remedy for all the little errors of childhood. It is the gentle, yet all-powerfully persuasive influence of love upon their tender, childish, and impressible hearts. The very name and essence of God is Love, and by it are all things to be subdued in gentleness, to his will. All-persuading love is alone sufficient for the governing of our household pets. If it should fail then, though the first instance has yet to be recorded, you will seek in vain for an antidote in the cruel rod. Do not then clip the little bright wings of childish thoughts, but make the air fragrant and balmy with love where first shall begin their puny flight; and in after years, when the many wintry storms of life have wrinkled the fair brows, and given in exchange for their chaplets of golden ringlets the silvery crown of age, even then the very atmosphere in which they live and move will be serene and redolent with sweet odors of love and good will for their fellowmen."

We think it will

BE ADMITTED

that corporal punishment in schools, in the family and by the state is productive of farther crime. It is not reformatory; it is not compensatory. It can do no good and will not even deter others from committing future crime. Inquire into the history of any of our criminals, and it will be found that they were punished by the use of the rod while young. They were not brought up under the genial influences of kind words.

Most people think it is time enough to educate the reasoning faculties when their children have arrived at the age of puberty, but that while young they must be whipped into obedience. When we hear a mother say to her child every five minutes, "Don't do so, or I'll whip you," or see her, instead of merely promising to whip, actually strike the child for every little offence, we think of the end of these children. Here is where our criminals are manufactured. We have known parents to cut the skin of their children by striking them with a raw-hide, or otherwise punish with unreasonable severity. We have brought legal action against such persons frequently, and here is a work for the humane society—the protection of our innocent children as well as animals. As a rule, the more children are punished by the use of the rod, in the family or while at school, the better will they be qualified to commit crime in after life. We are acquainted with a clergyman who believed it a religious duty to "spare not the rod." He had four sons and three daughters. He once said to us in conversation on this subject, "that he kept two instruments on hand for the proper government of his family—the Bible and a hickory rod." Two of this man's sons have been convicted a number of times for stealing, and one is now serving his time in the state's prison, while one of the daughters is unfortunate for life. As a means of ascertaining whether our account is true, let the judges of our courts and the justices of the peace question every criminal brought before them for one year, and it will be found that each will give a history in favor of our position, viz., that while young they received a regular amount of corporal punishment. It is not the severity of the punishment that makes children better, but judicious and certain means of correction which will do the work when administered in a proper spirit. The following narrative is copied from *Hall's Journal of Health*, on

PARENTAL CORRECTION:

"That man commits a crime, and so does the woman, who will send a child to bed with a wounded spirit, or who shall allow any vindictiveness of feeling to exist in consequence of anything the child may have done. Sharp-pointed memories have often driven men mad; multitudes are there who are more dead than alive, from the ailings of the mind, which is wasting itself away in vain remorses for the irrevocable past. The fault of most parents is over-harsh reproofs of their children; reproofs that are hasty, unproportioned to the offense, and hence, as to one's own child, helpless and unresisting, are a cruelty as well as an injustice. Thrice happy is that parent who has no child in the grave which can be wished back, only if for a brief space, so as to afford some opportunity for repairing some unmerited unkindness toward the dead darling. Parents have been many times urged in these pages to make persistent efforts to arrange two things in domestic intercourse, and to spare no pains and no amount of moral courage and determination, in order that they should be brought about. It may require a thousand efforts, and there may be a thousand failures, as discouraging as they are sad; still let the high resolve go out, "it shall be done!" and the prickling of many a thorn will be spared in after years and in old age. The two points to be daily aimed at are:

First. Let the family table be always a meeting-place of pleasantness, and affection and peace, and for the exhibition of all the sweeter feelings of domestic life.

Second. Let every child be sent to bed with kisses of affection, especially those under ten years of age.

All that is on this globe could not hire me to be put in the place of either the father or the mother in the following narration of the former editor of a monthly of deserved repute in its time. The occurrence took place in Boston, about the year 1850, and every detail is minutely and literally true:

"A few weeks before, L. B. H. wrote to me that he had buried his eldest son, a fine, manly little fellow of eight years of age, who had never known a day's illness until that which finally removed him hence, to be here no more. His death occurred under circumstances which were peculiarly painful to his parents. A younger brother, a delicate, sickly child from its birth, the next in age to him, had been down for nearly a fortnight with an epidemic fever. In consequence of the nature of the disease, every precaution had been adopted, that prudence suggested, to guard the other members of the family against it. But of this one, the father's eldest, he said he had little to fear, so rugged was he and so generally healthy. Still, however, he kept a vigilant eye upon him, and especially forbade his going into the pools and docks near his school, which it was his custom sometimes to visit; for he was but a boy, and 'boys will be boys,' and we ought more frequently to think that it is their nature to be. Of all unnatural things, a reproach almost to childish frankness and innocence, save me from a 'boy-man!' But to the story.

"One evening this unhappy father came home, wearied with a long day's hard labor, and vexed at some little disappointments which had soured his naturally kind disposition, and rendered him peculiarly susceptible to the smallest annoyance. While he was sitting by the fire, in this unhappy mood of mind, his wife entered the apartment and said:

"'Henry has just come in, and he is a perfect fright. He is covered from head to foot with dock mud, and is as wet as a drowned rat!'

"'Where is he?' asked the father, sternly.

"'He is shivering over the kitchen-fire. He was afraid to come up here when the girl told him you had come home.'

"'Tell Jane to tell him to come here this instant!' was the brief reply to this information.

"Presently the poor boy entered, half perished with affright and cold. His father glanced at his sad plight, reproached him bitterly with his disobedience, spoke of the punishment which awaited him in the morning, as the penalty for his offense, and in a harsh voice concluded with:

"'Now, sir, go to your bed!'

"'But, father,' said the little fellow, 'I want to tell you—'

"'Not a word, sir; *go to bed!*'

"'I only wanted to say, father, that—'

"With a peremptory stamp, an imperative wave of his hand toward the door, and a frown upon his brow, did that father, without other speech, again close the door of explanation and expostulation.

"When the boy had gone supperless and sad to his bed, the father sat restless and uneasy while supper was being prepared, and at tea-table ate but little. His wife saw the real cause, or the additional cause of his emotion, and interposed the remark:

"'I think, my dear, you ought at least to have heard what Henry had to say. My heart ached for him when he turned away with his eyes full of tears. Henry is a good boy, after all, if he does sometimes do wrong. He is a tender-hearted, affectionate boy. He always was.'

"And therewithal the water stood in the eyes of that forgiving mother, even as it stood in the eyes of Mercy, in 'the house of the Interpreter,' as recorded by Bunyan.

"After tea the evening paper was taken up; but there was no news and nothing of interest for that father in the journal of that evening. He sat for some time in an evidently painful reverie, and then rose and repaired to his bedchamber. As he passed the bedroom where his little boy slept, he thought he would look in upon him before retiring to rest. He crept to his low cot, and bent over him. A big tear had stolen down the boy's cheek and rested upon it, but he was sleeping calmly and sweetly. The father deeply regretted his harshness as he gazed upon his son, but he felt also the 'sense of duty;' yet in the night, talking the matter over with the lad's mother, he resolved and promised, instead of punishing, as he had threatened, to make amends to the boy's aggrieved spirit in the morning for the manner in which he had repelled all explanation of his offense.

"But that morning never came to the poor child in health. He awoke the next morning with a raging fever on his brain, and wild with delirium. In forty-eight hours he was in his shroud. He knew neither his father nor his mother, when they were first called to his bedside, nor at any moment afterward. Waiting, watching for one token of recognition, hour after hour, in speechless agony, did that unhappy father bend over the couch of his dying son. Once, indeed. he thought he saw a smile of recognition light up his dying eye, and he leaned eagerly forward, for he would have given worlds to have whispered one kind word in his ear and have been answered; but that gleam of apparent intelligence passed quickly away, and was succeeded by the cold, unmeaning glare, and the wild tossing of the fevered limbs, which lasted until death came to his relief.

"Two days afterward the undertaker came with the little coffin, and his son, a playmate of the deceased boy, bringing the low stools on which it was to stand in the entry-hall.

"'I was with Henry,' said the lad, 'when he got into the water. We were playing down at the Long Wharf, Henry, and Frank Mumford and I; and the tide was out very low, and there was a beam run out from the wharf, and Charles got out on it to get a fish-line and hook that hung over where the water was deep, and the first thing we saw he had slipped off and was struggling in the water! Henry threw off his cap and jumped clear from the wharf into the water, and after a great deal of hard work, got Charles out; and they waded up through the mud to where the wharf was not so wet and slippery, and then I helped them to climb up the side. Charles told Henry not to say anything about it, for if he did his father would never let him go near the water again. Henry was very sorry, and all the way going home he kept saying:

"'What will father say when he sees me to-night? I wish we had not gone to the wharf!'

"'Dear, brave boy!' exclaimed the bereaved father; 'and this was the explanation which I so cruelly refused to hear!' and hot and bitter tears rolled down his cheeks.

"Yes, that stern father now learned, and for the first time, that what he had treated with unwonted severity as a fault was but the impulse of a generous nature, which, forgetful of self, had hazarded life for another. It was but the quick prompting of that manly spirit which he himself had always endeavored to graft upon his susceptible mind, and which, young as he was, had already manifested itself on more than one occasion.

" Let me close this story in the very words of that father, and let the lesson sink deep into the heart of every parent who shall peruse this sketch:

"'Everything that I now see that ever belonged to him reminds me of my lost boy. Yesterday I found some rude pencil sketches, which it was his delight to make for the amusement of his younger brother. To-day, in rummaging an old closet, I came across his boots, still covered with dock mud, as when he last wore them. (You may think it strange, but that which is usually so unsightly an object is now most precious to me.) And every morning and evening I pass the ground where my son's voice rang the merriest among his playmates.

"'All these things speak to me vividly of his active life, but I can not—though I have often tried—I can not recall any other expression on the dear boy's face than that mute, mournful one with which he turned from me on the night I so harshly repulsed him.... Then my heart bleeds afresh!

"'Oh! how careful should we be that in our daily conduct toward those little beings sent us by a kind Providence, we are not laying up for ourselves the sources of many a future bitter tear! How cautious that, neither by inconsiderate nor cruel word or look, we unjustly grieve their generous feeling! And how guardedly ought we to weigh every action against its motive, lest, in a moment of excitement, we be led to mete out to the venial errors of the heart the punishment due only to wilful crime!

"'Alas! perhaps few parents suspect how often the fierce rebuke, the sudden blow, is answered in their children by the tears, not of passion, not of physical or mental pain, but of a loving yet grieved or outraged nature!'"

But why in this sad case should the mother be called to weep tears of blood, and be considered a partaker of the father's fault? It was for the criminal want of judgment and consideration on her part. The father had come home wearied and discouraged in connection with the business of the day, was sitting by the fire in a moody state of mind, and the mother bursts in upon him with the announcement of the boy's condition, without acquainting herself with the circumstances, and without uttering one word of extenuation, but presenting the case to the father's mind in the strongest terms of aggravation. No wonder, under all the circumstances, the husband should have fired up, and that he should have been driven on like one unpossessed of himself. Had the mother possessed but a small share of observation, and even a less amount of common sense, she would herself have inquired into all the circumstances of the case, and begun the history by extolling the nobleness of their son; then it would have had a calming, compensating effect on the father's mind; it would have been drawn away from business, and would have nestled itself lovingly amid the darling ones around him.

Even if there had been no extenuating circumstances, she ought to have had wit enough to have respected the humor of her husband; she ought to have seen in a moment that something had gone wrong with him, and should have studiously kept from saying or doing anything which could by any possibility have roused him into a tempest of uncontrollable passion. There are many other just such thoughtless, hare-brained women, who deserve neither the name of mother nor wife, who seem to glory in dashing at their husbands the instant they open the door, on their return from a hard day's toil, of body or of mind, and with amazing volubility, pour out the mishaps, vexations, and misfortunes of the day, and in a way, too, as if the husband was wholly to blame, although he may not have had the slightest connection with them, in the most remote manner possible.

Another inexcusable folly was in the father threatening to punish the child next day; leaving the little fellow's mind to exaggerate it in his fears, and be a living torture until the end came. Not long ago, we read an account of an editor who sent his little son to an upstairs room, and had the door locked, with the threat that he would be flogged at the end of a certain number of hours. True to his word, he went to the door at the appointed time, and in the unlocking of it the child was so alarmed that he ran to the window, jumped out and broke his neck. It is the limit of folly and the refinement of cruelty to threaten punishment to a child for a thing done. If punishment is merited, it should be inflicted and then dismissed; yet there are parents not a few who seem to have a malignant pleasure, after children have been reproved or otherwise punished for a specific fault, in reminding them of it on every possible occasion for months afterward; the certain effect of which is to induce a kind of desperation in the mind of the child, and a "don't care" feeling, which can not fail to have a most unfortunate influence on that child's character for all its life thereafter.

Let parents, then, who would avoid an old age of agony, in connection with harshness, injustice, and even cruelty to their children, remember never to punish or even threaten a child under the influence of a passionate state of the mind, because the morrow may bring death, and no other compensation can be ever made.

There is a physiological view to be taken of this case, which may be communicated with profit. Even if the child had been ever so much to blame, he should have been tenderly dealt with as to the present. His mind and body had been most intensely exercised, and the reaction had left the whole system in a state of complete exhaustion. In addition, the body was chilled. He should have been cleansed and redressed with all a mother's affection; a warm supper and some hot drink should have been given him, and he should have been put to sleep tenderly, in a warm bed. But instead of all this, he was cold, wet, hungry, "shivering," sent to bed, his feelings "hurt," to an extent which words can not express. We almost feel as if the father of the unfortunate boy was entitled to the designation of "savage," and his wife, a poor, hasty, weak-minded nonentity, worse than no wife at all."

It is not necessary to say that the parent who inflicted the unjust punishment, as reported in the previous narrative, was sufficiently punished, although not dealt with legally. How many thousand parents treat their children in a similar manner. Here lessons are instilled which culminate in crime.

Before closing this chapter, we will pen a few maxims, which, if strictly observed in the government of children, will render correction by corporal punishment entirely unnecessary:

1. Never require your child to do more than it is competent to perform.

2. Educate its faculties as fast as it is capable of comprehending. "Little by little lofty temples grow."

3. Never strike your child so as to inflict bodily pain: it will not reform it; it will not make it love you.

4. Never leave home without kissing your children, or on putting them to bed, or on rising in the morning. "Oh! how much there is in a kiss!"

5. Never act or speak in any other manner, in the presence of your child, than you would, under the same circumstances, if in the presence of the most distinguished person. "Respect your child, and it will respect you."

6. Appeal to the judgment of your child as well as present your own for its consideration.

7. Never correct your child while in an irritable mood: you will only set a bad example, giving the child practical lessons in the manifestation of angry passions. Remember, the child copies after the parent.

8. Never reprove or correct your child in the presence of strangers: this will only wound its feelings. Train your child to behave in the private nursery of the family as you would have it in the presence of strangers.

9. The father and mother never should differ in opinion as to the mode or necessity of correction in presence of the child. For the child will side with the one that is in its own favor. Concert of action

is necessary on the part of parents to have a correct family government.

10. Never let your child go to places of amusement while under age, unless you accompany it, or unless it is in the care of some trusty friend. Always introduce your child to strangers, just as you would a friend of your own years. You should go frequently with your children to proper places of amusement.

11. Never speak of your neighbor in the presence of your child in any other manner than you would in the presence of others. Never entertain visitors in the most genial manner and afterwards speak slightly of them. Do not invite them to be *sure* and call again, saying in the hearing of your child, after they have left: "Hope they never *will* call again." Do not promise to return their visit, but afterwards say, "I never shall call on them; they do not belong to 'our set.'" What can your child think of your double dealing?*

---

*To Train a Child.—A little tract issued for distribution by the Ladies' Sanitary Association of London, gives these wise suggestions for the nurture of children in health of body and spirit:

1. Never refuse a thing if it is harmless; give it, if you are able, without delay.

2. Never give anything because it is cried for that you have refused when asked for.

3. Be careful to observe real illness, and avoid causing bodily uneasiness from over-clothing or cold or unwholesome food, such as candy, sugar-plums, sour fruit, or giving buns or cakes to quiet the child.

4. Avoid false promises. They are sure to be found out false.

5. Avoid threats of all kinds. If believed, they make children

Let the principles set forth in this chapter be inculcated,—heralded broadcast over the land,—and create a popular sentiment in favor of the opinion that to prevent crime we must " strike at the root of the evil"—begin our work with the child ; and if we do our duty here, it will not be necessary to provide a halter for the adult.

---

timid, and injure both mind and body: if not believed, they are useless. Such threats as bogie, policeman, and black-man, are sure to be found out false, if the child lives.

6. Never say anything untrue to a child.

7. Do not wreak your own bad temper, or visit your own feelings of fatigue and trouble, on children, by being severe with them, or by saying, "You shan't have it" or "I won't give it to you," when there is no reason for refusal, except that you are yourself tired, or in trouble, or out of sorts.

8. Avoid giving orders, such as "Stand still," "Go on," "Hold your tongue," "Put it down," etc., unless you really mean that you should be obeyed; and the fewer orders you give, the better.

9. Neither give too much pity, nor yet be severe and unkind, when a child tumbles down and hurts itself.

10. Do not worry a child. Let it alone, and let it live in peace.

11. Teach it early to play alone, and amuse itself without your help. Let it alone, is a golden rule in nine cases out of ten.

To sum up all in a few words, try to feel like a child ; to enter into its griefs and joys, its trials and triumphs. Then look forward to the time when it shall have numbered as many years as you have seen, and pray for help and strength to do your duty by it. You may fail, as we all may; but if you sow the seed with humility and faith, you will have done all that is permitted to us imperfect creatures; and if you have reared up a cheerful, loving, truthful, and brave spirit, in a healthy body, you have been working with him who told us it was "not the will of our Father in Heaven that one of these little ones should perish."

CHAPTER XVII.

ON WEALTH, HEALTH, CRIME, AND THE LABORING CLASSES.—ORGANIZED CAPITAL AND THE EFFECT IT HAS ON SOCIETY.

"The tendency of wealth to accumulate in few hands, and the creation of giant power, and not disinclined to use it like giants, threatens to put the laws of state at the disposal of the highest bidder."—*Theo. Tilton.*

Subsistence and preservation of the vital integrity of the body is a law of nature. To insure such a state of enjoyment individuals have a right to make use of means which will provide for their physical wants. No law or condition of society should ever be allowed to infringe on one's rights to maintain an honorable subsistence. As subsistence is a law of the physical nature, so is education and the proper development of the mental faculties a law of the mind, and each individual has, therefore, a just claim on society to be permitted to acquire a mental subsistence as well as to maintain the body.

To accumulate wealth, position, and place, a giant power in the hands of a few, which is the tendency and the ultimate object of society, is not a law of nature. It is a perverted condition of the law of self-preservation, and its effect necessarily is to deprive a large portion of the people of an easy means of maintaining a subsistence. In consequence of this unadjustable condition of society with the laws of nature, some men resort to every means to acquire wealth, while, on the other hand, others are striving to preserve natural rights, honorably, if it can be done so; but money, men will have, though it may deprive some of the necessary means of subsistence. A man has a right to acquire a competency; but no one has a moral right by accumulating wealth to create a power that incites men to crime. Again, the education of man's capabilities, the moral, the intellectual, and the social natures, is a claim or lien which every child has on society by a law of nature which stands parallel with the first law of subsistence. Every individual child born into life should be sustained, and it is, at least, a duty, not to prevent it from acquiring a reasonable amount of education, which is a mental competency, and may be compared to that which provides for physical existence. In proportion, then, as one portion of society accumulates wealth by depriving the other of a needful competency, there will exist a lack of the proper intellectual development, thereby unbalancing the mental condition of society,—one portion rushing headlong after the things which will maintain position and wealth, and the other portion laboring under the weight of a benighted condition of the mind, and forced on by necessity of subsistence to often appropriate property that belongs to others.

For the purpose of increasing wealth, and holding a controlling power, men of capital have variously organized themselves. The condition of men unorganized is one comparatively void of power.

We will now consider the relative advantages which men have in acquiring moral and intellectual education and in the accumulation of wealth. It is a truth that to accumulate mental wealth, about as much labor and economy is necessary as to obtain houses, lands, and gold. The child learns early to supply its own body with the necessary food for subsistence, and gradually through life it continues to learn more and more,—how to make money, how to economize, and how to use all possible resources in making labor as profitable as possible. The same economy and ingenuity which is required to attain to an easy financial position is also necessary to be brought into requisition in acquiring a mind well stored with knowledge. In this last the common every-day laborer has but few advantages. During childhood and youth the laboring classes enjoy but few advantages for attending to an early mental culture compared with those who have sufficient financial income to support them during the most important period of life. The same cause that makes financial paupers make also paupers intellectual. The capital which controls labor also controls the education of the laboring classes. In this, capital is so far in advance that it is almost too late to remedy the difficulty. This unbalanced condition between labor and capital is productive of crime and much sorrow among men.

The faculty which governs capital is ever at work in devising means to maintain a supremacy. The love of money has already attained an alarming influence, and to counteract it is a matter of much study. Men are taught, in childhood, a few moral and intellectual lessons, which at manhood are almost entirely abandoned; the study is more how to make money. Instead of instituting a daily reading and studying of the sciences and endeavoring to master the true philosophy of human life, their leisure hours are mainly spent in reading the daily news, novels, and the most flimsical literature. Capital and men labor six days each week in the pursuit of earthly things; the churches, and other institutions, which have man's moral and religious welfare for their object, labor only two hours each week, giving capital and the business of every day life an advantage of six days, of ten to fifteen hours in each day, while the moral, intellectual, religious, and social nature of man receives only attention two hours in the week. Thus an unbalanced condition is gradually acquired by the individual. Society, of course, will be the same, for society is made up of individuals. Money is invested in public schools, whose labors, however, extend only to a short period; for, as we have already stated, all this work, as a rule, stops at adult age. The churches aim to counteract the tendency of wealth and labor to accumulate in the hands of a few, or even to carry away mankind in the direction of immoral or irreligious channels; but as capital labors six days each week, and ten and fifteen hours each day, and the churches labor only about two hours in each week, the church stands a very poor chance to gain much on capital. The capital employed in the direction of wealth, and in conducting the business of physical life, produces about thirty per cent. per annum, while the capital employed in conducting the business of man's developing and accumulating of that true wealth of the soul which only can eventually make men happy, produces comparatively no per cent. per annum. Take for example, the ten millions of property invested in churches in this city, and this amount of capital lies dormant for six days each week, and only really labors about two hours on the seventh. This ten millions of capital, invested in the business conducted by fashionable society, will increase during the same period of time from twenty to thirty per cent. Or, let us consider the ten millions invested in manufacturing business, and it will sway a power which it has been entirely incompetent hitherto to counteract, or to bring even a restraining influence to bear upon. The ten millions invested in manufacturing purposes, work men ten to twelve hours each day,— four hours longer than even the law of physiology would grant, to say nothing of the moral wrong,— and by this means an unbalanced condition is gradually acquired between the physical and mental ; and the ten millions employed by the church cannot compete in two hours with the efforts put forth in the sixty or seventy hours employed by the manufacturing interest each week. Here is an unbalanced condition of society—an antagonism between wealth, labor, and the intellectual work of man. In consequence of this unequal condition of society, corporal means are resorted to, to restrain the eating canker upon the body of society. Can it be longer a question whether society makes her own criminals? and is it not self-evident that by corporal punishment the difficulty can never be removed ? In consequence of this disproportionate condition of society, crime is prevalent, even in the higher as well as in the lower walks of life.

"Corruption in high places, or rather its exposure, is at present occupying a very large share of the attention of the public. We have had Tammany frauds, Credit Mobilier bribery, the corrupt election of senators, fraudulent contracts, defalcations of public officers, and almost every other variety of crime, dished up for our daily meal for months past. And still new exposures are being made, and new dishes are being set before us. The last is the discovery of forgeries by a prominent Pittsburgh business man amounting to seventy-five thousand dollars."

The strife between capital and labor is now being more and more agitated. In New York city the employers and workingmen are now beginning to discuss the proposed movement in various trades with reference to wages and hours of labor. Conflicting opinions prevail on both sides. The employers seem to be unanimous in their opposition to a reduction of hours, while the workmen are not united, and many regard favorably the ten-hour system.

Why this agitation and this great amount of friction? If all was rightly adjusted,—in harmony with the laws of nature (see Part III of this volume),—all would be more happy, crime would be less frequent, and men would seek after the things of the spirit, and employ the ten millions now invested in church purposes, in exercising the talents of the soul at least one hour and a half each evening, making about fifteen hours each week in place of two, thus bringing a reasonable amount of counteracting influence to bear on the ten millions employed in an opposite direction. We have aimed to be lenient when we compare ten millions of church property to ten millions of money invested in the opposite direction; but really the difference is by the thousands of millions, and hence we need not wonder that five hundred police are required in Chicago to keep men from tearing each other to pieces like wild beasts. Aside from the millions of organized capital employed mainly in what is called a legitimate business, millions more are invested in drinking saloons which are run about twenty hours each day, Sundays not excepted. Of these there are about twenty-five, on the average, throughout the state, to every church, and they manufacture at least five devils to one Christian made by the church. In the face of these facts, ministers of the gospel will rise in their pulpits and argue from the light of "divine revelation" that hanging our murderers is preventive of crime.

How shall we correct all this wonderful discord which pervades society? In addition to what has been said under the head of compulsory education, and of corporal punishment, we now call attention to one very important and too much neglected fact, which is,

THE LABORING CLASS

must be held in greater respect: they must be brought up into good society, and be permitted to associate with those of learning and of wealth. In other words, the line that now divides the laboring classes from the professional and the wealthy should be broken down.

It is a grand truth that labor is honorable, and without it we cannot exist. Think for a moment of the dignity and importance of labor; of the innumerable comforts the laboring classes are procuring for humanity; of the beauties they are elaborating all around us; of the mines of wealth they are developing in every direction.

> "Let not ambition mock their useful toil,
> Their homely joys, and destiny obscure;
> Nor grandeur hear with a disdainful smile
> The short and simple annals of the poor."

No, let us not "mock their useful toil," nor think less of "their homely joys," but give a helping hand to our common laboring classes, that all may together rise and progress in the pursuit of human happiness.

Have you ever contemplated the wonders which a faithful laborer's lifetime may accomplish, and yet not learned to respect the laboring man? I love to grasp the hand of a man that has felled a forest! It may be hard, it may be rough, but it is a brave hand and *I love it!* And when I think how that vigorous arm hath cleft in twain the proud hickory, how the lofty oak hath yielded to its ponderous blows,—I will persist in believing that the honest yeoman has accomplished a great, a noble work, the disparagements of the head-measurers notwithstanding. Yes, he who has redeemed a single acre from the fertile waste of nature, and subjected it to the work of feeding the millions, or has planted a tree from which posterity may pluck, has performed a noble act. I tell you it is for such as these that "the wilderness and the solitary places shall be glad, and the desert shall rejoice and blossom as the rose."

There are the "hod-carriers." Do you smile at the mention of the word? Stand a little while near a large building in process of erection and watch the movements of those busy men. Here they come, with hurried step, one after another, to the brick pile. For the hundredth time to-day they fill their hods and retrace their steps. Slowly, cautiously, they ascend the dizzy ladders. Their burdens dumped, they turn again to repeat that oft-repeated journey. But mark you! Those buttresses are growing. Upward, upward, toward the bright, blue heavens rise those massive walls! The roof is arched, the dome is finished, and now, as that noble edifice looms up against the sky, and you contemplate its stern solidity, its massive grandeur, its architectural beauty, does not a thrill of exultant joy vibrate within your inmost soul as you remind yourself that three or four brave fellows have absolutely shouldered that magnificent structure?

Away with that abominable dogma that the highly gifted only may accomplish great results. God can use the humblest vessel he has made.

Hands, heads and hearts should all be set to work to bless the world, and for the individual (I care not what may be the circumference of his skull!) who is willing to devote his triple self to the guidance of his Maker, I would not hesitate to predict an ample success in time, and a glorious career in eternity—

though all the craniologists in the world should shake their incredulous heads at once. It is not yours nor mine to say that such an individual might not, out of the abundance of his labors, actually double the hallelujahs of Heaven.

Think of the rebuilding of Chicago. Were it not for the laboring classes, the burnt district would yet be a barren waste. But as it is, hundreds of stately and noble edifices loom up against the sky, where one year ago was but solitary ruins.

Unless society makes proper provision for the working classes, by the universal education of all the mental faculties of every individual member of society, an unbalanced condition will continue between capital and labor,—between wealth and the moral and religious nature of man,—between the educated and the uncultivated faculties of the mind.

Society may be compared to an organization composed of a number of faculties the same as an individual. Now, where the faculty of acquisitiveness is the predominant power, the individual will measure everything by what money is worth. The chief end will be money. This faculty is even now the ruling force of society, supported by selfishness, revenge, and hatred, brought into activity by the faculties of combativeness and destructiveness. These are the forces which labor six days each week, and, in many cases, include the Sabbath day, while the faculties of reason, conscience, benevolence, friendship, love, and charity, are exercised only about two hours in the week. The majority of mankind "seek after the things that are temporal," rather than "after the things of the spiritual."

CHAPTER XVIII.

OUR PRESENT JURY SYSTEM.—PROPOSED REFORMATION. MURDER TRIALS.—WOMEN AS JURORS— CONCLUSION OF PART II.

We would not consider our task complete in what has been said on crime and punishment, if we were not to give a passing notice to the present jury system. In the first place, we remark that we believe the Grand Jury to be a useless body of officials which should be discontinued. We give the following reasons:

First. It is a secret trial of a person supposed to be guilty of a crime, where the criminal is not permitted to be present, and has, therefore, no opportunity to defend himself.

Second. The Grand Jury, after deliberation, renders a verdict which is no more descisive than if twelve men, not empowered by any legal authority, were to meet in secret and pass resolutions that a certain person in the neighborhood is guilty of some crime or misdemeanor, and would recommend an arrest, and that they be committed for trial. How many persons have been found not guilty by the court, even after the Grand Jury passes a verdict of guilty, and many have been set aside by the courts.

Third. Any one may go before the Grand Jury and give in testimony against their neighbors, and no one is allowed to know who the complainant is, making it altogether a one-sided trial, giving credence only to the story of one side of the question. Here much injustice is done; and if there were none, it is entirely useless, as the decision is not final; a useless expense, a sham trial, and may be dispensed with without in the least impairing our resources to deal out justice. The justice of the peace, or any judge, may give an opinion and cause one to be committed to farther trial, after hearing the preliminary testimony. What use is there, after a coroners' jury has found a verdict, that the Grand Jury should again consider the case, and proceed to trial of the criminal.

Trial by jury we believe to be just and a verdict by a two-third vote is all that is necessary to arrive at a just decision. Instead, however, of decreasing the number, as the Attorney General of England proposes, as a radical means of reforming the jury system, which is not looked upon with much favor, however, we are in favor of increasing the number to twenty-four in all trials for murder and treason. To show that the subject of reforming our present

JURY SYSTEM

is already being agitated in this and the old country, we copy from the press opinions which explain themselves:

"The evils of the jury system, as developed by modern experience, are of a nature too serious to be ignored. The subject has been agitated to considerable extent in this country for some time; and the English journals have shown the same state of things in Great Britain. At last the attorney general of that nation has proposed a very radical measure, which is not looked upon with favor, and will hardly succeed in becoming a law.

"The principal features of this proposition are a reduction of the number of the jury from twelve to seven, except in trials for treason and murder, and the principle that a majority shall be allowed to vote a verdict. The first change is recommended in order to decrease the number of persons withheld from their occupations to attend court where they await summons as jurors. The attorney general argues that there is no magic in the number twelve, and that the number might just as well be seven. In reply to this, it is answered that there is no more magic in the number seven; that the evil complained of can be remedied in some other manner, and that it would be dangerous to change the number constituting a jury when the people have learned to regard that number as necessary to their protection.

"The principle that a majority shall be allowed to vote a verdict, is assailed still more strenuously. The proposition is similar to one recently introduced in the Illinois Legislature, except that in the latter case a vote of two-thirds is required for a verdict.

"It is hardly probable that either of these propositions would work an improvement on the present system, and we think the views of the public, are expressed in the following terse extract from an article on the subject in a morning paper in this city, which says: 'Both plans seem to be inconsiderate and dangerous. In the organization of juries, two-thirds of the members are as apt to be stupid blockheads as one-third, and the proposed change would give them the opportunity of determining a verdict whenever such a division should occur. It would simply be an application of the majority rule to jury verdicts, as it exists now in politics. The principle is carried far enough already, and it would be especially dangerous and objectionable to apply it to absolute judicial verdicts affecting life, liberty, and property. The principle of unanimity has the constant advantage of securing deliberation and consultation more apt to result in a just verdict than a hasty, inconsiderate vote of the majority.'"

We cannot see a good reason why a two-thirds vote is not as near true justice as when one-third stand against the rest and are finally persuaded to "give in" and return a verdict by a unanimous vote. As before stated, we are in favor of increasing the number of jurors to twenty-four in all murder trials and for treason. Twelve men and twelve women. After the trial and the usual charge given by the judge, the jury should then retire to a suitable room where each is provided with a seat so isolated from each other that no private conversation can be had: in no case should it be allowed. We do not believe that discussions are proper by a jury. The case has been sufficiently discussed during the trial, and each member of the jury should be allowed an individual vote, and not be influenced by the knowledge of how others vote. The sheriff, or the clerk of the court, should act as chairman of the jury. At the sound of the gavel, each juror should be required to step to a private desk, and write his or her verdict on a suitable card, and deposit it in a box. A two-third vote to be decisive; if, however, a two-third vote is not the result of the first ballot, then a second ballot may be ordered by the chairman; should there be no decision, he may call for a third, but this should be the limit, and, however the ballot may then stand, a verdict of guilty or not guilty is rendered, after which, the jury should be discharged. We oppose all discussions by juries, in the jury-room, for the following reasons: First, the best talker can carry those who are easily persuaded. Secondly, many persons, though having clear minds, are not competent to bring rebutting arguments, having had no practice in speaking or debating, and yet would render a just verdict.

We hold it to be just and necessary to require, by law, certain

QUALIFICATIONS

of jurors before they are considered as fit to sit on a jury. First, we mention age. No male should be allowed to sit on a jury under thirty or over fifty; no female under twenty-five or over fifty. Between these two periods of human life, the judgment and mental capacities are at the highest degree of vigor, and are available more than at any other time, and hence the most just decisions may be arrived at if this precaution is taken in the selection of jurors. The second qualification should be that each juror be in possession of knowledge of our common branches of education, at least. The third qualification is, that each juror should be a freeholder, and in pursuit of some honorable vocation, by which to maintain a subsistence. Some may object to our idea of permitting women to set on juries.

We ask, has she no power to judge of human affairs? Can she not understand right from wrong, and is not woman more moral than man, as a rule? And if she is to be governed by law, why shall she not have a right to say how she shall be ruled? And again, has she not as much interest in the welfare of the opposite sex as men have in hers, and is it not a moral duty that she should interest herself in matters of law as well as in domestic affairs? Let women be permitted to take their place in the jury-box, and we affirm that our courts of justice will not be conducted as too disreputable a place for a respectable lady even to appear in as a witness. In all trials for crimes less than murder or treason, twelve jurors are sufficient,—six men and six women,—but a two-thirds vote should be requisite for a verdict, and the same rule should be observed as before mentioned.

In trial of disputes in regard to property or money, the present system is as good as need be. Minor cases of crime, such as justices of the peace are now allowed to decide, may be continued. For example, a person is arraigned for vagrancy. It is not necessary to decide by jury; but if the evidence is sufficiently conclusive, the justice of the peace may at once decide the case, and send him to the reformatory institution, where such persons are further disposed of by a competent board of educators.

We do not believe in the right of appeal from one court to another; after a trial has been had according to law, it should be decisive. As it is now, so long as parties have a dollar to spend, they continue to law one another until justice is defeated. This creates a spirit of revenge. Men declare that they will have satisfaction if they have to spend their last dollar. This is a great evil, though it may be remunerative to officers of the law and lawyers. The question is, has ever an appeal been made with a view only to gain justice, or was it mainly through a spirit of revenge and an object to dishonorably win the suit on some technical point in law? Remove, then, the right of an appeal after the case has been regularly tried, according to law, and then the poor will have justice done, as well as moneyed monopolies, or those that have money enough to carry on a law suit until their opponent has exhausted all his resources.

Take away the right of appeal, and the pardoning power from the executive, make justice the imperative power in the land, and people will shun the law as they would a prison, attending to their legitimate business rather than trying to defeat the ends of justice.

We believe that no court has a moral right to require men to take upon themselves a solemn oath. Affirmation by one's own word of honor, as they hope to answer to men and this court,—not to God,— is stronger than the oath now administered. Most people who swear falsely fear hell less than they do men, as the majority believe there is time enough for God to forgive their sins; and they will risk the indefinite hereafter rather than incur the nearer punishment of the law established by man. A person who will respect his own honor less than an oath, is not a proper subject to sit on a jury or to testify as a witness.

In conclusion of this chapter and Part Second of this volume, we take occasion to review briefly the leading ideas advanced in support of the total abolition of the death penalty. History shows that the severity of the death penalty inflicted upon criminals is growing less, and it is now only used as a punishment for murder and treason, while in former ages it was administered for many crimes of lesser magnitude. Formerly executions were held in public: now only murderers in the first degree are executed, and this is done in private. This favors the idea that it will soon be abolished. History further shows that the death penalty has never prevented crime, and that it had its origin among heathen nations and is not a command of God,* nor was it ever suggested

---

* THE PUNISHMENT OF MURDER.—*To the Editor of the Chicago Tribune:*—SIR: Why is it that our clergy, as a general thing, are so clamorous for the bloody code? These heralds of the gentle Jesus—that Jesus who never uttered a syllable approving the taking of human life as a punishment—one would expect to be the last to call for the old Mosaic ukase of "A life for a life."

As an instance how the most adverse texts of Scripture are used by clergymen to enforce their notions, the sermon of the Rev. Mr. Helmer on Sunday evening was remarkable. His theme was Cain, the first murderer; and, in some way, from that he drew an instruction in favor of capital punishment.

Now, Cain was not put to death by God, but separated from his fellows; and, to prevent his fellowmen from killing him, God put

by a righteous person or an enlightened nation. It is therefore a relic of barbarism adhering to our civilized institutions, which long since should have taken its place in oblivion.

We have also maintained the great necessity and right to punish crime, and contended successfully for the strict enforcement of the three primary objects of law and punishment, namely: first, reformation of the criminal; secondly, reparation or compensation to the injured party, and thirdly, prevention of future crime. We have shown that the first object can only be obtained by sending the criminal to a reformatory prison,—murderers to prison for life, withholding the

---

a mark on him, and threatened seven-fold vengeance upon any one who should kill him.

Not much capital punishment doctrine here.

That so candid and able a man as Mr. Helmer could fall into such a line of deduction, seems singular.

I, for one, have long been opposed to the death penalty. The arguments of its advocates seem to me fallacious, and the secret of the desire for its infliction to be in the natural feeling of vengeance in case of murder.

That the restraining effect of executions on crime is a vagery, is proved by the fact that, in each of the recent executions in this city and in New York, murders were committed within a single day thereafter, within cannon-shot of the scaffold.

The *Tribune* of this morning, to my mind, struck the right note, and for the first time, to my notice, has the thought been clearly put forth, "that at present, and until we abolish the pardoning power, there is no such thing as imprisonment for life."

We must have the death penalty for murder till we can imprison for life. Let us take away the pardoning power from the executive in case of murder; and, until we can do that, let murderers hang, say I. CHIVEX.

CHICAGO, March 24, 1873.

pardoning power from the executive, as also the right to appeal to higher courts or for a new trial on the part of the accused.

These principles can never be attained by enforcing the death penalty. After death, no reparation can be made by the criminal; nor can we call back the innocent and restore life again. Neither science, nature, or divine revelation teach that it is a Christian duty to hang murderers; but, on the other hand, they teach us plainly that as long as God and nature lets the criminal live we should certainly be willing to do so, and—as God did with Cain—separate them from society, and imprison them for life. It has also been successfully argued that the death penalty does not deter men from committing crime, but rather induces crime, and is therefore not a sure prevention. The only true means of preventing crime is the certain enforcement of the law, and the punishment being made reformatory and compensatory; compulsory education of the masses, and in placing a high estimate on life, educating mankind to the belief that "the chief end of man" will be to look after the proper culture of the child, in order that the future generation may develop into healthy, intellectual, and moral men and women, rather than to acquire wealth and mere earthly possessions, which are at any time liable to "take to themselves wings and fly away."

Let labor be looked upon as honorable, and the working classes have as many advantages in acquiring an education as those who have wealth, and our young men will not despise to learn a trade, or make farming their profession. As it is now, young men aspire to some

PROFESSION

rather than to learn a trade. A few years ago we penned a short article on this subject which is here inserted:

"Some mothers and sisters, and perhaps fathers, may be mortified because one of the family chooses to be an artisan rather than a clerk in a counting-room. So far as education goes, perchance, "the honors are easy," but looking to the future of life, and supposing no capital but brains and character, who has the greatest chance, a young man who wears out the best of his years in posting books, collecting debts or making sales, with little or no hope of promotion, and who considers a salary of two or three thousand per annum large pay—or another who learns a trade thoroughly, and is an expert in a a handicraft always in demand, at the highest wages, making as his own master, even when a journeyman, from fifteen hundred to two thousand dollars per annum, and as he gets known, taking contracts and gradually passing from the position of operative to that of superintendent, and finally that of "boss?" There are many illustrations of this fact around us. There are two brothers here now, for example, one a physician and the other a mechanic; the last could buy out the first and not feel it; he is received, as he deserves to be, in quite as good a social circle; and his children mix with their cousins in the same associations, notwithstanding some of the "social status" shoddyites, whose progenitors were coal-heavers, may turn up their noses at them.

"The whole question of his supposed inferiority lies in the question of education and manners, and nothing else; for, other things being equal, that is the best pursuit which, faithfully and intelligently adhered to, furnishes steady occupation, affords a reasonable chance of promotion as the result of industry and enterprise, and, above all, leaves the man independent, and not the servant or slave of a corporation or individual upon which he is dependent for his daily bread.

"It is a melancholy sight to see a gray-haired book-keeper, or a vigorous clerk, cringing and fawning to suit the whims or caprices of some fancied superior, often his junior in years and experience, who has inherited the "silver spoon," but is his inferior in intellect and all the attributes that make a man. If any one supposes these employes do not feel the humiliation and recognize their slavish condition, he is mistaken. Hard and stern necessity compels the "hated utterance" and submissive mien. The knee is too often crooked "that thrift may follow fawning," and so the man's life ebbs out; and at last he leaves, perhaps, a widow and children stranded on the bleak shores of the world's charity, to shift for themselves as best they may. How many of our readers will respond, "true, we know it," and would gladly, if they could, take up a trade, and thus work out their individual freedom.

"We do not suppose that in this wide country there

is really any energetic man suffering, if he will work, but every one who has been in California or the far west, or any new country, knows that doctors, lawyers, store and office clerks are a comparatively useless class as contrasted with those who understand the tilling of the soil or are skilled mechanics. Your professional man, while he is usually respectable, has one great drawback in the necessity of doing all his work himself. You can not preach, try causes, physic, or edit a newspaper by deputy, unless you are a quack —a humbug. The limit of your income is your own ability to earn it, save in the exceptional cases of good fortune of the successful merchant or tradesman, and it is worthy of note that it is only recently that commercial pursuits have been allowed to class with professions, and that even now, in Europe, the merchant, unless he has wealth enough to buy his way into society, is as much under the ban as the mechanic.

"How much better, then, would it be if our young men, instead of yielding to unworthy prejudice, and frittering away their time and efforts in over-crowded, and in most cases unproductive, pursuits, would go to work at what promises prompt and certain support, and, with skill, sobriety, and industry, insure competence.

PART III.

THE LAW.

CHAPTER XIX.

ON THE LAWS OF NATURE.

Our first effort will be to define the laws of nature, and then make our deductions applicable to human life. By the laws of nature, we understand a constant and regular order of facts, by which God governs the universe; a regular order of facts which are presented to the reason of man through the five senses, and which are common rules for the guidance of his actions, without distinction of person, age, or sect, and a close observation of which will ultimate in happiness.

By the word, law, we understand "an order or prohibition to act, with the express clause of a penalty attached to the infraction or of a recompense attached to the observance of that order." Literally it signifies a *lecture*, translated from the Latin word *lex lectio*, which took its name from the practice among the ancient nations to proclaim, in the form of a lecture made to the people, all ordinances and regulations, in order that they might observe them, and not incur the penalties attached to the infraction of them. This is the most comprehensive definition that can be given either of the law of nature or of the word law itself.

Blackstone divides law into the "unwritten and the written." The unwritten law is that which is cognizable only in the workings of nature. It is a fixed law of nature that water flows downward; that it endeavors to find its level; that it is heavier than air; that all bodies tend toward the earth; that flame ascends toward the heavens; that fire disorganizes vegetables, and destroys the life of animals; that air is necessary for existence; that water will drown all air-breathing animals; that certain plants will poison and kill, and certain minerals attack the organs and destroy life when taken into the system; that the sun illuminates successively every portion of the surface of the terrestrial globe; that its presence causes both light and heat; that heat, acting upon water, produces vapors; that those vapors, rising in clouds in the regions of the air, dissolve into rain or snow, and renew incessantly the waters of fountains and of rivers; and so on, in a multitude of other instances. The unwritten law may be further defined as common law, which is a rule of action deriving its authority from long usage or established custom, which has been immemorially received and recognized by judicial tribunals.

The written law is a rule of action prescribed or

enacted by the legislative powers, and promulgated and recorded in written statutes, ordinances, edicts, or decrees.

Natural laws are always right: they are fixed, and do not change so as to create discord. To make the legislative acts of man a success, they must agree with nature's laws and thus only can the written law become a blessing to man. For man to accomplish this, a thorough knowledge of nature, or what is termed the unwritten law, is requisite, for the laws of man must be adjusted strictly in accordance with those of nature before we can hope to arrive at a just determination of the right and the wrong. We will now

PROCEED TO EXAMINE

some of the laws of nature which have a bearing in governing the actions of men.

Prof. W. Fishbaugh says: "The starting point of all thought and investigation with every human being is his own interior consciousness. This is to every one the most absolutely fixed of all facts—the most positively certain of all certainties. Hence it is the position from which all other certainties and uncertainties, probabilities and improbabilities, possibilities and impossibilities, are estimated. But as, from our individual centers of consciousness and intellect, we open our eyes and look without us, we find ourselves surrounded by various forms and conditions, near and remote, which act upon our physical, intellectual, and moral natures, and are reacted upon by us.

These active and reactive influences are, in some sense, at a constant equipoise. There is thus a universe *without*, and a universe *within* us,—a universe of cognizable forms, principles, and conditions, and a universe of cognizing faculties,—the one being related to, and corresponding with, the other. It is a legitimate object and privilege of every inquiring mind to understand, in some degree, both of these universes; and in order to do this to the fullest extent, one must investigate each with a constant regard to its analogy with, and relation to the other."

The forms of the outer universe are included in a few simple and comprehensive classifications, arranged above or beneath each other in the scale of creation. Those beneath man, and which at present form the special subject of our investigation, are embraced in the comprehensive divisions of animal, vegetable, mineral, geological, astronomical, or cosmical forms. Of these, singularly and in united groups, together with their more superficial properties, the interior soul gains a preception through some one or more of the sensational channels, known as *touch*, *taste*, *sight*, *hearing* and *smell*. Proceeding upon the basis of the impressions received through these avenues of sense, the ratiocinative faculty becomes the medium of some knowledge of the purposes and mutual relations of these, and of the laws by which they are governed; and availing itself of the contributions of both *sense* and *reason*, at the same time that it draws from its own interior and independent resources, the faculty of *intuition* decides upon their causes, their life forces, and their more interior significations.

The universe, or rather the material world, makes an impression upon our senses, without which there can be no existence. This contact with physical nature creates a certain feeling, or, in other words, makes an impression upon the interior cognizing faculties, which are so constituted as to be impressed by the cognizable forms, principles, and conditions of the surrounding universe. We form ideas in connection with what we see, hear, touch, taste, or smell; and we say how rich, how beautiful the heavens and the earth, when exposed to our sight. The senses combine and create within us wonder and amazement when we contemplate the movements of the universe, animated, as it were, with a soul, as our own bodies are, and we speak of nature in a sense mysterious,—"the intentions of nature; the incomprehensible secrets of nature,"—all operating on every being in various ways so as to create a peculiar condition, both in the external conformation as well as in the mental operations.

As we study the peculiarities of individuals, we often say, "The nature of man is an enigma; every being acts according to its nature." As we examine the nature of things, and inquire into the actions of each being, or each species of beings, we see that all are subject to constant and general rules, which can not be infringed without interrupting and creating discord in the general as well as the particular order of things. These are rules of action, and constitute what are called natural laws. It is a law of nature that not two individuals existing are precisely alike in external conformation, neither in mental organization; at least, various conditions of individual peculiarity exist in a relative degree of activity. Now, as there are a great number of different tissues, organs, and filaments, which constitute the physical organization, and a great variety of articles of diet, and agencies and conditions necessary to sustain life, so the mind is made up of a great many different faculties, and each faculty has its own peculiarities which operating together, constitute an individual character which manifests itself in an infinite variety or degree of activity, and thus each person furnishes a particular element, which, when organized, constitutes what is termed society.

In order, then, to reform an individual, it is necessary first to understand the nature and peculiarities of the individual and the natural laws by which a change may be wrought. So in regard to society. To bring about a radical change in any of the customs of society, it will be necessary to co-operate with the primary principles of nature, and to be successful in this, it is necessary to analyze society, as well as the individual, into ultimate parts or elements.

After we have ascertained the ultimate elements of which society is composed, we are prepared to extend our attention to the proximate elements, or those conditions which have been created by a combination of the primary or ultimate principles, and having inquired into the effects of all, we can easily retrace our steps into the examination of the causes. The same course of reasoning is applicable in our investigations of any of the mysterious workings of nature. First, to understand the nature and the peculiarities of the primary elements; then, to inquire into the nature and peculiarities of the proximate elements, and the conditions and the effect of these elements when comprehended. To understand the harmonious operations of these elements, when compounded, or, in other words, to determine whether the effect of all is right or wrong, is wholly a matter of experience, and, by reasoning analogically, we are enabled to form a correct conclusion as to the right actions of men.

To understand the various conditions, and fully comprehend the natural order which ends in right action, is our present object, so that we may be enabled to adjust or harmonize man's laws with the laws of nature. In the first place, we find that man is so organized as to require support from the external world to maintain his existence. In the second place, there is no demand made by the interior organization which is not even bountifully supplied by nature. Man has but to use proper means to possess them to maintain harmony between the interior and the exterior, to aid in which, two universal forces are established in man, which attract or repel him in his dealings with the existing corporal surroundings, which are *pleasure and pain.* Pleasure attracts and pain repels. The primary object of pain is the protection of the organic integrity, while pleasure produces a love of existence. For example, under certain conditions, cold will produce an unpleasant sensation, and the being is thus admonished to use means by which to protect itself, by maintaining an equilibrium of temperature. The same of heat. Under certain conditions, where the temperature has been raised to a burning heat, the being is immediately warned on coming in contact with it, by pain, to protect itself, and thus avoid being destroyed. This condition first gave rise to the necessity of clothing the body, and also to the construction of houses, for protection against cold and heat, in order to maintain that equilibrium of temperature which is necessary for the proper expansion of life. While man is thus engaged in clothing and protecting the body against violence from whatever cause, a sensation of pleasure is produced, which creates a satisfaction, and is the reward of labor.

Hunger is the messenger which informs the being that the body is in need of food for the purpose of maintaining the internal integrity of the organization. Were it not for the pleasure experienced in eating, it is doubtful whether people would supply the body with nourishment, simply from duty, receiving no other reward than mere existence.

These are, then, the forces which cause men to act in a physical sense, and we shall show that all human actions have their starting-point in man's endeavor to flee from pain, unpleasantness, and sorrow, and to attain pleasure, satisfaction, ease, and happiness. These are natural laws; and while nature inflicts pain under certain circumstances, she also provides the means by which to avoid or overcome such circumstances, and rewards the being by giving pleasure in place of pain. Pain, then, is a teacher rather than a chastizing or condemning power. When certain circumstances exist which are contrary to the nature and welfare of man, this force teaches him how to use means to the end of overcoming the difficulty, and thus leads him to happiness. Here we see no malice, no revenge; nor can we find that nature ever outrages her own laws. Pain, in truth, may be considered an angel of mercy,—not a "fiend from the regions of darkness." We have stated that the starting-point of the actions of man is in pain and pleasure. This is true in a physical sense; and now let us see if the same course of reasoning will not apply in regard to the mind. It has been stated that the exterior world makes certain impressions upon the five senses, and thence an impression is conveyed to the mind, arousing certain faculties, or producing certain impressions upon the cognizing powers of the interior. Intellectuality proceeds in regular order as the external impressions are conveyed. We will take pain again, for example. The first impression made on the physical, as well as on the mental, is a feeling of resistance, and the first mental faculties which are called into requisition are combativeness, destructiveness, and the selfish propensities. These are the executive powers, and immediately bring into use such measures as the nature of the difficulty may indicate. These faculties, however, are subject to the higher faculties of reason, caution, acquisitiveness, and conscientiousness, or, in other words, the moral and intellectual faculties, which proceed analogically and in accordance with previous experiences.

Thus the mind is interested in the welfare of the physical organization through which it operates in providing for its wants; to relieve when distressed, to feed when hungered, to clothe when naked; and even to provide for future necessities by laying up a store of provisions, acquiring property, and to pursue happiness, which is the ultimate object of all human action.

There can be no physical sensation without a corresponding impression being made on the mind, or, at least, on one or more of the faculties of the mind which correspond to the nature or kind of impression conveyed through the physical communicating channels. The physical wants of the body are constantly making demands on the faculty of acquisitiveness, and this calls into requisition the executive faculties, which go to work to supply the necessary means of support or give protection. Sensation does not end here. The higher tribunals are impressed which judge of the right, the propriety, or the possibility of consummating or complying with the requisition that is made. The same is true of the social and of the sexual propensities, which make a constant demand for the exercise of their functions, wholly for the pleasure which such exercise affords. So in regard to other propensities or faculties of the mind. In regard to the mind rendering a just verdict in deciding upon the right or the wrong of any of the demands or requisitions that are made, we will find that this is done in accordance with a previous knowledge acquired through experience or by being educated through the experience of others, conveyed to the mind by means of one or all of the five senses. In this manner man acquires knowledge of the fixed laws of nature, and also of the penalty which follows any actions which are in disregard of such laws. There are many real and regular orders or laws which may be stated to illustrate how man gains a knowledge of the laws of nature to which he must conform. For example: if man pretends to see clear in darkness; if he goes in contradiction to the course of the seasons, or the actions of the elements; if he pretends to remain under water without being drowned; to touch fire without burning himself; to deprive himself of air without being suffocated; to swallow poison without destroying himself, he receives from each of these infractions of the laws of nature a punishment proportionate to his faults. But if, on the contrary, he observes and practices each of these laws according to the regular and exact relations they have to him, he preserves his existence, and renders it as happy as it can be.

We find, further, that it is a law of nature that man, under certain circumstances, is severely punished; or, in other words, he suffers pain in gaining knowledge by practical experience. Under other circumstances, knowledge is acquired by the reward of pleasure, the opposite force, which is the attractive while pain is the repelling force of man's actions. Thus man is endowed with the power to judge according to the kind of impression that is made upon him, whether such impression produces an unpleasant sensation or a feeling of pleasure. He says, "This is pleasant to me; this I will pursue; or, "This is unpleasant, and this course I will shun." Now, without a knowledge of the right road to happiness, man is liable constantly to incur the infliction of pain. Even in his endeavor to relieve himself, he often makes bad worse; but by the long experience of men, through the many and progressive ages of human existence, much has been learned in regard to the laws of nature, and the intimate relation which man sustains to them. This knowledge is transmitted to the rising generation by precept, by tradition, by record, and, if properly inculcated, will enable the future generation to pass along through life without having to go back and learn by practical experience. Hence, we see how necessary it is to institute laws and institutions of learning to benefit the race by the experience of those who lived before us, continuing to add little by little to the previously acquired store of knowledge through our own experience; for it is impossible to exist scarcely a moment without being impressed by our surroundings, and we form an idea as to the nature of such impressions and judge of the pleasant or unpleasant sensation which is made on the cognizable principle within us. It is easy to perceive how to construct laws which will insure to every individual a happy physical existence. The revelations that have been made by physiology, give us a correct idea concerning how to feed and how to clothe the body, how to exercise, sleep, bathe, and how to educate each mental faculty, in order to live a healthy and happy life. It has been determined that a crude, unreformed, animal-like organization has a corresponding effect on the mental organization, and we have a gross, unregenerated, beastly character to deal with; while, under opposite condition, where persons understand and live strictly in harmony with the principles of physiology, an enlightened and highly refined character is manifested, one, too, highly moral and religious; for we shall claim for physiology the starting-point of all correct human action. All other branches of education are really and only collaterals.

HUMAN LAWS

must be in harmony with the laws governing physical life before we can expect to adjust them in harmony with the higher nature of man, or rather the laws of nature which govern moral action. For example, it is a law of physiology that time, practice, and favorable surroundings are necessary to develop, to educate, and to regenerate a gross organization. To facilitate a healthy growth, all obstacles must be removed, and the agencies that support a harmonious exercise of the capabilities of man be supplied. This can not be done by laws which only exact a forfeiture of money or property with a view thereby to cure a condition of depravity. As well take the clothing from a man already too poorly clad, to protect him against cold, bread from a child sparingly fed, in the endeavor to support its physical existence. Any law where "might makes right" is contrary to nature, and we can easily see the true philosophy of our argument, in the fact that a man, before he will freeze, will steal. This is only obeying a physical law, and man's law, instead of taking that which the offender has, should supply him with an extra garment; and the moral effect will be obvious. We see, therefore, that all legislation which is intended to govern the actions of men must first be in harmony with physiological laws, or we shall never be enabled to do so correctly. So long as man's laws continue to disregard the physical laws of nature, just so long shall we fail in creating laws the infraction of which will bring a just punishment upon the transgressor. We have stated that human action begins with physical existence, and that though our ideas have their starting-point in the things of the corporal or cognizable universe, pain and pleasure, the primary forces, which cause men to act physically, so to speak, as well as mentally, that we are endowed with a principle which is the cognizing or a universe within; that pain repels and pleasure attracts; that pain is an admonishing principle or force, which teaches the being to avoid that which is wrong, and pleasure is that which rewards as well as creates a feeling of right; that the mind calls into requisition every available means to enable the being to flee from pain and attain to happiness; that physiology is the only reliable science or branch of education which teaches the plain road to health and happiness, and all other branches of education are auxiliary, and all join in rendering man's physical existence harmonious with the general and special laws of nature; that the mind reasons on all subjects analogically, and decides between the right and the wrong, by a knowledge previously acquired, either through personal experience or from being taught by precept, tradition, or by reading the records of the experience of others;

that human laws must agree with the laws of nature, and especially with the laws of physiology, in order to be successful in regulating the actions of man; that criminals require treatment on the same principle that a person who is in a physically diseased condition is not indisputable, and the treatment must be in harmony with physiology; that might does *not* make right, nor is the old Mosaic law, which taught "an eye for an eye or a tooth for a tooth," any reason whatever why we should so legislate at the present day.

The question may now be raised, "Can man, by the study of nature alone, arrive at a just conclusion as to what is right and what is wrong?"

Speaking from a

MORAL STANDPOINT,

we answer, that nature is the only source whence we derive any truth, and that a moral action is strictly defined by nature as well as by Divine revelation. We derive from the light of nature the same idea that is declared in the New Testament, namely: "Do unto all men as you would have them do unto you." In the first place, we remark that it is very easily ascertained from our own feelings whether, under certain circumstances, we are in pain or having a pleasant sensation. If the sensation experienced is painful, we say it is wrong, because it is contrary to our own nature, and we resist it. If, however, the sensation is pleasant, and perfectly congenial with our nature, we say that is right, and we pursue it.

Thus far our argument will be admitted. Now, if this is good reasoning in regard to the physical sensations produced through the physical senses, then, as it has already been stated that a corresponding impression is made on the mind, do we not derive a correct idea of right and wrong? As the body is thus guarded and instructed, as it were, by the sensations of pain and pleasure, when we are in discord or inharmonious relation to the laws of nature, then are we not so organized mentally, also to draw a moral conclusion from such action? What sensation is to the body, conscience is to the mind. Conscience, therefore, always decides whether an act is right or wrong. If it is decided that a certain act is wrong, a feeling of remorse is produced, and we are morally in pain; or, if it is decided that such an act is right, then we are morally happy. If a feeling of remorse is produced upon the mind, then the first impression is a feeling of resistance, and the intellectual faculties are implored to assist in providing means to overcome the difficulty. If a feeling of right is produced, then all is happiness.

Conscience also proceeds to decide between right and wrong, in accordance with a previous experience and education, brought about variously by our senses combining and creating knowledge. The starting-point of all is in the physical sensation that is produced on the bodily senses, the mind drawing an analogical conclusion, and by so reasoning a moral feeling is produced. We will illustrate our idea. For example, we come in contact with a red-hot iron; we find that it will burn us; a feeling of pain is produced, and we use means to avoid further contact. Our contact may have been accidental or intentional—the effect is the same; the hot iron will burn us. Here we have learned a very important lesson, yet so far no moral feeling is produced. But we see a child advancing, who knows not that the hot iron will burn it, and if, without giving the child instruction, we allow it to take the hot iron in its hand, its hand is burned to a crisp, and it is crippled for life, and we know, from previous experience, that the iron would burn it, as also that we might have prevented such a calamity, a moral feeling is now produced in us, and we are having moral pain while the child is suffering only physical pain. We will illustrate our idea still further. Suppose you have no knowledge of the iron being hot, and your neighbor does know, but neglects to instruct you so as to save you from a sad experience, the first feeling you will have toward him will be that of revenge, and you will call him to account for not instructing you in regard to the iron being hot. Now reverse the case, and, without the knowledge and experience you have, another advances whom you might save from meeting with the same fate, but you neglect to do so,—a moral feeling is produced in your mind, and conscience will say, under the circumstances, you ought to have done as well by this man as you wished the other to do unto you. Thus a moral action is produced, and a moral lesson is learned from the light of nature alone. If it were not for the wise provision which was made by our Creator in creating the faculty of conscience, *might would make right;* or, in other words, the strongest would rule, and there would be no moral accountability, and consequently no law would be necessary to regulate the actions of men. Before the moral and the intellectual faculties were educated, man was in a savage state, and even now approximates to the brute in exact ratio as his moral education is neglected. The person who possesses a well-balanced physical organization, and a correspondingly well-balanced moral education, requires no law to restrain or force him into right doing. But since such persons are rarely to be found, and the majority are comparatively in an unbalanced condition, legislation is necessary, only however with a view to educate on the one hand and to restrain on the other.

"How may we know that we 'shall not steal?'" asks one. "Does nature teach us that we must not appropriate to ourselves that which

BELONGS TO ANOTHER?"

We answer that it does, from the fact that every human being is endowed with the faculty of acquisitiveness which says, this or that is my own, and you must not take it from me without compensating me for it. Having such a feeling ourselves, then, when we steal from another, conscience and reason will chide us, and we know that we have not done as we wish to be done by. From this same standpoint we reason, also, that when we have lost property, we have a desire to bring the perpetrator to an account, and if we can get a majority of the community to think as we do, we can have a law enacted by which the thief may be tried and punished. The punishment should be, first, to make reparation of the stolen property, or we bring the criminal to account mainly through a feeling of revenge; and, secondly, to reform the criminal, that he may never commit a like crime again. This question has been sufficiently argued in Part II. of this volume. No one, therefore, can appropriate property, knowing that it belongs to another, without feeling that he has stolen, though he is entirely ignorant of the command, " Thou shalt not steal."

We will now consider how men run into

ECCENTRIC CHANNELS,

while in the pursuit of happiness. Men's organizations differ in regard to temperamental condition, or in the various combinations of the elements of nervous susceptibility, and manifest as many different dispositions as there are individuals. On the subject of nervous sensibility we wrote an article, a few years ago, and think it quite proper to reproduce some of the ideas:

"The action of the nervous system is always addressed to our senses. This is so decided, when the moral feelings are greatly agitated, as to effect the exercise of the other functions. The dynamic conditions of the organism, being no longer in just proportion, all the springs of life share in the activity of the nervous system. It is remarkable, indeed, that the metaphorical language of all languages, accurately represents the effects produced on the body by an exalted sensibility. The blood freezes—the eyes sparkle—the heart burns—we tremble with fear or hope—we are pale with fright, swollen with pride, panting with desire—these are examples of truthful metaphors in all languages. In a word, organic disturbances and the agitations of the mind are in perfect correspondence, evidently because the source of both is identical. When these truths are considered, we shall cease to wonder that the rules of æsthetic art have been referred to feeling, or that Abbot should say, 'Sensibility is the source of all our genius.' Montaigne has already observed that 'a man is of no account until he is aroused.' This is so true that a boor may become eloquent under the excitement of strong emotion. Certainly, the spirited personifications of savage oratory, such as, '*Shall we say to the bones of our fathers—rise and march with us?*' or the mournful and stirring watchword of the Vendean peasants, '*Long live the king!*' are as powerful and startling as the words which Massillion thundered in the ears of the Court of Louis the Fourteenth: '*I think this very hour your last, and the end of the world.*' No one is ignorant of their effect on his auditory. So we may perceive how feeling contributes in the reply of Buffon to La Cardamine, where he describes him wandering over 'mountains covered with eternal snow, through immense solitudes, where Nature was habituated to a silence so profound, that she herself would have been startled at the human voice that dared to interrogate her secrets.' The audience struck with the sublimity of the figure, sat a few seconds hushed and breathless, when a thunder of applause greeted the orator. Whatever may be the reason, high moral and intellectual culture adds little to the effect of eloquence; all its power is due to profound emotion. Speak to my soul if you would have my soul give ear—that above all others is the precept the orator should heed. M. Villemain, one of the most distinguished among our men of letters, declares Tacitus to be the greatest historian, precisely because 'while he is the most candid and impartial, he is, I dare avow, at the same time, the most passionate; because he decrees like a judge, and testifies like a sworn witness, though excited and indignant at what he has seen.'

"It is now an easy matter to explain by an application, the

LAWS OF THE SENSIBILITY;

the moral peculiarities of men, the most remarkable for their labors and genius. Predisposed by nature to feeling, to lively emotion, because in their case the impressions received surpass in intensity and duration, the occasions that give rise to them; they are eager for these impressions and the sensations they produce, and store them up from their earliest years. On account of the variety of ideas they acquire in a brief space of time, they very early learn to judge and understand; then endowed with the capacity of expression, carried away and enraptured with their own thoughts, they experience an irresistible craving to communicate them, to cast them into the world of intelligence. And these thoughts we must say impose laws on the world; they are the life-giving energy that emanates from those powerful souls that civilize the nations, elevate them, sometimes degrade them, or regenerate or enable them to accomplish their destiny. The force of circumstances in the social world is only the force of ideas. Cromwell was in his age 'the visible destiny of that time.' Napoleon was the destiny of the opening epoch of our century. But how is it possible to believe that such vital and intellectual activity can co-exist with the regular and tranquil exercise of the functions of the organism? Is not life here in excess, in the moral as well as the physical economy? Consider, indeed, that agitation which is never stilled, that impatient and never-resting activity, that inward turbulence of emotion, which constantly disturb the organic forces, that feeling of abounding life so intense and, at times, so painfully oppressive, which gives to the character of distinguished men an air of violence and disquietude, a something feverish and inexplicable entirely alien to ordinary experience. This restless and disturbed condition ceases, or is at least in a measure subdued, when life is very active, or even when by literary labor, the torrent of thought and emotion is able to find vent. This crisis is ordinarily beneficial. The master works of art are produced, the treasures of feeling and imagination are poured out to relieve the over-burdened spirit, and satisfy a burning aspiration; this is in accordance with a law of the organization. The poetry is in the poet, just as sound is in the lyre; this is a truth of positive physiology. The man of genius has often labored without a thought as to what should become of his work, simply for self-gratification, happy in his success. A multitude of inferences might be deduced from these principles, applicable to science, art and education, but such details are inconsistent with the object of this work; its purpose is fundamental positions, and these I am anxious to establish.

" Perhaps it will be said that the above reflections apply to artists alone, in whom the imagination is generally more ardent than with men of science; this is an erroneous impression. The savant whose highest capacity is simply to understand, is a man of erudition merely—he knows what has been, but endowed with higher intellectual gifts, he desires to extend to boundaries of science; he investigates, he invents, he imagines. If facts do not accord with his imagined explanation, it remains a vague theory or hypothesis; if on the contrary, facts agree with it and the theory is their only fair exponent, progress has· been made, whether reached by synthesis or by analytical and inductive processes. To apprehend a general principle, to perceive its most remote consequences, and trace them out with such vigor, boldness and pertinacity of thought as to reach immense and valuable results, and next to state and formalize that controlling principle as to render it intelligible, and explanatory of whatever may be legitimately deduced from it—this is certainly a work of intellect to be performed only by the aid of a powerful imagination. So far as regards invention, Homer and Archimedes may justly be said to occupy the same rank. That keen sensibility of soul, moreover, which animates one with enthusiasm for ideas, is a characteristic of savans, as well as artists; they have the same passion, the same fanaticism for their works, their conceptions, their theories or systems.

"There is in the nerves, the veins, the blood, the very fibres of the man of genius, whether he be savant, artist, poet, or mathematician, something which predisposes him to extravagance, either in ideas, sentiment or action. Thus the man of vigorous and active imagination, must always appear a kind of enigma to one of a cooler temperament. Which of the three was the most demented—Archimedes, the mathematician, running naked through the streets of Syracuse, shouting 'I have found it!' Peter of Cortona, saying to the bronze statue of a horse, 'Well, why do you not move, do you not know you are alive?' or the mineralogist, Werner, ever ready to dash in pieces the finest statue, to examine the structure of the marble of which it was made? Such generous frenzies of the soul evidently depend upon a sensibility capable of excitation from the slightest imaginable causes.

"Sometimes owing to

EXCESSIVE EMOTION,

agitation or excitement, the faculties are stunned into a sort of impotence or stolid apathy. The individual then feels the want of inordinate moral stimulus, the soul's vitality seems exhausted and burnt out, as the body of the voluptuary becomes wasted and worn.

The cause of this exhaustion and need of stimulus is the same, and is easily explained. However superior the nervous system, taken as a whole, may be to the other functions of the organism, it is confined to certain limits of action compatible with the entire human constitution. The intellectual and moral life is the highest, the inner and true life of man; but like every vital energy it must act within prescribed bounds. If we give to the functions of feeling and knowing unlimited range, the organism will soon be unable to respond to such action, and will be deprived of its vigor with greater or less rapidity. In that case, the higher man becomes a victim to chimerical and fantastic ideas. He still desires, but what does he desire? what would he have? for what does he sigh? He knows not. This excessive aspiration of the faculties towards something undefinable and uncreate; this soul sometimes rapt away to the third heaven, and again cast down and grieved to death; these flights of a dreamy and morbid imagination, without apparent aim or determined object, "heaving its restless waves in a sea without shore," have been very well described by many writers. It is a state which has a real existence in certain individuals endowed with great moral energy, too early and inordinately developed. I will only observe that romance writers usually describe it as a condition peculiar to youth, while on the contrary, medical observation has shown me that the man who has had some experience of life is more frequently afflicted with it. The fresh and vigorous sensibility of the youth, and the grandeur of his hopes, give sufficient scope to the activity of the spirit. Another proof that this singular state is a consequence of a premature exhaustion of the sensibility, is that the imagination no longer finding adequate aliment in the external world, turns in upon itself, and revolves in the circle of its own creations, making incredible exertions to combat the weight of thought and the pressure of despondency. Fleeting from abstraction to abstraction, from chimera to chimera, it ends with that fancy so often repeated by Rousseau, " Naught beautiful save what is not so." But the original impulse to such fantasies is always found in a remarkably susceptible nervous system, in an inordinate and ever excited sensibility. In this way we ascend from effects to the law that explains them. Whoever takes a different course, deserts the path of observation and reality to wade in the vast region of hypothesis. The most ultra asserters of the innate powers of spirit, have been often brought back to it in spite of themselves. Pascal said with great good sense: " Let us not mistake, we are as truly body as spirit." Do you not in a manner admit it yourself, my divine Plato, when you declare that every pain and every pleasure has, so to speak, a nail with which it fastens the soul to the body, renders it like itself, and persuades it that there is nothing true but what the body tells it? (*The Phaedo.*) Nature has then wisely ordained that the harmonious play of our sensations should be successfully called out in gradations of activity, of different force, and style; that our desires, our emotions, our passions should be developed in proportion to that activity; but she at the same time admonishes us by the feeling of weakness and disgust, that it is folly to crave superhuman impressions in connection with actual organic weakness, and demand from life more than life can give. She seems to say to us with a certain philosopher: 'Thou are but a limited creature desiring a perfection thou canst not attain. Do not waste thy strength in vain endeavors; obey my laws and follow out the career appointed thee; in the beyond thou shalt find that abundant well-spring of delight, which can alone satisfy thy thirst.'

EFFECTS OF THIS LAW ON THE SPECIAL ACTIVITY OF THE INTELLECT.

"In stating the general laws of the sensibility, I observed that among the first of these was the tendency to concentrate itself upon a particular point of the organism, when that point was unduly excited. The states of health and disease, the physical and moral condition furnish a multitude of illustrations of this great law. This demonstrates that physiology, pathology, and psychology are connected together by phenomena substantially the same, because they all coalesce in one direction in the sensitive unity. Stimulate a single point in the organism strongly, and all the movements of the system at once gravitate to it, because there is an undeniable sympathy between all the organs. In the same way, also, let a person be intensely pre-occupied with one idea, and the energies of the understanding will immediately take that direction. Around that fixed idea all others will group. If in the physiological or pathological state, this law is seen to assume many degrees of development, we may likewise observe gradations in the concentration of conscious emotion. Following an ascending scale, we find attention, reflection, meditation, contemplation, and finally ecstacy—or *raptus animi extra sensus*, an elevation of the mind beyond the senses. At this point, the sensibility abandons, so to speak, the external organs and the body so closely with the moral being, that there results a purely pathological state. The coldness of the extremities, the paleness of the skin, a general trembling, spasms, or the convulsive rigidity of the muscles are its symptoms, and indicate its several stages. It should be remembered, that in this faculty of concentration is involved the power of abstraction, a characteristic of human intelligence; man owes to it, of course, his superiority to the brute. Further, it is precisely the power of attention and depth of contemplation, which place certain men on a level superior to others. Has it not been asserted that genius is nothing more than the capacity of attention? Has it not been compared to a burning mirror, the focus of which illumines with intensity but a single object? In truth, the more earnest the attention—that gaze of the mind—the more vigorous and sprightly will be the imagination. Our power is commensurate with our intelligence; and the intelligence is equal to the force of concentration. If man, the frail creature of a day, has been able to measure the heavens, calculate the mass of the heavenly bodies, seize the thunderbolt in the cloud, and subdue the ocean; if by the aid of the telescope and microscope he has been able to reach two infinities; if it has been given to him to wrest from nature some of her secrets; to establish sciences; to assign to motion its laws; to the universe its progress; to determine the limits and origin of reason, beyond contradiction he owes it to this faculty. According to Avicenna, the Arabian physician, all things obey the human soul when elevated to the ecstatic state. The meaning of this oracular statement is now understood. The fertility of invention, the creative energy of the fine arts, the elevation and compass of thought, power of execution, the magnificent gift by which life is imparted to marble, bronze, and to the canvas are entirely due to the concentration, to exaltation of mind, to that ecstatic intuition in which the body no longer exists. It is, so to speak, to pass during this life from the sphere of gross matter to that of essences. The essential point is to have that strength of brain which renders one capable of grasping and holding under a single point of view, the objects, with which the mind is occupied, in order to consider it in its parts and in its totality, to examine it closely, to control it at will and become master of it. A truth well known is but the copy and production of a model long since elaborated in the intellect of a man of genius. There is a type pre-existing in the soul of the poet and artist, which comes to light only under the fire of thought. The pencil, the pen, the chisel, and the burin are but instruments employed to bring out what has been first contemplated and finished in the lofty region of the intellect. Before calling their aid, the inner genius has already realized the ideal, that is, what no one has before seen and conceived.

"To recapitulate; the sensibility is the distinguishing characteristic of bodies which are organized, living and animate; it attains its maximum of activity in man; it exists, acts, and lives only in and by itself; in a word, the sensibility is the *stuff* of which life is made. Meanwhile, this property is not merely the prime mover in organic action; by means of sensations and consciousness, it is the source of our pleasures and our pains; it influences the character, the inclinations and the will—the warmth and coolness of the imagination, the violence or moderation of desire, the activity or sluggishness of the intellect. Considered physiologically, we may say, that man is what the sensibility makes him. This function or property is so important, so necessary, so radical, that the philosophers had made of it a special soul—the sensitive soul. Bacon distinguishes the science of the soul, into that of the divine breath, whence the rational soul was derived, and into the science of the irrational soul, which is common to us with the brutes, and is regarded as the product of the dust of the earth. According to Plato in Timæus, 'the gods having taken the principle of an immortal soul, created a mortal body within which to place it; but they joined to it a mortal soul subject to the passions by the necessity of its nature.'"

As men are differently organized, so do they differ in the emotive principle, according to the sensibility of the nervous system through which impressions are conveyed to the cognizable, and again reflected in the form of actions of which we judge as to whether they are in harmony with the general or special laws of nature and with the laws established by man.

CHAPTER XX.

THE LAWS OF PHYSIOLOGY THE ONLY RELIABLE STARTING-POINT FOR THE ENACTMENT OF HUMAN LAWS.

Whatever may be the theory of men, or however many different stand-points may be assumed, outside of the laws of physiology, in reasoning and deducing proper data, from whence to start in the construction of governmental laws, it will be found, after a thorough investigation, that physiology is the only science which points out to men the right direction. Any law enacted by man which disagrees with the laws of physiology,—which are also the laws of nature,—can not stand, and men will not obey it.

Every thing in the universe contributes to man's happiness, when in its proper relation. The starting-point of all human action is in the physical. Even the very thought, to have an existence at all, must be associated with some existing thing. To convince any one of the truth of this statement, let it be put to a test. Any person can make the experiment. You have only to endeavor to think of something that does not exist, or to form a definite conception of an object of which you know nothing,—which has not been presented to your understanding through the nerves of sense,—and you will find it an impossibility. Now, if even thought is dependent on the objective world for its support, may it not be reasonable to conclude that the moral nature of man is also indebted to the exterior world for its existence? There can be no action unless some feeling of consciousness is aroused which is either pleasant or unpleasant to our sensitive nature. Whatever we learn, or whatever we do, the ultimate object of all is a happy physical existence. In this we are often disappointed; yet we have a peculiar nature, which enables us to try again. In the study of physiology, we learn the road to physical perfection; and I claim, as we approximate to physical perfection, we are also approaching moral and spiritual perfection; for the spiritual of man is so intimately connected with the corporal that it is impossible to separate the two. I affirm, therefore, that all successful legislation must first agree with the laws of physiology; and I may further affirm that there never was a moral code of law given by Divine revelation,—in the last dispensation, at least,—that may not be harmonized with the same laws. For example, take the ten commandments. Each is most positively sustained by the teachings of physiology. But some one asks the question, "How does physiology teach that we shall worship only one God—the ever-living God of the universe?" "Thou shalt have none other Gods before me." The theological as well as the scientific version of this command is that God is omnipresent,—that he pervades the universe; and hence, to form an idea of a God consisting of a single substance—a single object—is physiologically dangerous; for when the mind becomes intensely occupied in the pursuit of a single object, or study, the faculty through which such exercise is carried on becomes unnaturally developed, and an unbalanced condition among all the faculties is thus created. Such a person is in danger of becoming deranged. For example, consider the miser, whose sole aim in life is to hoard up money. In time he becomes a monomaniac. The faculty of acquisitiveness has been fostered to such an excess that every thing in life appears subordinate to riches. Such a course is forbidden, by the command of God which we have quoted. It is worshiping a false god instead of the true God of the universe. It is likewise forbidden by the teachings of physiology, for it is not reasonable to suppose that God would give a command for the government of man, and then create fixed laws in nature that do not harmonize with it. It is a law of the body that a mixed diet is necessary, in order to supply the various ingredients of which it is composed. This has been ascertained by persons making the experiment of trying to live on a single article of diet. Animals have been fed for months on a single substance of food, and it has been found that such animals soon lose that natural integrity necessary to health, become demented, emaciated, and, if the process is continued, soon die. A great number of different substances enter into a chemical combination to form a healthy body. Everything in the surrounding universe contributes to man's welfare. Let him have a separate God,—living on a single article of diet,—and he will waste away and die. God is in one sense a "wrathful God," for his laws are immutable, and ever require obedience to their mandates. As it is with the laws of the body so is it with the laws of the mind. For any one to pursue persistently a single study, without investigating collateral ones; to foster passions which are already in excess; or to cultivate a single faculty, or even a group of faculties, to the exclusion of the rest, will so unbalance the nature, if not corrected, that destruction is imminent. A variety of studies, and pursuits, embracing the whole of our surroundings, is the only safe course in life to insure a healthy condition of mind and body. Thus physiology, as well as Divine revelation, declares that we are not to worship any god save the God of the Universe. In like manner each and every law of physiology will, when investigated, be found to agree with the commands of God, and I am justifiable in making the statement that they all aim to render man happy during his physical existence, as well as to point him to a glorious future.

In this connection, it may be well to state a few familiar facts which will serve to impress

ON THE MIND

the observance of such regulation of habits of body and mind as will enable the man of letters, as well as all others, to maintain a degree of health and vigor that will tend to subserve the higher purposes of life. Where is the artist, savan, statesman, administrator, etc., who will not assent frankly to the truth that they are now victims to their negligence in regard to sedentary habits? The multiplicity of business affairs, the want of method in working, the idea that they have not exceeded certain bounds, and that a little exercise will be sufficient; the secret hope that they will be strong enough to resist leads them on, until at last nature admonishes them, by some aiement more or less severe, that they must change their course of life. Is there any more certain means of producing a multitude of diseases than to keep the mind constantly employed and the body inactive? The blood was made to circulate and the members to be exercised: life and action are almost synonymous terms. Tycho Brahe had a house erected with a high tower, upon the Island of Huen, in Denmark. This retreat he called *Urainsburgh.* Here he lived twenty-one years, scarcely ever going from home, and laboring assiduously upon his astronomical observations. It was probably in this way that he contracted the disease of the bladder of which he died. How many analogous examples could be cited. We live upon food and air, but we require food only at certain intervals, while we need air at every respiration.

The principles of life which we extract from the latter must, then, be constantly renewed. Now, when the atmosphere is heavy, dense, mephitic, unchanged, it is evident that instead of rectifying the blood by respiration, we corrupt it deeply, and there is no more abundant source of disease than this. Its effects are more particularly apparent in large cities. I am aware that the progress of civilization has diminished the evil, but not so much as is generally believed, especially for men devoted to the labors of thought. One should guard against judging by those upon whom fortune has lavished her gifts. There is now more than one poet singing of the beauties of nature and the delights of the country who habitually breathes only the unhealthy air of the obscure street where he resides; and many an artist has painted Aurora opening with her rosy fingers the golden gates of the Orient, who never saw the sun rise. Savans may also be found in smoky laboratories and narrow cabinets, who are busied with experiments upon the purity and salubrity of the air. All, however, with but few exceptions, complaining of the bad state of their health. If you induce them to consider the cause, then come objections and difficulties without end. The celebrated Hellenish Dansse de Villoison labored upon Greek fifteen hours a day. La Harpe having asked him what his relaxations were, he replied that when his brain was fatigued, he went to the window a short time. He resided in Rue de Saint Jean de Beauvois, one of the most remote and dirty streets of Paris, especially at that epoch.

Let us bear in mind constantly, that pure air is an indispensable to man as a bright sun is to vegetation.

PROLONGED AND REPEATED WATCHFULNESS.

Leibnitz sometimes passed three consecutive days and nights in the same chair, resolving a problem that interested him; an excellent custom, as Fontenelle observes, to accomplish a labor, but a very unhealthy one. The Abbe de La Caille, a famous astronomer, had a fork invented in which he adjusted his head, and in this position passed the night in astronomical observations, without knowing, as a man of wit observes, any other enemies than sleep and the clouds, without suspecting that there could be any more delightful way of employing these silent hours which revealed to him the harmony of the universe. Thus he contracted an inflammation of the lungs which carried him off in a short time. Girsdet did not like to labor during the day. Seized in the middle of the night by a fever of inspiration, he arose, lit the chandelier suspended in his studio, placed upon his head an enormous hat covered with candles, and, in this strange costume, painted for hours. No one ever had a feebler constitution, or a more disordered state of health than Girsdet.

Man, and especially enlightened man, is, of all animals, the one most subject to disease. What must this predisposition be in men who have in them the active and progressive principle of civilization? All that affects the social man re-acts upon his physical and moral constitution with an energy almost always prejudicial to his health and well-being.

A delicate organization, extreme sensibility, habitual excess of the same sensibility, a vivid imagination, the functions of the brain in continual action, negligence and forgetfulness of the proper means to preserve the health; what a number of means to weaken the springs of the economy, to undermine its strength, to render the body languishing, sickly, exposed to the attacks of morbific agents, and to make of life a fever, an agony of perpetual strife! All diseases, then, to which the human kind are subject may manifest themselves among men whose labors of the intellect are excessive.

We lay this down as an incontrovertible truth for this reason: that the elements which form their constitution, their being, their proclivities, are also the sources of a host of diseases; irritability being the primitive element of inflammation, as well as of the nervous affections. However, as every temperament has a special tendency to some particular class of diseases, it will be observed that among studious and meditative men, certain pathological affections are more frequent than others. Let us now consider the morbid effects of a prolonged application of the mind, without flattering ourselves in the meantime, that we can traverse the entire circle of so many miseries.

In following the order of the organs as closely as possible, we find in the first class,

AFFECTIONS OF THE BRAIN.

As I have already remarked, their shades of difference are infinite. Sometimes the disease is rapid in its course, as in inflammations and cerebral fevers; at times the stupifying influence of prolonged study produces diseases which are slow in their development. Apoplexy itself, which destroys so many thinkers, presents these various phases. Before the victim is stricken down, how many times has the brain been excited and overstrained? how many rushes of blood to the head, flushes of heat in the face, dull pains, sudden vertigo, accelerated arterial pulsation, uneasy slumber, have plainly indicated a sanguine repletion, a cerebral excitement above the normal degree! But these symptoms are dissipated and forgotten; again they return, and the delicate structure of the brain is irremediably injured, often in the very commencement of the career. "I will begin to die at the head," said Swift, and he was in fact attacked by a species of mental alienation. La Bonyere died of apoplexy at the age of fifty-two, on the 10th of May, 1696.

Habit, enthusiasm for a labor, the desire for celebrity, entices the thinker beyond the limits prescribed by reason. On the 18th of July, 1374, Petrarch was found in his library dead from apoplexy, with his head lying upon a book. Copernicus, Malpighi, La Clerc du Fremblay, known in history under the name of P. Joseph, Richardson, Linnæus, Marmontel, Rousseau, Daubenton, Spallanzani, Monge, Carbanis, Corvisart, Walter Scott, and many other celebrated men have been struck with apoplexy. Napoleon, who dreaded apoplexy, asked Corvisart, his first physician, one day, what positive ideas he had of this disease. "Sire," answered the physician, "apoplexy is always dangerous, but it has premonitory symptoms; nature very rarely strikes without giving warning. The first attack, nearly always light, is a summons without costs; the second much more severe, is a summons with costs; and a third, is a *death warrant*." Corvisart himself was a melancholy illustration of the truth of his theory. The gradual action of the causes of this disease, may be explained in the following manner: The permanent excitement of the brain augments its activity. This excessive activity often repeated, gives rise each time to an afflux of blood into this organ; the stimulation then becomes congestional.

The misanthropy of which I have just spoken leads insensibly

TO HYPOCHONDRIA.

It cannot be doubted that the seat of this affection is in the brain, or in the abdomen; hence, it is always characterized by a great activity of the nervous system—it is the distinctive trait of this disease. In the physical sense, a feeling of perfect health and comfort will be succeeded suddenly by some unaccountable distress, some imaginary pain. The same inconstancy and instability is observable in the moral sense also. A mind and a disposition always changing. The vigorous play of a strong intellect, and a puerile weakness; flashes of the brightest reason and inconceivable littleness; generous thoughts and traits of a strong egotism; a soul with heavenly aspirations or groveling in the commonest sphere; moments of wild enthusiasm, then of frightful depressions; strong attachment of the heart, then cruel doubts; a deep disgust of praise and of all that appeared sublime to them; a sad feeling destroying all bright illusions, all pleasures; such are the singular contradictions which characterize the hypochondriac; and this incredible change of the feelings often occurs suddenly, because the normal physiological state has ceased to exist. Joyous and confiding, sad and suspicious, a fool or a man of wit, a Socrates or a madman, the victim seems to be transformed every moment. This is not to be wondered at; all these variations of mind and character, proceed evidently from morbid nervous sensibility, of which I have so often spoken. The entire economy is disturbed by the slightest cause, by the most fleeting impression. It will be seen that sad affections predominate always in hypochondria. I have known a hypochondriac who lived in perpetual fear of a comet striking the earth. Men of genius are often victims of incurable hypochondria, which throws a lugubrious pall over their lives and their works. Lichtenberg, who was attacked by this pathological disease, makes this remark, "My hypochondria," said he, "is, properly speaking, the faculty of extracting, for my own use, the greatest possible quantity of poison from every event of life. I am often grievously tormented because I have not sneezed three times in succession for twenty years. Pusillanimity is the true name for my malady; but how can I cure it? Ah, if I could once pluck up the resolution to be well!" There is much sense in these light words. As it has been remarked, if one could see the puerilities which traverse the brain of the brightest genius at the time when it performs its greatest work, one would be seized with astonishment. The case is different when there is a morbific cause continually acting upon the brain.

Since I have already noticed the causes of this affection, it will be unnecessary to recur to them. I will merely repeat that it is almost always characterized by one fixed idea, which ordinarily takes absolute possession of the soul. The sentient principle, pursuing this ruling thought, to its farthest limits, leads inevitably to the marvelous, to the incomprehensible, to the *ægri somnia*, or to the pure truth, to the discovery of a fundamental law. In both cases two things happen, and these tend equally to melancholy. This strength and continuity of attention which belongs to superior talent, fatigues and destroys the springs of the economy; and the soul transported into the lofty regions of the intellect, separates itself as much as possible from the flesh and blood. To free the bonds of the probable, to enjoy all its spirituality, it quickly attains the limits of humanity, and descends afterwards unwillingly to material interests, often after having broken the fragile organ of good sense. Ah! rest assured that this intellectual superiority is inevitably accompanied by melancholy, and, as an almost immediate consequence, by several maladies more or less severe, and nearly always chronic. The age, the kind of work, the social position, or exterior influences, determines the kind and the form of these maladies. Melancholy never loses sight of its favorite idea, misfortune. It places itself face to face with its trouble; it irritates the wound, increases it, exhausts all the cutting pleasures of grief; it takes delight in the langour into which they plunge it.

SOME DEGREES FURTHER,

and we reach the point when the personal identity is

lost,—where there is a discord between internal perceptions and exterior impression. The despotism of one idea, deeply rooted in the imagination, absorbs all other thoughts, or at least destroys their harmony. The perpetual irritation of the brain unhinges the intellect while it stimulates it.

Hence, arise illusions, hallucinations, phantoms, deceptive images, which delude the minds of these unfortunate beings. When the empire of the faculties is overthrown, they create a realm in which they reign supreme, and are sometimes happy in this imaginary world. But this cruel happiness is denied intelligent and reflective men who are attacked by this malady. Notwithstanding this indefinite prolonging of one idea which happens in monomania, there is nearly always a depth of reason, accompanied by memories and regrets, which unite in forming their torment. Delirium exists, but it is generally incomplete; the victim has a consciousness of the disorder of his mind, and at the same time feels his powerlessness to restore its harmony. Is not this the acme of human misery? It was thus that Pascal saw an abyss ever yawning beside him, and that Tasso heard voices whispering his own thoughts.

This is what the great man wrote to his friend Cataneo, in regard to his malady: "When I am awake, I see fires burning in the air and sparks issuing from my eyes, which become so inflamed that at times I have fears of losing my sight. At other times I hear terrible noises, whistling, the tinkling of bells, a sound like a clock ticking or striking the hour. While sleeping, I imagine that a horse is about to trample me under foot, or that I am covered with unclean and repulsive vermin. All my joints are full of pain, and my head is heavy. In the midst of so many pains and fears, sometimes the image of the Virgin, beautiful and young, appears to me with her son, surrounded by a halo of colored vapors; sometimes it is a foolish sprite, which torments me and pursues me in a thousand ways." Unhappy poet! how wearisome! what miseries! Oh! who would desire glory at such a price? Who would covet this crown of thorns which encircles the heads of those who are called the kings of thought? We will extend no further this rapid survey of the diseases peculiar, so to speak, to the temperament and habits of thinkers. Our intention has been to notice only the principal ones, for there are a great many affections classed among the indispositions which daily attack those whose intellects are ever active; such as megrims, pain and heaviness in the head, hemorrhoids, partial paralysis, spasms, trembling, and a host of nervous affections, which make of the entire existence a sort of perpetual disease. It must also be remarked that, without being sick, it is felt that certain parts are habitually sensitive and painful —the chest, in some, the kidneys in another, etc. The Emperor Napoleon, having a very sensitive head, disliked new hats, and wore the same ones a long time, and he was accustomed to have them wadded. This is the origin of the little hat so famous in the history of this great man. Independently of these morbid affections, there are many more, peculiar to certain classes of savans or artists.

OF ORGANS ESPECIALLY AFFECTED BY EXCESSIVE LABOR.

If there is a positive fact in pathology, it is that all causes capable of producing irritation and inflammation commence by exciting and augmenting the sensibility. The synergic propagation of nervous irritation is therefore particularly observable in the constitution now under consideration.

It is then upon the general and primitive nervous system, that all causes of disease act. Now, when this system has acquired an exclusive and unnatural predominance; when the economy is saturated with sensibility, so to speak, it is evident that all the organs over which it distributes itself, must be in a state of morbid imminence, and much predisposed to all pathological affections. This is precisely the case with many artists, men of letters, statesmen, etc., who deliver themselves to the tyrannical infatuation of intellectual pursuits. However, there are certain organs which seem more exposed to the action of these causes. It is to these the attention should be directed.

We will place the brain and its accessories in the first rank. The incontestible supremacy of this apparatus is the same in all the different modifications which the economy undergoes: it is always the primitive power of organic association. But here this superiority, and the dangers which accompany it, are augmented by the excessive activity to which the encephalus is subjected. It is undoubtedly in the brain and its functions that the source of happiness is to be found. It is the creator of the ineffable pleasures,—the inconceivable delight of these men who dwell only in the realm of thought. Unhappily here, too, is found the veritable *atmion mortis*, the origin of the evils to which they are exposed. Certainly if one considers the high importance of the functions of the brain, the extent of its relations, the energy and diversity of its sympathetic connections, one is no longer astonished at the number, variety, and gravity of the maladies produced by its extreme and prolonged excitement. The integrity of its actions forms the basis of health; if this is disturbed, all is thrown into disorder. It should be observed that there is much diversity in the diseases of the brain. The shades of difference are often imperceptible, for we recognize only those which are extreme. It can be readily conceived that this prolonged reflection, this earnest application of the mind which strains the springs of thought, absorbs the life, devours it by fractions, keeps the cerebral forces in a continual state of excitement, must end in producing a general weakness, which is the source of serious diseases. But it must be remembered that these affections are sometimes slow, sometimes rapid in their course. Latent irritations, dull inflammations, partial congestions, the softening of many points of the cerebral substance, often manifest themselves only by the doubtful and equivocal symptoms of a morbid excitement. When the evil has made some progress, serious disorders indicate the cause more plainly; but it is then too late to remedy it. This is one of the fatalities of the medical science. The peculiarities of temperament, age, etc., have an evident influence in cerebral affections. The young are more liable to inflammation of the meninges. Old persons who have a tendency to venous plethora, often experience organic disorders, congestions, ruptures of blood-vessels, softening of the brain, etc. I repeat, that at all times, pathological affections of the brain are particularly dangerous by reason of the active, and continued excitement of this viscera. Let us add that the moral, as well as the physical sensibility, acquires in this instance, an increase of activity. If it is true that among civilized men the imagination increases the causes and results of disease a hundredfold, what effect must this imagination produce in men who concentrate their existence upon the exercise of the intellectual faculties? Then one may expect to see the most serious disorders produced by very slight causes. The poet Santenil almost lost his reason at finding an epithet that he had sought for a long time. A picture by Raphael produced such a paroxysm of admiration in the painter Francia, that he fainted and died. One of the principal effects of the continued tension of the brain, is to weaken all the organs more or less immediately depending upon it, in depriving them of a part of the nervous influx necessary for their exercise; hence, a number of maladies more or less serious,—more or less varied.

The stomach is, perhaps, the organ most exposed to this deprivation. The weakening of the digestive apparatus seems peculiar to illustrious men. The opinion of Zacutus Lusitanus upon this subject is well known. In our days, some have pretended to value the genius according to the state of the stomach. While acknowledging the exaggeration of this assertion, we must agree with Fissot, " that the man who thinks the most, is he who digests the worst, all other things being equal; and he who thinks the least, is the one who digests the best." Take blockheads, and ignoramuses, and compare them with thinkers. The daily practice of medicine, and the history of celebrated men, furnish superabundant proofs of our theory. But why is the stomach generally so delicate in deep thinkers? It has been attributed to a sedentary life; this may have some influence, but only to a certain point; for do we not observe some women and artisans who lead a very sedentary life, and yet who digest admirably? Napoleon, whose remarkable activity astonished his cotemporaries, had, on the contrary, a very susceptible and irresistible stomach.

Orators, musicians, actors, anatomists, chemists, physicians, etc., are exposed to maladies relative to their occupation, and to the organs most fatigued in the exercise of their profession. The greater number of these affections can be referred to the general principles I have already laid down. As for the rest, I am able to say, notwithstanding this lugubrious picture I have just presented, that many illustrious men would avoid these evils by habitual sobriety, and even regain their constitution if they knew how to stop in time to preserve their strength; if they were all convinced that the muses are not always homicidal sirens, according their favors only to those who sacrifice their health and life to them. But far from this, there are but few among them who know how to put bounds to their labors, their enterprises, and their ambition. Exhausted and breathless as they are in their career, they continue their efforts and toils.

Weakness, uneasiness, sufferings are nothing, provided one can say *eureka*. Juste Lisper, like many others, labored until his strength was entirely exhausted. Canabis tells us of the contempt this celebrated man had for physical pain, pretending to shake it off as he did moral pain. At the opening of the states-general he had the jaundice. He did nothing to cure it. He even settled several important questions while the fever was upon him. In fine, he neglected himself completely; for, as his physician remarks, "this impetuous man felt himself to be immortal at too many points, to believe himself subject to the common laws of infirmity and death." It is known that he died young, and that excess of all kinds was the true poison that killed him. It must be observed that the more frequent maladies are in the nervous constitution, the more this constitution augments in intensity. That is to say, the sensitive strength increases in activity, while motive forces decrease. It is certain that when one is no longer young and full of vigor, after a long and serious illness, sensibility becomes more active, the body more impressible, the strength of vital resistance lessened. This even happens to individuals the most strongly constituted. It is generally known that maladies nearly always leave behind them a remarkable predominance of the sensitive system over the motive forces, and that it increases more when it has existed previously. No one assuredly ever received from nature a more vigorous body than this same Mirabeau, of whom we have just spoken. By the effect of diseases, his muscular strength was reduced to nothing, as it were. The most robust man became susceptible of being moved by the weakest impressions. His muscles remained always like those of Hercules in volume: his nerves were almost as weak as those of a delicate and sensitive woman. Having reached this point of weakness and irritability at the same time, it is easy to presume what would become of his health and happiness. A nervous irritation and a prostration of health alternately succeeded each other. No function acted regularly, although without any notable pain. Often there was even a species of interior ardor, of incipient fever, which, excited, undermines and destroys the economy.

Efforts may be made to re-animate the vital powers; but the progress of exhaustion is such, the organs are so fatigued, the thread of life so worn, that existence becomes a labor of each day, of each moment.

Yet one should watch, armed with redoubled precaution, lest a premature old age, or frightful diseases, soon cover the altar of glory, that faithless shelter against attacks of physical pain, with the funereal cypress.

In addition to what has been said on this subject, we deem it quite proper to extend our remark to the study of

PHYSIOLOGY OF MAN.

In a general and comprehensive sense, physiology is the science of the elements, properties, and phenomena of organic bodies and of the laws which control their condition and action. Human physiology is that branch of medicine which has for its special object the investigation of the nature and life-phenomena of the various functions and operations of the body while in a state of health. Man, like other bodies in nature, is a collection of matter existing in a separate form.

Though such an infinite variety and number of forms are presented to the senses in the world of matter, it is a singular fact that matter exists only in two forms, (generally classified as organic and inorganic,) based simply on two distinct constitutional differences. An inorganic body is composed of a mass of matter destitute of distinction of parts, or one in which every fragment retains all the characteristics of the original body. A drop of water is as completely water as a lake or an ocean. A particle of air in a drop of water possesses all the characteristics of the atmosphere. A fragment of granite differs not from the grand mass that underlies the Rocky Mountains. The same is true of every fragment of all mineral forms. Hence the whole mineral world is enclosed in inorganic bodies. An organic body, on the contrary, is made up of distinctive parts, each one of which is essential to the completeness of its existence. A root, a bud, a leaf, or a flower is not a plant or a tree. All, however, are essential to the existence of the plant or tree. Wool is not a sheep; yet a sheep is not complete without wool, or a bird without feathers. The foot is not like the head; the eye like the ear; the brain like bones; yet all are absolutely necessary to complete a man. Any one part marred, mars the whole. The completeness of the whole is found only in the completeness of each individual part. Such is an organic body. Chemical laws govern inorganic bodies in all their changes and phenomena, generally denominated physical force. But organic bodies, though molded by the same law of combination, are also controlled by an unseen power which we call vital force. Chemical force takes hold of the crude, inorganic material, reduces it into infinite minute particles or atoms, whence the vital force collects it, digests it, and appropriates it to the building of an organic body. The chemical constituents of the human body embrace all of the ultimate elements of the outer world, such as Calcium, Magnesium, Potassium, Sodium, Iron, etc., all exist in the body in a combination of one form or another, generally denominated proximate principles. They are introduced into the system by the food we eat, the water we drink, and the air we breathe. A proximate principle is a distinct compound, ready formed in animals and vegetables, such as albumen, fat, sugar, etc. They are of inorganic and organic origin.

The proximate principles of inorganic origin, are the first to present themselves for investigation; they are derived from the exterior, are found everywhere, in unorganized bodies, always found under the same form, and with the same properties in the interior of the animal frame as elsewhere.

They are crystalizable; they comprise such substances as water, chloride of sodium, carbonate and phosphate of lime, etc.

The second class are of organic origin, crystallizable, and comprise such as the different kinds of sugar, oil and starch.

The third class includes such substances as albumen, fibrin, casein, etc., and comprise a very extensive and important order of proximate principles, strictly of organic origin, are not crystallizable and of a definite chemical composition. Water, of the first class of proximate principles, is universally present in all the tissues and fluids of the body, comprising about two-thirds of the entire bulk, which must be regularly supplied, as the solid materials are held by it in solution, assisting them to pass and repass in the animal frame. The system suffers more rapidly when deprived of water, than when solids only are withheld; hence it is an important ingredient of the food, and should be supplied with constancy and regularity. Water is the only natural drink for man; all other beverages may be considered medicated, such as coffee, tea, spirituous and malt liquors, which should only be imbibed as a medicine prescribed by a properly qualified physician.

Milk contains nearly all of the principles of the body, and is the next most natural drink, holding many of the solid materials of food in solution, and yet not enough of solid matter to supply an adult, or sufficient water to supply the system with enough fluid to perform the functions of its office, hence while milk is sufficient food and drink for the babe and young animals, it would not answer the purpose in the adult. Water, pure water, may be drank freely, and he who is the most prompt and regular in supplying nature with such an indispensable agent to the well being of the animal economy, certainly enjoys physical life in the most perfect sense. All other inorganic material, such as calcareous salts, alkaline, phosphates, etc., occur naturally in sufficient quantity in most of the articles of food, except chloride of sodium, (common salt,) which is usually added to food and requires to be supplied with tolerable regularity. The proximate principles of the second class are sugar and oily matters, and are derived from both the animal and vegetable kingdoms.

Starch is converted in the system into sugar, and to a great extent sugar is converted into fat, hence the articles of food that contain the greatest amount of starch are the best to nourish the body. Sugar may be taken in its purity, as certain vegetables will yield it, also fat and starch, for the system craves and must have them in some form; yet there is not a single article of food yet known that would supply us with all the system requires; hence a mixed diet is necessary if we would be healthy. Wheat, rye-meal, oatmeal, corn, rice, barley, potatoes, and all kinds of fruit, will supply the system with the greatest amount of this class of proximate principles.

The articles of food that contain the greatest quantity of proximate principles of the third class, are all those mentioned under the head of the second class, but in addition to them, meat contains the greatest quantity of fibrin; eggs, albumen, and milk, casein. No article of food void of these principles will nourish the body any length of time; neither does the nutritious character of any substance, as an article of food, depend simply upon its containing either one of the alimentary principles in large quantities, but its containing them mingled together in such proportions as are requisite for the healthy nutrition of the body. These proportions are determined by observation and experience, and up to this time but little is known on the subject. The total quantity of food required by man has been variously estimated. But the habits and constitution of the individual must be taken into consideration, and the kind of articles employed; as corn, wheat, rye and meat contain more alimentary material, in the same bulk, than fresh fruits or vegetables, and hence the quantity must necessarily vary. It has been ascertained, however, that an extensive diet of bread, fresh meat and butter, with water for drink, the quantity of food required during twenty-four hours by a man in full health, and taking free exercise in the open air, is: meat 16 oz.; bread 19 oz.; butter or fat $3\frac{1}{2}$ oz.; water 52 oz. This is about $2\frac{1}{2}$ lbs. of solid food, and rather over three pints of liquid food. In selecting the required quantity of food, we must take into consideration the digestibility of the articles chosen; also the proper time and regularity of introducing them into the system. This, however, is generally best regulated by the demand of the system, and if the natural promptings are obeyed, generally no violence can be done, for nature does her work well. She will not let the system starve nor be overcharged with food, or allow even any thing to enter that may cause a disturbance of the harmonious operation of the bodily organs within.

The body is endowed with five senses, for a twofold purpose; first, for the protection and preservation of the integrity, and secondly, that through these channels the true man that dwells within may gain an earthly or material experience. By the eye we behold God's great and glorious universe, enjoy the beauties of nature's garden, and also behold the approaching danger. Through the ear, we enjoy harmonious sounds, and sweet music; also the approach of danger; this assists the eye, and in case the eye fails, will preserve and protect the body, though not so perfectly.

The sense of touch, taste and smell, are important guardian angels and messengers of delight, which, if not prostituted by violence and disobedience, are a correct guide to health and happiness.

NUTRITION

consists in the introduction into the stomach and intestinal canal of proper nutriment; its formation into blood; its changes in the lungs; the transformation into tissues; their re-absorption into blood; and the excretion of effete matters from the system. In reference to the first stage, we must select such articles of food as contain albuminoid, fatty, and mineral principles, as no one alone is sufficient to nourish the body; then combine them so as to form tissues and organs. Regulate the amount according to the state of the atmosphere; if cold, more oxygen is consumed; there is greater waste, consequently the system demands more food than if the air be warm; also in proportion to the amount of physical or mental exertion, those laboring requiring a greater supply than those of sedentary habits.

Food, when taken into the system, undergoes various changes before it nourishes the body. The changes are brought about by a set of organs commonly denominated the digestive apparatus, and before speaking of the digestive process proper, it would be well to give a brief description of the organs immediately concerned in the work. The first in order is the mouth, which is endowed with three salivary glands on each side, a set of grinders or teeth, a tongue and palate. The throat or gullet connects the mouth with the stomach; the second department, situated immediately below the lungs, separated from them by a partition called diaphragm. The stomach is flask-shaped, guarded by valves or circular muscular bands at the entrance and outlet, which open and contract as the food enters or passes out of the stomach. Then comes the small intestine, different parts of which, owing to the varying structure of their mucous membranes, have received the different names of duodenum, jejunum and ileum.

In the duodenum—the department of the small intestines next to the stomach—we have the opening of the bile duct which conducts the bile from the liver, also, the opening of the duct which conveys the juice from the pancreas, a small gland situated back of the stomach. Finally, we have the large intestines

THE LAWS OF PHYSIOLOGY. 337

separated from the smaller by a valve called ileocæcal, constituting a canal about twenty-eight feet in length, commonly called alimentary canal, composed of a mucous membrane and a muscular coat, with a layer of fine skinny-like tissue between the two. The muscular coat is every where composed of a double layer of longitudinal and transverse fibers, by the alternate contraction and relaxation of which the food is carried through the canal from above downward. The mucous membrane differ in kind in the different departments of this canal; in the mouth it is hard and smooth, in the stomach it is soft and thrown into minute folds, in the small intestines it assumes the form of small sparigoles like the small absorbent vessels situated at the ends of the rootlets of plants, in the large intestines it is smooth and shining. Again, the juices secreted also vary in these different regions. In its passage downward the food meets with no less than five different digestive fluids. First it meets with the saliva in the mouth; second, with the gastric juice in the stomach; third, with the bile; fourth, with the pancreatic fluid; and fifth, with the intestinal juice. It is the most important characteristic of the process of digestion, as established by modern researches, that different elements of the food are digested in different parts of the alimentary canal by the different digestive fluids. By their action, the various ingredients of the alimentary mass are successively reduced to a fluid condition, and are taken up by the vessel of the intestinal mucous membrane.

CHYLIFICATION.

Formation of the Alimentary Matters into Blood.—The nutritious portion of the ingesta passes through the cell-walls of the epithelial covering of the intestinal villi into the lacteals. This milky fluid, or chyle, flows continuously through the lymphatic glands towards the thoracic duct. The chyle, examined microscopically, consists of a multitude of small molecules. After passing the mesenteric lymphatic glands, it mingles with the lymph and chyle corpuscles, and subsequently is converted into blood corpuscles by the action of the blood-glands.

The blood-glands, widely distributed through the body, are very vascular, in which are found vast numbers of colorless nuclei and cells, richly supplied with lymphatics. The lymphatics exercise a great influence over the fluid which passes through them, and serve to perfect it for the changes it is to undergo. The fluid passing through the mesenteric lymphatic glands, being milky is denominated chyle, that found in the other lymphatics is limpid, constituting lymph. These lymph corpuscles also enter the thoracic duct, and each contributes to the formation of the blood.

The chyle supplies the fatty, albuminoid, and mineral principles, reduced to a soft mass; while in the blood-glands are formed the corpuscles, which become gradually developed as they flow along the lacteals, and through the lymphatic glands are sent through the right side of the heart into the lungs, as soon as they reach the blood, and are converted into blood corpuscles.

CIRCULATION OF THE BLOOD.

The blood passes from the left ventricle of the heart by the aorta, through the systemic arteries into the capillaries, and is distributed throughout the body. It is then carried back by the veins to the right auricle of the heart passing into the right ventricle, which sends it to the pulmonary artery, then to the capillaries of the lungs, and then back through the pulmonary veins to the right auricle and ventricle.

The blood is propelled by contraction of the muscular walls of the heart, and by the changes which it undergoes during its circulation through the body. The heart is so formed that by the union of contractile cavities and valves, the blood is constantly distributed through it only in certain directions.

SOUNDS OF THE HEART

The first sound of the heart is long, deep, and dull; and the second, short, sharp, and more superficial; the impulse or striking of the apex against the thorax, rushing of the fluid through the aortic orifices, flapping together of the auriculo-ventricular valves coinciding with the former; and the rushing of blood through the auriculo-ventricular valves, flapping together of the aortic valves, and contraction of the ventricles produce them. The action of the heart is readily excited by exercise, increased respiration, and mental emotions. The left ventricle contracts much more forcibly than the right, owing to the greater thickness of its walls, and the greater resistance to overcome.

The arteries are tubes composed of elastic and fibrous tissues, which convey and distribute the blood through the body, and change its wave-like movements into a continous flow. It flows the most rapidly when forced into the left ventricle, owing to the great resistance of all the tubes. The length and thickness of the artery is consequently increased, but soon recovers its usual size. These actions constitute the pulse, whose vibrations number sixty to seventy in the adult.

The capillaries, consisting of fine membranous contractile tubes, sub-divide the blood so that it may be influenced by the constant attraction exerted by the tissues. The veins arising from the capillaries, are similarly constructed as the arteries, excepting the elastic tissue is not so thick. The passage of the blood through them is assisted by internal valves and respiration; the former being so arranged as to prevent the fluid returning through the capillaries.

RESPIRATION

is carried on by the lungs, whose structure is so arranged as to expose a large number of the capillaries to the action of the atmosphere, in inspiration owing to the contraction and descent of the diaphragm, while ordinary expiration is owing to the elasticity of the lungs and walls of the chest, aided by abdominal muscular contractions.

During health, the number of respirations vary from fourteen to sixteen per minute; in disease they may range from seven to one hundred. The inspired air is constantly absorbing a portion of the oxygen, and giving off carbonic acid gas to the expired air; and as the absorption of the former is far greater than the production of the latter, it follows that the oxygen serves not only for the oxidation of carbon, but also of hydrogen, in the organism; and if the air be already charged with carbonic acid, the quantity of oxygen is much decreased, the air becomes very impure, and if proper ventilation be not made, dyspnœa, and even asphyxia may result from exclusion of atmospheric air.

TRANSFORMATION OF BLOOD INTO THE TISSUES.

The blood must be of a healthy quality, which implies that digestion, assimilation, respiration, secretion, excretion, etc., must be performed properly; a proper quantity in a part is also necessary; the mind must be free from fear or anxiety; and the part to be nourished must be in a healthy state. If the growth be too great, hypertrophy results; if too diminished, atrophy exists.

RE-ABSORPTION OF THE TISSUES INTO BLOOD.

At the same time that particles of matter are assimilating from the blood, others are constantly entering it from those textures which have completed their work; the new substituting the place and form of the old. The blood, therefore, is composed of organic matter formed by the alimentary canal and blood-glands, (primary digestion) and those obtained from the tissues and gaseous fluids through the lungs from the atmosphere, (secondary digestion). The constituents thus derived are changed and transformed during the circulation, and are carried to the various excretories, where they separate and are removed from the body.

ANIMAL HEAT.

Animal heat is produced by the combination of the oxygen and blood in the lungs, and the formation of carbonic acid gas in the capillaries. The quantity generated corresponds with the activity of the respiration and the supply of food. If respiration be rapid, the heat evolved is greater than if slow. In northern climes where the oxygen is more abundant, more food is required than in the tropical regions. In order to maintain a constant temperature, the amount of fuel consumed must vary according to the supply of oxygen. The natural temperature of the body estimated at 98 to 100 deg. Fahr., seldom varies, owing to the evaporation through the skin. In fevers, it may rise to 107 deg., and in Asiatic cholera, may sink to 77 deg.

EXCRETION OF EFFETE MATTERS FROM THE BODY.

These matters are removed by means of the lungs, liver, kidneys, skin, and intestines. The amount of water daily exhaled from the lungs varies from six to twenty-seven ounces, that of carbonic acid, six ounces.

The venous blood supplying the liver by means of the portal vein, mostly originating from the intestines, differs from other blood in containing fat, dextrine, and sugar, (principles obtained from primary digestion) and fibrin, (the result of secondary digestion.) When the blood reaches the liver, it breaks up into a number of minute capillaries, and the secreting cells which fill up the spaces between them, attract and select from it matters which form bile, viscid, greenish, or yellow fluid, having a strong, bitter taste which is discharged through ducts to the gall-bladder. The daily quantity formed varies from seventeen to twenty-four ounces, part of which is excreted through the alimentary canal, although a greater quantity is absorbed into the blood, and removed from the lungs in the form of carbonic acid; thus proving that although useful as a secretion in operation upon the chyme, yet its main function consists in purifying the blood of hydrogen and carbon.

The liver also secretes a large quantity of free fat and glycogen, (a substance containing all the properties of hydrated starch,) which decomposes and disappears upon coming in contact with the oxygen of the air in the lungs. If the action of the lungs be imperfect, that of the liver is prone to be especially disturbed. Thus, if more non-nitrogenized aliment be consumed than can be exhaled in the form of carbonic acid, the liver secretes more bile into the duodenum, which gives rise to bilious symptoms.

The kidneys separate from the blood a large quantity of the water taken into the body, as drink, certain matters resulting from a primary and secondary digestion, particularly urea and uric acid in the latter, and a large amount of earthy salts. These, together with the excrementitious fluid secreted by the cortical substance of the kidneys accumulate in the urinary bladder, and are expelled from time to time from the urethra; the daily amount discharged being thirty-five fluid ounces in a healthy individual.

The skin is continually excreting watery and fatty matters; the former being removed in the form of vapor by the sudoriparous, or sweat glands, and the latter by the follicular, or sebaceous glands, in the form of an oily fluid. The quantity daily excreted varies from one to five pounds. That removed daily from the intestines amounts to five ounces, which consists of undigested food, and of various secretions poured into the alimentary canal.

I have now briefly stated a few facts, giving the outlines of the laws of physiology, which the reader is advised to embrace, as part of his daily study, and pursue the subject in perusing the writings of other authors. No person is qualified to assume any responsible position who is ignorant of the laws that govern physical life. Those who enter the holy bonds of matrimony, who are parents, teachers, preachers, savans, laborers, business men, and especially those who make our laws, are benefited in their undertakings by consulting the science of physiology. " True knowledge," said a celebrated philosopher, "is better than riches." "First seek ye the kingdom of God and his righteousness, and all things else shall be added unto you." I believe this to be a physiological truth, as well as religious or moral, for it is demonstrated almost every day that those who seek first after a proper knowledge of the laws of nature, and who obey them in their daily practice, are the most happy, the most successful in business. If you have a knowledge of the truth, "all things else will be added unto you," demonstrating the truth of the saying, "for unto every one that hath shall be given." Those who seek not after a knowledge of the laws governing life, have a hard road to travel in their search after those things which contribute to man's happiness; therefore, "from him that hath not shall be taken away even that which he hath." It is evident that when we live in obedience to natural laws, we are blessed; and when we disobey them, we are cursed. If this is true in regard to the individual, it is true in regard to the nation. Governmental law, to be right, must agree with the laws of physiology, or the natural laws, which govern the life of the individual. The starting-point is with the individual rights, and the natural relation one human being sustains to another. I attach so much importance to the study of physiology that I would have it required, by

A LAW OF THE LAND,

that every person who has arrived at the age of maturity, and especially those who vote on governmental affairs, should be possessed of an average amount of physiological education. The immortal Dr. Mott said: "I have no confidence in man's efforts to reform the world so long as the governmental laws disagree with the principles of physiology." The great Ex-Governor Talmadge, of Michigan, said, in a speech, " To purify the nation, and to enact laws which will render the greatest amount of happiness to the greatest number, we must require certain qualifications in property and education of every voter of the country." I have long been in favor of a law requiring at least a certain degree of educational qualification in our voters, withholding the right of elective franchise from all persons of a doubtful moral character, those engaged in an unlawful business, and those of no business, trade, or visible means of support. It is certainly in keeping with common sense to prohibit those from voting who take no interest in their own welfare, or those who are too ignorant to know their own good, for such persons can never contribute to the happiness of the people. Our laws to become harmoniously adjusted with the laws of nature, must be philosophically considered, in order to incorporate true principles, by which to govern human actions, in all forms of civil and political rights, laws, remedies, and governments; and not until then may we expect the glory of Heaven to come on earth,—when human laws and institutions harmonize with the just and immutable principles of cause and effect.

CHAPTER XXI.

MENTAL CULTURE, OR THE LAWS WHICH GOVERN MENTAL TRAINING.

I do not propose in this chapter to enter into a full discussion of the subject, so far as quoting authority is concerned, but simply to state a few facts as they have appeared to merit attention, and as I have observed them during a number of years of my professional labors.

No one disputes the impressible character of a child's mind, and that it is just as easy to make a bad impression upon it as a good one. In the first part of this volume, we showed how persons are by nature inclined to evil, and require only conditions favorable to such inclination to show its development. The fact that such a tendency exists must be the basis of our remarks.

The pliancy of the mind is readily observed in the young child, as well as the avidity with which it receives impressions. It is suggestive that there is a store-house within the soul to be filled, and at a very early period the mind begins to collect its treasures for futurity. It is well to consider the character of the receptacle, its comparative fragileness, and its susceptibility to fatigue.

Any material of nature possessed of the philosophical principle, pliancy, we are well aware, has a tendency, from its elastic quality, to yield under the pressure of a constant strain. This effect is sure to follow in the case of the overtaxed mind. A board constantly bent, not only assumes the bent position, but does not return to its wonted state. The bent twig, when forced into an unnatural position, if the strain is continued for a sufficiently long time, never returns to its previous erect posture. This principle applies just as forcibly to the mind; and the training, during its commencing period, should be just as carefully conducted as that of the young tree; yea, far more so. If the mind is to live forever, it is of much more consequence than a tree; yet how many will spend unwearied care over a little bush, which will seem to bear upon their minds as of far more consequence than the intellects of their children.

They are left to themselves, as if of a spontaneous character, and all that is necessary for their proper development is to leave all the cultivation to natural circumstances.

This should not be, nor is it so with those who have a true conception of the work to be done, and the great end to be accomplished. The endless questions of the child, as before stated, show that the mental storehouse is waiting to be filled, and the constancy with which they apply themselves shows that the work is all sufficient for them. The two-year old prattler does not need the constraint of a school-room in order to avoid being a blockhead; but learning the names of different objects, the process of associating and comparing them with each other, is sufficient to keep so young a mind busy.

They must learn the idea as well as the *fact* of

obedience, and though they may not take to it instinctively, yet its importance requires that it be established. Compulsion in this matter is hardly out of the question; but to learn what the sounds, home, tree, man, dog, etc., mean, seems almost a part of their nature. What good can it do a child to be constrained to look upon the letters m-a-n, when it has but just learned the import of the sounds they convey, and when its powers of association have been so feebly called into action? It has all it can possibly learn to become familiar with the names of the myriad of objects in the world around, and this is just the foundation for future development.

The tree requires the rain to give it moisture; the sunshine to give it health and vigor; alternate day and night to perform its respiration—absorb oxygen and give off carbonic acid gas, etc.; the wind to give firmness and strength to its body and roots; all of these are necessary to accomplish what is requisite for a perfect tree. Yet it is not best that the storm should continue to beat upon the tender sprout just spreading above the ground; rather should it be sheltered down in the deep wood, where the mighty parent trees cast their shadows over it until it lifts its head far up among those parent trees, when it has secured a sufficient strength to resist in its own behalf.

So the young mind needs to send out the roots of advancing strength in obtaining the fundamental principles of its nature. There are some bright geniuses, which, like glowing meteors, dazzle the eye with their brilliant corruscations; but such geniuses are often, like the meteor, soon gone. Those children who in early youth receive all the prizes and medals for brilliant scholarship, are not generally the ones who make a mark in the world. Such children possess temperaments of an extreme nervous character, and are like transparent boilers of glass, though by-standers may hurrah and spur them on, their minds can stand only a certain tension—they burst and are gone.

One of the most inconsiderate acts of fond parents, possessed of one of these fragile characters, is to press it on. "Crowd it on" is only a faint expression for the course pursued by some of them. If a prize is offered, they wish them to get it, no matter what the sacrifice may be. It would not be such a pleasant scene to parents and friends, if, upon examination and exhibition days, they could see how nearly the fuel in their darling's brain has been consumed in trying to obtain that phantom of mental worth, and what a wreck of mentality is just behind a thin curtain of the future, which they, in their present blindness, can not see through. Frequently the truth bursts upon them when too late. It is strange that parents and teachers do not more readily understand what forms the true

BASIS OF A STRONG

mind. Often the apathy caused by nature refusing to shower a brilliant exotic intelligence upon the child, is taken to be laziness. But when, in after years, the child comes forth a man, with a fully developed brain and a sound, rugged body, possessing an energy of character sufficient to control an army of those early lights, the fact appears that nature knew her own business best, when, instead of lavishing the vital principle, or nerve stimulus, in producing a premature growth, she built the mind a house not founded upon the sand, but upon a rock—a sound body.*

Some parents lament exceedingly that their boy or girl is not as bright as their neighbor's. The minister, perhaps, wishes his son to be a minister also; but the son cares as little for Greek, Latin, or Hebrew, as an elephant would to try to imitate the antics of a monkey, and, perhaps, if forced to them, would succeed just about as well. But the boy loves to ride a horse, or crack a whip as he drives in his neighbor's carriage, and his mind can not be taken from it. That boy may or may not, in after years, when the body has become matured and the brain enthroned over an established kingdom, become one of the mighty men of our land. Thousands of just such men are to-day wielding a wondrous power over the destinies of mankind, who, under other developments, might have been but striplings when compared with their present giant intellects. But if the boy chooses to continue his career in the way he has started, it would only be lost labor to try to fashion his character otherwise.

At what age the child should go to school has been extensively discussed, and perhaps with as indefinite results as would naturally be expected. Laws have

---

* Watts on the Mind.

been passed in some states restricting to certain ages, though these high authorities are disposed to differ. Parents are often actuated by different motives in regard to the matter. Some are so extremely anxious to see their children making advances in the road to learning that they urge them away to school at a very early date—to private schools if forbidden in the public. Others are desirous that their children should get all the knowledge they can before they are old enough to work, thinking their services will be of advantage after they have passed their infancy. Another class, possessed of only an unhappy, fretful spirit, wish to get the noisy little ones out of the way. This is acting from a most contemptible, mean spirit. They can not govern their children at home; therefore they wish to throw the responsibility upon some one else. Generally they care but little for the impressions made upon their minds and characters, nor do many of them care even whether they go to school as ordered, if they only keep their noisy selves away from the house.

With such a spirit acted out by the parents, what shall we expect from their children?—only an augmented looseness of character, a far more debased, brutish mind, and a general sinking to a selfish, sensual kind of life?

But in all this there is no mental training; it is only the spontaneous growth of the wheat choked by the weeds of an uncultivated soil. But little good comes from it, yet evil reaps a rich harvest.

From six to eight is quite early enough to commence the stern realities of cultivating the mental powers. But how often we see those parents who have some of those sparkling little gems entrusted to their care,—"those brilliant little spirits," said Dr. Burrows, in a lecture on mental training, "who are living in advance of their years, and who are the products of parents of over-heated imaginations, urging them into the arena of science, while scarcely able to speak without the lisping voice. It seems hard for them to deprive these tender plants of the noonday sun, since it is so delightful to themselves; yet they do not think of the fragile character of the just expanding bud, and how easily it may wither when exposed in the spring of infancy, to the fierce rays of a midsummer's sun."

"The teacher catches the spirit of the parent," says Professor Venton, "and the desire is to please the parents, and therefore they urge them on."

The great Dr. Thomas remarks, "there is something endearing in those sparkling eyes, those tender and sympathetic affections, that ready wit and quick apprehension, which causes the tenderest feelings of the teacher to twine around such rare spirits." No, there is nothing unnatural in this. Yet for a reflective mind—a mind that perceives causes and effects—there is something sad in the picture. Not that the less favored ones are neglected, but that the "exalted ones are setting fire to their own funeral pile."

"It is easier to write upon the sand," said a distinguished teacher and author, "than upon the flinty rock," and so the teacher's work is more delightful while laboring with those whose minds are, like tinder, to be kindled with the merest spark." Such a work may be delightful, but it is more like taking the water from the shallow mud-puddle, than boring into the depths of the earth for the clear living spring. Those who thus labor, however, finally have the pleasure of drinking the pure waters from a never-failing well, and have a greater satisfaction than he who takes the surface drainage. Happy the teacher, who has with much labor turned up a precious gem, and, after great efforts to polish, sees the shining surface beginning to appear. The stone which was rejected for many years by the builders, at last became the "key-stone" in that grand arch of King Solomon's Temple. The priceless stone is kicked and trodden down by the multitude for many years perhaps, but, by and by, through persevering efforts, the sparkling surface begins to dazzle all around, and people wonder that some one had not discovered it before. Such experience is a pleasure of the most exalted kind. Professor Crumbaugh reports a case in point, one which came under his own care :

"A boy of about fourteen was almost wholly bent upon history, geography, and such studies as required the memory only, but mathematics he had no taste for at all. Anything that could be repeated from memory he would learn with the greatest ease. Page after page he would repeat, after reading them over once or twice, but anything in figures would hardly claim his attention for a moment. I used every means I could invent to get him to consider the principles upon which the rules of arithmetic were founded, but all seemed of no use. Almost every lesson would set him crying, and cause my own heart to fail, as for nearly three months I plied every sort of stratagems to capture his mind and fasten it upon this important branch. The term of school was nearly out, and to all appearances I had not made the slightest progress towards accomplishing my object.

"One day there seemed to be something buoyant in the atmosphere—something that had an exhilarating effect upon the animal spirits as well as upon the mind. The mildness of the weather—for it was winter—the soft rays of sunlight, and a gently sighing breeze filled the school-house, and all within seemed to catch an inspiration from the visible presence of nature around. One particular example in his arithmetic seemed to take the attention of my backward scholar. He called for help. My own head felt clearer than usual as I endeavored to unfold the principles involved, and all at once, with a sparkling eye and a beaming countenance, he almost jumped for joy, exclaiming, 'I see it! I know how it is done!'

"How beautifully the joy of his as well as of my own heart contrasted with that beautiful morning! The hour of triumph had come, as his after course proved. From that very moment his attention was so strongly fixed upon his arithmetic, that 'recess' might come and go; boys be merry at their plays without, yet he would be bending over his slate as if transfixed with the magic power of figures, seeming almost to forget that he even needed a little rest from severe mental labor."

Great evil however may arise from such an absorption of mental power, and the course our good professor pursued in the foregoing instance is not always advisable. One who is in the quick-sands cannot lift himself out, since he has no sure foundation to stand upon. The sudden transition of the mind from a dark picture to an extremely light one, may cause a momentary blindness.

The teacher's work is to manage so delicately formed an engine so that too great a pressure may not produce a terrible disaster. A powerful ambition may keep up even a weak body for a long time, but re-action is sure to follow. He who can govern himself in this matter is a wise master.

A thorough understanding of this subject is of

IMMENSE IMPORTANCE.

Those children who learn rules by rote are in danger of becoming little better than parrots; for correct mental discipline should enlist the understanding.

Candidates for the position of teacher, and children undergoing school-examinations, are judged as to their qualifications by questions which are mainly intended to puzzle rather than to find out whether they have an understanding of the subject. Many of the former are rejected, as unfit to be teachers; and the latter to receive a prize, on the most trivial mistakes,—mere technicalities,—while, at the same time the best teacher loses the position sought, and the child that has real understanding, the prize; while those who are rewarded can scarcely bound correctly the town in which they live,—happening merely to be posted in such insignificant details as the examiners select for a standard by which to measure educational standing. In this, doubtless, many of our boards of education are woefully deficient. Graduates of colleges often make the poorest teachers. To understand how to teach so as to make the greatest progress with the pupil is a fine point, and little is as yet known on the subject. To merely hear the pupil recite his lesson, or require him to speak a piece, is not, in my judgment, teaching. Many children learn their lesson at home, where they are assisted by their parents; the next day they repeat it at school. To teach is to explain, to analyze, to illustrate, to lecture, to question, and allow the pupil to propound questions, to be answered by the teacher, and thus a mystery may be easily made plain to the child. If the pupil is required to learn alone, from books, it may take months to acquire all this. A knowledge of Greek, Latin, the higher mathematics, and everything that belongs to a classical education does not always make profitable teachers. A piano may be perfect, and our performer well dressed, good looking, and college educated, with finger rings, breast-pins, etc., and we may think we have a right to expect delightful music. But oh, horrors! Those fingers do not go to the right place; the instrument does not give forth charming sounds. What is the trouble?—is the fault with the piano? Another performer, rough in appearance, educated only in the commonest branches, but knowing how to produce harmony, having a higher knowledge of music, approaches the instrument, and how different the notes which now fall on the gratified ear! The secret is, the one has caught the true spirit and meaning of his art; the other has not. So it is with the teacher. It is not always the one who makes the biggest noise that understands the business best. Many who are unpretending are often the most successful, and impart more information to a class of learners than scores of the more inflated ones can. Teachers, superintendents, and committees should be careful how they are carried away by hobbies in discharging a duty requiring the utmost candor.

The question may now be asked

HOW SHOULD

it be done? This is a question easily asked, but not easily answered; especially by merely yes or no. I remember, on one occasion, the graduating class in a medical college, in Philadelphia, was about to undergo a final examination by the different professors, whose merits were pretty freely discussed by the students. One of the professors was noted for his eccentricities and his rough exterior bearing, and was set down as the one to be most dreaded. This dread was not lessened by the instruction to the class to meet in his parlor at an appointed hour, or they would not get his signature to their diplomas. At the appointed hour, with trembling steps and beating hearts, they wended their way to the supposed cheerless spot. The class had planned to move together, and on entering found things more cheerful than they had anticipated. The professor, in his easy chair, dressed in his evening-gown, leisurely reclining with his feet elevated, all plainly bespoke a degree of indifference that made them feel much at home. The conversation was free, about the weather, health, business prospects, studies, etc., and before they were aware of it the examination was rapidly advancing. It was remarked afterwards that this was the most satisfactory examination they ever passed.

In this way each student had been led to produce the treasures of his mind, and had not been treated as an automaton—a mere machine to move in a prescribed circle to satisfy the fogyism of stereotyped domineering customs. The course pursued in the examination showed, also, that the professor understood his business, without books or papers. The object of these examinations are simply to inquire whether the candidates understand what is requisite for them to know. A few questions printed on a slip of paper, requesting the pupil to answer them in writing, does not give us an idea of the real knowledge the pupil possesses. The teacher who can comprehend at a glance the proper method of arousing the child's mind, and who is capable of unfolding to that mind what he knows himself, be it much or little, is the most successful.

The richest man that walks the earth, if cast alone upon a barren island, would die of famine just as surely as would the poorest one; nor would it be any help if he should pompously walk around counting over his houses, lands, bank-stocks, railroad-bonds, etc. What he now wants is the substantial—the food for the stomach. So may the mind of the child famish for want of proper food, though the teacher is abounding in the languages, mathematics, and fine arts, but lacking in a proper knowledge of how to impart them to others. Thus we want more practicability. The picture must be painted in durable colors, and not be simply a shadow thrown upon the wall, as quick to vanish as it was in making its appearance.

The more we study the mind, the more we see its constitutional frailty, and the more impressed we must become with the wondrous care needed in moulding it in its formative stage. If we wish to make it a flower filled with the sweets of a virtuous character, the cultivation must be faithfully attended to. Evil principles in the mind, like weeds in a garden, are destructive to all good, and will grow down everything desirable. If the cultivation and dressing is not prompt and constant, so much headway is made by the weeds that all good is in danger of being rooted up. It is a sad time when the garden of the mind must be left disfigured with vicious growths, just because both good and evil have been so allowed to take root together that the eradication of the one will disturb the other. It is virtually acknowledging that the weeds have the mastery and must therefore be left untouched.

When we consider the pliancy of the mind, need we wonder that boys and girls, scarcely out of the nursery, are so easily lead from the path of virtue, when the moral principles are but imperfectly impressed upon the mind, especially since the seeds of temptation are scattered so thickly over our land. Our station-houses are full of them, and large prisons are multiplying for them. Our country is groaning over the increase of crime of every shade, for boys and girls, men and women, who have minds crowded with the rank weeds of discord, are beyond the reformatory power.

Therefore, mental training should be so conducted as to deprive the king of darkness of his terrific power. But many times, where, in the matter of general education, the child is driven, at a very early age, to tasks he heartily despises, or is so long and steadily confined to them that his whole nature revolts, the mind gradually becomes weakened, and finally yields to the cold advances of the relentless usurper. When once a distaste for study has been created, it is far more difficult to restore such a one than to gain one who has never before visited the field. The pet bird if once wounded will no more sit upon the hand that feeds it; the whipped dog will not obey the will of him who gave the blow; and, as the overloaded stomach revolts at the thoughts of the food that has made it so, so the mind, when doubly bitted and whipped into an ill-fitting harness, only tries to keep as far off as possible.

One of the greatest misfortunes arising from a misguidance in mental training is the

LOSS OF REASON.

Professor Denton remarks on mental training:
"A bright, intelligent being, one who has been the

pride of parents and society, and whose ready wit and buoyant manners have been sought for as of inestimable worth, through a mysterious transformation becomes an imbecile! The brain is just as large now as ever, the stature has not diminished in the least, but the intelligence has suffered from some invisible effect. This is more generally the consequence of overwork in those of middle life than among children. The child, especially if it be one of those premature developments, puts forth all its intellectual beauties before the body has sufficiently matured to support so much mental fire, and as the strife goes on between body and mind, the one or the other must yield, and generally the physical being is conquered and the child dies. The mind is still strong, and even while death is undoing the ties that bind the immortal to the perishable, the soul shines forth as strong and brilliant as ever, and the consoling thought is seized upon by the bereft parents, that *the child is too good to live.* How often such a remark is made, yet how imperfectly understood. Everyone knows that a safe without a lock is no more burglar-proof than the merest sham made of wood; but the idea is at once forgotten when we look upon the body as a safe to contain the priceless soul.

"The matter of physical training in colleges and schools is a good one, but perhaps it is in a crude state at present, or its importance is unfairly considered by the people at large. The contrivances for lifting, pulling, leaping and such like performances, may be better than nothing, but what does it avail, though a man by persevering effort may enable himself to lift a thousand pounds! It is only an overgrowth, and entirely unnatural. For properly developed men and women we must look into rural life, where, instead of lifting just for the lifting itself, the strength is applied for the accomplishing of some other valuable object. The full chest, the well developed lungs, the ruddy and sun-browned cheeks and the naturally expanded waist, all tell how securely enclosed is the mind of such people.

"Look the world over and see how facts and figures trace out the birth-places of genius and intelligence, tracing them to rural districts among the mountains and wilds of the outlying country. The farmer's boy, after he becomes his own man, seeks out the city where he can bring the treasures of his mind into action, and his strides are gigantic, because there is power in his physical being to drive him through all opposition. With proper care he lives to bear his gray hairs to extreme old age, and when called to die, can leave a record of years spent in the vigorous pursuit of the great end of his earthly existence.

"Let us turn for a moment from these interesting reflections and enter yonder alms-house to make observation upon the different classes of those inmates living upon public charity. There is a young lady who still bears some of the beauties of a once lovely face; symmetrically proportioned, and still bearing charms that captivate the eye and heart. Were she only as richly attired as when she moved in the grand circle of a father's mansion, she would surpass the whole class of village belles in personal attractions.

But why is she thus meanly clad, and debarred from the society of others? How can such a beautiful creature be contented with such common fare when the world is open before her? Why does she not seek the pleasures and amusements of life while her youthful days are passing? She is never heard to utter one word of complaint, or express a desire for a different life. See how she tosses herself from side to side, gazing here and there with a wild and frantic look! See how she laughs at her own wild thoughts! Now why does she cry? Every trifle pleases, but she scarcely notices anything that transpires. Why does she not notice or speak to us? Alas! her mind is gone! She is a maniac—an idiot—a town pauper! She still retains that exquisitely beautiful form, but she appears to differ from a beast only in shape. The beast may be frightened at its shadow and she may laugh at her own ungovernable fancy.

"Now we may apply to ourselves the questions: Why are we not all there under similar circumstances? Why is not our summer table the sunny hillsides or the smiling valley? Why do we not seek the refreshing shade of the leafy grove as our only retreat from the burning sun? Why are we not at the command of some celestial being, as the lower order of animals is to us? Because the liberty of the mind calls for a higher position, and a more benevolent status obtains among us.

"Then, is not a correct mental training one of the most important features of our existence? Do we not see that there is too much conformity to prescribed rules? Anything possessed of the pliancy of the mind, requires the peculiar adaptation of every circumstance in order to promote its growth.

"As every face differs in some respect from all others, so does the training of different minds require every available means that can be brought to bear in the work. In passing through a crowd where thousands have congregated, we can sort out our friends, and no one can deceive us in our work. The slightest difference in the contour of the face, every expression of the countenance, every ray that shoots forth from the soul within, bears some mark which we take in at a glance, and deception is next to impossible. Why can not the teacher read just as readily the peculiarities of his pupil, and thus be enabled to sort out all the appliances that will assist in the proper development of the mind he is training? It is sometimes done, and such teachers or parents are the successful ones. It is for the purpose of obtaining such teachers that superintendents and committees of schools should so order their examinations as to discover who has and who has not these sterling qualities. If a political or a partizan spirit is the prime mover for the official work, the consequences will still prove to be as disastrous in the future as they have been in the past."

Training is not only confined to schools, nor to parental care; neither must it be confined to the early period of youth, as if it were the only time when the mind is receiving impressions from surrounding circumstances, for this work is constantly going on through life. I must speak of a very important subject before closing this chapter, which is on the wonderful power

OF THE PRESS.

It is, like everything else, capable of accomplishing much good, and may also be made to do a great deal of harm. In the work of mental training perhaps there is no other means which can compare with it. Thoughts and vocal sounds are invisible. Sound, touch, taste, and smell, make a single impression on the mind,—then are no more; sound especially can not be heard the second time. The press places upon paper those ideas in a durable form, where the eye can see them as often as it chooses, even though the writer has slumbered beneath the sod of the valley for centuries. His words are still living. Think of Homer, away off in those dark ages of time of which we have scarcely an echo; listen to his wonderful words as he speaks of wars, of heroes, of heroines, of gods, and of nations, who, but for the immortality of his verse would now be entirely lost in oblivion. A writer said:

"As we read his graphic descriptions, we can almost hear the clashing hosts; we can almost feel the shocks of contending gods; we can seem to hear the crash of falling walls and bursting gates; the groans of the wounded and dying; and yet all this was in long, long years ago, though keenly alive to our senses to-day."

If the work of the press thus lives, then, is it not important to ask what is the character of the matter that is thus immortalized? The cottager, with a beloved wife and half a dozen children, far in the backwoods, where a newspaper only occasionally disturbs his peace, and where he can pursue undisturbed his vocation, and the study of the wilds of nature is, perhaps, the happiest of mortals.

The dark deeds of murder, robbery, oppression, licentiousness, and the great catalogue of crimes that overflow, like a deluge, the clustering abodes of men, do not annoy him. The storm may howl around his cabin, the torrents pour upon his thatched roof; but his home is cheerful even in the cheerless storm. Even though the winds roar, the mighty trees rock like so many toys, and the lightnings rend them into a thousand splinters, yet all is the work of Him who sustains the great universe. There are furious storms in nature; but what storms are also raging in the moral world! Who will deny the growing tendency of the press to obscenity? Professor Venton, in commenting on this subject,

CONCEIVED THE CORRECT

idea, when he remarked:

"We can not pass the bulletin boards of our city news-stands, or the bar-rooms of country hotels; nor even fences, rocks, trees, barn-doors or house-fronts of country wilds, but what exciting pictures sent out by some of the novel papers of the day must stare at us like so many demons to infuriate the minds of the young. Do we ever think of it as we see them, and consider how rapidly we are drifting to the vortex of iniquity that has proved so destructive to a once proud France? Pictures of feminine beauties are unblushingly displayed in such positions and with such exposures as will arrest the unwary youth from that purity of mind which should always be the object of a perfect mental training. But it is not the object here; therefore the more indecent the exposures, the more debased the mind becomes, and will run after all such tempting baits. The stories themselves are the strongest that can be made to excite just that one passion that should be held in mastery above all others. The day laborer as well as the millionaire will fill his pockets, of a Saturday night, with these inflammable documents, for his family's amusement during the tedious hours of the holy Sabbath day. He says he does not get much time to read, and he wants something light to cheer him up. It makes his fireside brighter, during the winter evening, to hear some exciting story, for he *knows* it is not true. Oh! what a delusion a mortal can fall into! Even if it does not materially injure his own mind, can he not see the mighty power of fascination such idle tales are throwing around his children? All other books are quickly thrown aside for the delightful romance. Yea, it is far more pleasing to read them than to fulfill the necessary duties of the day. Often the hour that should be devoted to such duties is stolen, and in some secluded place the absorbing story is consumed by an enfeebled mind lost to almost everything of a holier nature, until it becomes the most agreeable food it can swallow. Yea, it soon becomes the master of the whole mind, and daily duties or religious devotions are almost entirely forgotten or neglected.

"Observe a very common fashion among young ladies! A book in the hand is apparently made to be a mark of intelligence and literary refinement. In cars, in by-ways, and on the street, these emblems are held up to view, as if they would certainly convince passers-by of the notable fact of their high standing; but did you ever notice the character of any of them? It needs but a glance over the shoulder of yon fair miss, who is all absorbed in her reading, to see what food her mind is taking in. One of the most attractive novels of the day, with the whole force of its plans and devices arranged and put forth by one of the most powerful writers is inflaming, to the most disastrous extent, that passion of her mind which will lead her astray. It matters not whether it be a book or a paper, yellow-covered or no cover at all, if the spark is there, it will soon set the whole soul on fire. Is it any wonder there are so many elopements? Married men running away with young girls; married women with young boys; husbands and wives exchanging partners, and other such heterogeneous mixtures? There is nothing that will destroy the proper balance of the mind quicker than the undue excitement of the amorous passions. How many there are who have almost lost their individuality from the complete absorption of the nerve stimulus of the body, to support the furious flame of Cupid's kindling! Such intensity of mental emotion rapidly drains both strength of body and mind until the individual is unfit for the necessary duties of life, since one single passion has been fanned into a general conflagration."

These things are poisoning the minds of our youth, and what more is needed to bring the law upon them? "But they make the papers sell," is the cry, and it tells a fearful tale of what the tastes of the people are becoming. While a paper of an honest, upright, literary and scientific character, can hardly be kept alive, these publications, so poisonous to virtue and pure mortals, are scattering their leaves over the country thicker than the snows of winter. Why? Simply because fathers and mothers buy them or allow them to be bought for their children, and so eagerly are they sought for, that prices will be paid for them that would forever sink from sight a sheet of a more upright character. How often the punishment comes home unawares to the paternal head of the

UNGUARDED HOUSEHOLD!

The fair daughter, the promising son, by reading an inflammable novel pass completely into the hands of an infuriated passion.

Nor is all the evil centered in this single condition of life, for often the seeds of discord are seen springing up through the stage of wedded life. When those in tender youth have urged themselves forward so far as to have entered the married state, having followed only the promptings of a spirit excited by the many fictitious stories read, with no other understanding of its holy orders, do we wonder that there are so many unhappy homes, unnatural associations leading to runaways, murders, suicides, drunkenness, and the long list of evils that make up newspaper gossip? What does the young miss of fifteen or sixteen know of the steps she is taking, when, all excited,—yes, almost to insanity,—she complacently receives the overtures of A. B. or C., regardless of character or standing? Sometimes their minds are so wrought upon that they would rather make love to a baboon than none at all, or why will they so often forsake caste and all personal regard, and elope with some inferior servant of the house? Look at these cases and usually they are the ones who have lost their mental balance, and have been swallowing love-novels as their choicest food.

This is no picture—it is a simple account of what is every day occurring, and now must we see one of the consequences? Jealousy instigates the man to furious acts, and if he feels a fear to follow the suggestions of the dark spirit within, the fiend *alcohol*, or what is worse, *drugged liquors*, are at hand to banish every thought of fear. The man may become the sot in the gutters until buried in disgrace beneath the sod, or hanging from the gallows, a guide-board in the highway of justice.

Can novel reading produce this? I will not answer more! I leave the sketch already drawn to speak for itself. I can seem to see the mind of the reader just now calling up similar cases, and I seem to hear a silent assent, as if the great fact were far from half told.

In all I have said in regard to the press I do not arraign it as a useless thing: by no means. It does a world of good, and is one of the most powerful means we have to use in combating the evils already spoken of. Because a razor or butcher-knife has cut so many throats, we do not say they are only for evil, for they admirably fulfill the purposes designed, and are harmless when kept in their place. So with the press. All stories are not bad, nor do all pictures inflame the mind. If the boy plays with his sunglass, there is no harm, provided he uses it in a proper manner; but what would we say if we saw him drawing a focus upon a quantity of powder that communicated with a barrelful underneath? The thoughts of a boy flying in a thousand pieces in the air would be sufficient to cause us to act instantly to prevent so sad a catastrophe.

If you will, call the mind this barrel of powder; the amorous passion the most inflammable quality of all the compounded ingredients; the novels the sunglass, and the writers of them the half-witted boy, then the picture is complete.

In the proper training of the mind, it is a duty we owe to the rising generation to close up by law every avenue through which even a single member of the human family is unfavorably effected. All that comes within the social attraction of a single infractious child, man or woman, in a neighborhood, is subject to contamination by such evil influence. If the mind is pliable as we have shown, then why not give it the attention that you would the little sprout of your garden. If you would have a beautiful tree, you must cultivate it in accordance with the laws of nature. So in regard to the mind. A constant impression must be made until the subject is mastered;

then only will the child or adult make that proficiency which crowns effort with success. All excesses must be avoided, and the laws of physiology strictly obeyed.

During this age of electricity,—this newspaper epoch,—it behooves every parent and teacher to be vigilant, always on the alert to guard the young mind against the alluring evils of to-day. Let correct principles be instilled in the young mind, and instead of wrecked homes, visible growths of immortal excellence and moral goodness will lead the rising generation on to glory. That would, indeed be a happy household where all should have the highest motives to prompt them to walk in the paths of virtue and happiness. That home will not be a stranger to the refinements of the age; but poetry, music, stories, games, etc., will help to make it the highest type of all that is cheerful, refined, and Christian-like. In it there will be a joy enduring as eternity,—that arising from a consciousness of having acted from pure motives, and in accordance with the principles taught in the great book of nature. "Prepare to live, and we shall be prepared to die." So said an eminent philosopher. Those who are happy in life have the best assurance that the same will be their reward in the glorious future. It can not be that this earth is man's only abiding-place. It can not be that life is a bubble, cast up by the ocean of eternity, to float for a moment on its waves, and then sink into nothingness. Else why is it that the glorious aspirations, which leap like angels from the temple of our hearts, are forever wandering about unsatisfied? Why is it that the rainbow and the clouds unfold to us a beauty that is not of earth, and then pass off and leave us to muse upon their faded loveliness? Why is it that the stars which hold their festivals around the throne of chaste Diana are set so far above the grasp of our limited faculties, forever mocking us with their unapproachable glory? And finally, why is it that the bright forms of human beauty are presented to our view but for a moment, and then taken from us, leaving the thousand streams, of our affections to flow back with the turbulency of Alpine torrents upon our hearts? We are born for a higher destiny than that of earth. There is a realm where the stars will be spread out before us like the islets that slumber on the ocean; and where the beautiful beings that here pass before us like shadows, will live in our presence forever.

I can only say as a last reflection: Train for it the human mind. A mind filled with such glorious hopes will keep above the miry slough, and away from the dangerous pitfalls, where those allowed to play carelessly on the brink are on the way to destruction.

Happy unbroken household in Heaven! Every member a star! What a glorious sight! Not a wail, not one sound of sorrow, for a missing, erring one! United and happy in the expanding glories of the transcendent life they commenced in a world of temptation. The thought should be sufficient to stimulate us on to virtue, to the proper development of the mind, in order to secure such unbounded fulfillment of joy. The shipwrecks that lie so thickly around us are a result of the unfaithful performance of so important a duty.

> " O wailings still the winds of heaven bear,
> And every hour they pass some cast away,
> Some foundered ship on life's unsteady sea,
> On billows of temptation tossed, so fair
> As seemed at first from every danger free,
> But lost at last, and gone—we ask not where!"

There is a time when all must "render up this earthly clay," and the time of reckoning will surely come. Let us not be deceived on this matter. Let us diligently strive for correct mental training, for this has much to do with our eternal peace; neglected, it will be impossible to remedy the evil when once the day of probation is past.

> " There is an hour
> When all things known must meet a final doom;
> And, too, so sure no man can find the power
> To give delay. Into the solemn gloom
> Of Time's oblivious depths, as darkly swell
> Its tides with all we love, we, too, must go,
> And in eternal light the long past tell,
> Enwrapped with pleasure, or o'erwhelmed with woe."

CHAPTER XXII.

ON THE LAWS OF PHYSICAL CULTURE.—TEMPERAMENTAL HARMONY THE BASIS OF PHYSICAL PERFECTION.

"Among the important topics that should command our attention, in the course of human observation, is a study of the temperaments."—*Howard.*

"It is the law of formation, that the development of any part of the body is in the direction of the vital currents which, by means of exercise, are brought to bear upon it."—*Theophile Gautier.*

The subject of temperaments is so little understood by the general reader that I am persuaded a chapter devoted to that subject will be of great interest, and assist much in enacting correct laws for the government of man. I believe that every person who has arrived at adult age should have a knowledge of the temperaments, at least so much as is known of them, and taught by scientific men. "Bodily conformation," says Professor Lawrence, "gives us an intimation of the character of the individual." As long ago as the days of Hippocrates, human temperaments have been considered by distinguished physiologists a subject of great moment. Some have looked upon the study as little more than a pretty speculation. "It is my conviction that if it be a speculation, all departments of natural history and physiology fall into the same category."* My own

---

* Professor Powell on Human Temperaments.

observations, during seventeen years of medical practice, have convinced me, beyond a doubt, that the temperament is as much a physiological condition as life itself, and that it indicates to us the quality and tone of the intellectual capacity, as well as the activity and power, of the whole individual organization.

By the word temperament we understand a certain state of the constitution, depending upon the relative proportions of its different masses, and the relative energy of its different functions. Some distinguished author defines the temperament as "that portion of us which we live the most." It is a constitutional condition with respect to the predominance of any quality denominated as the temperament of the body. Every condition of the bodily organization bespeaks an individual character which is peculiar, and when we compare man with the other animals we observe that he is distinguished by characteristic features which do not permit us for a moment to confound him with any of them; so when we compare man with man we are struck by the no less obvious fact that there exist between individuals differences analogous to those which mark the different species. One is tall and muscular; another, small and plump; a third, small and slender. We observe also that the functions of life are not performed in all with the same degree of force or rapidity, and that their likes and dislikes have neither the same direction nor an equal intensity. These differences are the results and indications of what we call temperament, which has already been defined.

I will not stop to notice the old

CLASSIFICATIONS

of temperaments, as given by Hippocrates, George Combe, Powell, and others, but mainly give the reader the latest and most scientific classification, as recognized at the present day by our best physiologists. The temperaments are presented for our examination as existing in a variety of forms, and in different degrees of development; numerous and varied as the individuals of the race, no two persons being found with precisely the same physical constitution. Tracing them back to their simpler forms, however, we shall find them all to result from the almost infinite combinations of a few simple elements.

To facilitate our study of the temperaments, and to make my explanation comprehensible to the reader, I shall here devote a few pages to the structure of the human body.

From a classification of the natural system of anatomy, we are enabled to derive a clear idea of the temperaments. In this, I am largely indebted to Professors Jacques, Wells, Walker, Florence, Wilson, and others, whose systems of classification I regard as the most scientific ever given to the world.

The human body consists of three grand classes or systems of organs, each of which has its special function in the general economy. They are denominated:

1. The Motive or Mechanical system;
2. The Vital or Nutritive system;
3. The Mental or Nervous system.

These three systems, each naturally sub-dividing into several branches, include all the organs, and perform all the complicated functions of the physical man.

THE MOTIVE,

or mechanical system, consists of three sets of organs, forming, in combination, an apparatus of levers, through which locomotion and all the larger movements of the body are effected. They are: the bones, the ligaments, and the muscles.

The bones form the framework of the body. They are primarily organs of support, sustaining and giving solidity to every part.

The ligaments help to form the joints, and are properly called organs of connection. Their strength and toughness is so great, that it is hardly possible, by means of any ordinary force, to tear them asunder. "It is wonderful," a late medical publication says, "to see how admirably the ligaments are arranged to answer the purposes for which they are intended!" Where the ends of two bones meet, as in some of the joints, ligaments pass across from one to the other; and so firm are they in their structure, that they never allow the joint to become loose, however much it may be exercised. The provision for keeping the joints constantly oiled, so that they never wear out, and are never injured in any way by friction, is not less wonderful or less efficacious than the arrangement by which they are held together.

The muscles are simply bundles of red flesh, growing tougher and more compact toward the extremities, by which they are attached to the bone, and terminating in white tendons or cords. The muscles are, *par excellence*, the organs of motion. It is by means of them that the indwelling mind, telegraphing its mandates through the appropriate nerves, effects any desired movement, by causing a contraction of the fibers of which they are composed, thus drawing the parts to which they are attached toward each other. They present a great variety of forms, and are of all lengths, from a fourth of an inch, as in some of the muscles of the larynx, to three feet, as in the sartorius, or tailor's muscle, which is used in crossing the leg. The muscular system, in its development and organic condition, is more completely under our control than any other part of the body,— a circumstance of vast importance in connection with the subject of human physical perfectibility.

THE VITAL

or nutritive system, consists of three classes of organs, forming a complicated apparatus of tubes, which perform the functions of absorption, circulation, and secretion, and incidentally of purification. Their principal seat is the trunk of the body, and they exercise a minute peristaltic or pulsatory motion. They are designated as: the lymphatics, the blood-vessels, and the glands.

The lymphatics are small, transparent tubes, furnished with valves at short intervals, and connected with the ganglia or glands which are distributed over the body, but are most numerous on the sides of the neck, the armpits, the groins, and the mesenteric folds of the intestines. Their office is to absorb nutriment and pass it into the circulation. They convey the lymph from every part of the system to the descending *vena cava*, where it mixes with the venous blood returning to the heart.

That all-important function, the circulation of the blood, is effected by means of a system of tubes, or, rather, two interwoven systems of tubes, which carry it to every part of the body, and then return it to the center of circulation. This center of circulation is the heart, a muscular organ, situated in the lower part of the thoracic cavity, between the two folds of the pleura which form the central partition of the chest.

The glands, or filters, are the organs which secrete or deposit not only the various substances of which the different organs are composed, but the fat, milk, hair, and other animal products. They are composed of two sets of capillary vessels, the one for the circulation of the arterial blood, and the other for secreting their proper materials. The lungs, stomach, intestines, reproductive organs, and especially the liver, are mainly glandular in structure and function, and so far are included in this system.

The lungs present to the view a spongy mass, made up of air-tubes, air-cells, and blood-vessels, all bound together by a cellular tissue. Of the air-cells there are many millions; and the internal surface presented by the combined air-cells and air-tubes is probably more than ten times the external surface of the body. Around each of these minute cells is woven a net-work of hair-like tubes, through which come and go the venous and arterial blood. It is through the coats of these that the air acts upon and vitalizes the blood, giving it oxygen and receiving carbonic acid in return.

The liver is the largest gland in the body. And its office is to secrete bile from the blood, which is poured from the gall-bladder into the duodenum a few inches below the stomach.

THE STOMACH

is a musculo-membraneous reservoir, continuous on the one side with the esophagus, and on the other with the duodenum. It is situated beneath the diaphragm, liver, and spleen, and occupies the epigastrium and a part of the hypochondrium. Its office is to convert the food into chyme.

The intestines, or bowels, comprise the duodenum, or second stomach, the jejunum, and ileum, which collectively are called the small intestine, the cœcum, the colon, and the rectum. The duodenum, or second stomach, leads from the pyloric orifice of the stomach to the jejunum. Its length is about twelve fingers' breadth, and hence its name. The jejunum, so called from being generally found empty, forms the upper two-fifths of the small intestine, leading from the duodenum to the ileum. The ileum, which signifies to twist or convolute, forms the remaining three-fifths of the small intestine, ending in the colon. It is smaller, paler, and thinner than the jejunum.

The kidneys are hard, glandular bodies, lying on each side of the spine near the last ribs. The office of the kidneys is to separate the urine from the blood and convey it into the bladder, by means of its long tubes called ureters.

The spleen is also a glandular body, and is situated at the left of the stomach. Its function is not well known. The intimate relation and sympathy between the glands and the brain give rise to some singular phenomena, as will be seen further on.

THE MENTAL SYSTEM.

It is by means of this system that sense, thought, and impulse to action, and consequently all connection between the soul and the external world, takes place. It consists of a series of globules, bound by membraneous investments into fibers of various forms, the motion of which is invisible. The chief seat of this system is the head. It admits, like the other systems, of a division into three orders of organs:

1. THE ORGANS OF SENSE.—These are the organs through which we receive impressions from external objects.*

2. THE CEREBRUM.—The human brain, speaking of it as a whole, is an oval mass filling and fitting the interior of the skull, and consists of two substances —a gray, ash-colored, or cincriterous portion, and a white, fibrous, or medullary portion. It is divided,

---

* See author's work on the Human Five Senses.

both in form and in function, into two principal masses, called the cerebrum and the cerebellum. At its base there are two other portions, called the annular protuberance and the medulla oblongata. The cerebrum is the organ of perception, reflection, and all the other essentially human faculties and sentiments.

3. THE CEREBELLUM.—The cerebellum is the organ of permanent action and of physical life. It lies behind and immediately underneath the cerebrum, and is about one-eight the size of the latter organ. There are generally reckoned eleven pairs of nerves arising from the brain, and thirty-one from the spinal marrow. It is thus seen that the whole nervous apparatus is included in the mental system, as we have defined it, and that the brain is omnipresent in the human body.

With these briefly stated facts, which form the outlines of the system of anatomy, the reader will be measurably prepared to read with profit what is to follow. Those who have access to anatomical and physiological works, and leisure for their study will do well to pursue the subject further.

In the natural system of anatomy, the outlines of which we have just briefly given, it is shown that the human body is composed of three grand classes or systems of organs, each of which has its special function in the general economy. We have denominated them, the motive or mechanical system, the vital or nutritive system, and the mental or nervous system. On this basis rests the true doctrine of the temperaments, of which there are primarily three, corresponding with the three systems of organs just named. We shall call them,—

1. The Motive temperament;
2. The Vital temperament;
3. The Mental temperament.

It is the predominance of the class of organs from which it takes its name that determines each of these temperaments. Thus the first is marked by a superior development of the osseous and muscular systems forming the locomotive apparatus; in the second, the vital organs, the principal seat of which is in the trunk, give the tone to the organization; and in the third, the brain and nervous system exerts the controling power.

The simple or primary temperaments are, however, practically, little better than abstractions; but they serve as points of departure from which to arrive at their various combinations.

THE MOTIVE TEMPERAMENT.

The bony frame work of the human body determines its general configuration, which is modified in its details by the muscular fibers and cellular tissues which overlay them. In the motive temperament the bones are proportionately large, and generally long, rather than broad, and the outlines of the form manifest a tendency to angularity. The muscles are well developed, but only moderately rounded, and correspond in form with the bones. The figure is commonly tall, elegant, and striking; the face oblong;

the neck rather long; the shoulders broad and definite; the chest moderate in size and fullness; the abdomen proportional; and the limbs long and tapering. The complexion and eyes are generally, but not always, dark; the hair dark, strong, and abundant. Firmness of texture characterizes all the organs, imparting great strength and endurance. Men of this temperament are naturally vigorous, active, energetic, and impassioned, and possess strongly marked, if not idiosyncratic, characters. They manifest great capacity for conception, and are constantly carried away, bearing others with them, by the torrent of their imaginations and passions. They are leaders, rulers, and conquerors in the sphere in which they move. This is the temperament for rare talents, great works, great errors, great faults, and great crimes.* An abnormal development of the motive temperament, in which both the vital and the mental systems are sacrificed to mere animal strength, forms what the ancients called the athletic temperament. It is marked by a head proportionately small, especially in the coronal region; a thick neck; broad shoulders; expanded chest; and strongly marked muscles, the tendons of which are apparent through the skin. The Farnese Hercules furnishes a model of the physical attributes of the abnormal constitution, in which brute force usurps the energies necessary to the production of thought, and leaves its possessor decidedly deficient in all the higher mental manifestations. This temperament does not occur in women.

---

* Cabanis.

THE VITAL TEMPERAMENT.

As this temperament depends upon the predominance of the vital or nutritive organs, which occupy the great cavities of the trunk, it is necessarily marked by a breadth and thickness of body proportionately greater, and a stature and size of limbs proportionately less than in the motive temperament. Its most striking physical characteristic is rotundity or plumpness. The face inclines to roundness; the neck is rather short; the shoulders broad and round; the chest full; the abdomen well developed; the arms and legs plump, but tapering and delicate, and terminating in hands and feet relatively small. The complexion is generally rather florid; the countenance smiling; the eyes blue; and the hair soft, light, and abundant. Persons of this temperament are characterized mentally by activity, ardor, impulsiveness, enthusiasm, versatility, and sometimes by fickleness. They have more elasticity than firmness, more diligence than persistence, more brilliancy than depth. They are frequently violent and passionate, but as easily calmed as excited; are generally cheerful and amiable, and almost always very companionable and fond of good living. An undue and abnormal preponderance of the absorbent system, and a sluggish action of the circulatory, give rise to what has been called the lymphatic temperament, which presents forms even more rounded and softer than those we have been describing, but lacking their well-defined and graceful outlines. A feebler color of the skin, a lack of expression in the countenance, insurmountable sloth, and a general weakness and apathy, both of body and mind, characterize this state of the system, which is so evidently the result of disease that we see no propriety in setting it down as one of the natural temperaments. When perfect health shall have become universal, we shall have no lymphatic people, and no lazy ones.

THE MENTAL TEMPERAMENT.

This temperament, depending upon the predominance of the brain and nervous system, is characterized by a slight frame, and a head relatively large and of a pyriform appearance. The face is generally oval; the forehead high and pale; the features delicate and finely chiseled; the eye bright and expressive; the hair fine, soft, not abundant, and commonly of a light color; the neck slender; the chest rather narrow; the limbs small; and the whole figure delicate and graceful rather than striking or elegant. In persons of the mental temperament, the brain and the nervous system are active, the thoughts quick, the senses acute, and the imagination lively and brilliant. It is the literary and artistic, especially the poetic temperament, of which Byron, Shelley, Keats, and Poe, furnish good examples. There is at the present day, and in this country, an excessive and morbid development of this temperament, especially among women (to whom, in even its normal predominance, it is less proper than the preceding), which is most inimical to health, longevity, and happiness. It answers to the nervous temperament of old classification, and is characterized by the smallness and emaciation of the muscles, the quickness and intensity of the sensations, the suddenness and fickleness of the determinations, and a morbid impressibility. It is caused by sedentary habits, lack of exercise, and a false system of education, inducing a premature and disproportionate development of the brain; the immoderate use of tea, coffee, and tobaco, and habits of sensual indulgence. We shall show farther on how this state of the system may be prevented, or, if already existing, remedied, at least.

The three primary temperaments, combining with each other in different proportions, and being modified by various causes, form sub-temperaments innumerable, presenting differences and resemblances depending upon the relative proportions of the primitive elements. The simplest combinations of which the three primary temperaments are susceptible give us six sub-temperaments, which may be designated as:

1. The Motive-Vital temperament;
2. The Motive-Mental temperament;
3. The Vital-Motive temperament;
4. The Vital-Mental temperament;
5. The Mental-Motive temperament;
6. The Mental-Vital temperament.

The names of these compound temperaments sufficiently indicate their character. The motive-vital and the vital-motive differ but slightly,—the name placed first in either case indicating the element which exists in the larger proportion. The same remark applies to the motive-mental and the mental-motive, and to the vital-mental and the mental-vital.

It is evident that perfection of constitution must consist in a proper balance of temperaments. If any one of them exists in great excess, the result is necessarily a departure from symmetry and harmony, both of form and character. Whatever, therefore, has a tendency to promote the disproportionate development of either of them, should be carefully avoided.

Each person is born with a particular temperament, which there is an inherent tendency to maintain and increase, since it gives rise to habits which exercise and develop it; but this tendency may be counteracted and changed entirely by external circumstances,—by education, occupation, superinduced habits, climate, etc.,—and more particularly by special training instituted for that purpose. George Combe, in one of his valuable works, points out the important changes produced in the temperament by a continued course of training. "It is common," he says, "for the bilious (motive) to be changed into the nervous (mental) temperament by habits of mental activity and close study; and on the other hand, we often see the nervous or bilious changed into the lymphatic (vital) about the age of forty, when the nutritive system seems to acquire the preponderance." Spurzhiem was accustomed to say that he had originally a large portion of the lymphatic temperament, as had all his family; but that in himself the lymphatic had gradually diminished, and the nervous increased; whereas, in his sisters, owing to mental inactivity, the reverse had happened, and when he visited them, after being absent many years, he found them, to use his own expression, "as large as tuns."[*]

---

[*] Hints toward Physical Perfection.

ON THE LAWS OF PHYSICAL CULTURE. 391

To cultivate or to restrain the temperaments according as they are deficient or in excess, is a matter of great importance, and, to assist our readers, I give here a few rules which, if persevered in, will accomplish the desired end and, other things being equal, lead to health and happiness.

If the vital temperament is found to be deficient, the first thing to be done is to strengthen all the organs of vitality. The lungs should receive daily exercise, by a special effort to expand them by breathing clear up full at every inspiration, and empty them well out at every expiration. This will aid also in the circulation of the blood, in the digestion of the food, banish sadness, and create a buoyancy which will make life a glorious holiday instead of a weary drudgery. "Away with melancholy." Avoid all gloomy associations. Alternate rest and sleep with exercise. You should watch and follow your intuition or instinct, and if you feel a special craving for any kind of food or pleasure, indulge it. Especially be regular in sleep, exercise, eating, and all the vital functions, as well as temperate in all things; and, above all, keep your mind toned up to sustain the body.

To restrain this temperament, practice rules opposite to those which are required to cultivate it. Those who manufacture vitality faster than they expend it are large in the abdomen; too corpulent, too sluggish, to expend vitality as fast as it accumulates, and hence should work—work early and late, and with all their might, and, as much as possible, with their muscles, and out of doors; should eat sparingly, and of simple food; avoid rich gravies, butter, sweets, fat, and pastry, but live much on fruits; sleep little; keep all the excretory organs free and open by a laxative diet, and especially the skin by frequent ablutions—the hot-bath, etc. Fleshy persons, especially females, never should give up to indolence, for this will end in disease and insanity,—never should lounge in a rocking-chair or in bed. "What is wanted," says an author, "is to do,—not to loiter around." Inertia is your bane, and action your cure.

To cultivate the motive temperament, take all the muscular exercise you can endure. Make yourself comfortably tired every day. Choose that kind of exercise most agreeable, but practice some kind assiduously. Dance more and sit less.

To restrain, use your muscles less, and brain more.

To cultivate a deficient mental development, it is well to exercise the mind more than the body; to read much; attend lectures, church, debating societies, commit to memory each day a verse or more, and cultivate the intellectual faculties by making daily observation, and trying to remember what is learned each day. Think over your experience, as thus you will strengthen the mind and create a balance between the mind and body.

Where an excessive mental development exists, to restrain it, exercise the body more than the mind.

In the study of the human temperaments, you must make

DAILY OBSERVATION

and learn something of every person with whom you

meet. After you have mastered the first part of this chapter, you will be enabled, by and by, to recognize any complication of the temperaments. All that is necessary, is to be able to define the predominating quality, or discern which of the different systems has the controling power, and you have a sure index to character. Of course a knowledge of the shape of the head and the physiognomical developments will help you to form a correct idea of the temperament. By the bodily conditions we can read character more correctly than by phrenological or physiognomical science alone.

I will now consider temperamental condition when variously compounded. It is a demonstrable fact that a good, well-balanced body is requisite to a correspondingly well-balanced mind. "The worst of souls is the better for being in the best of bodies," says St. Augustine. No one can cultivate the body otherwise than by the strict observance of the laws of physiology, and in this it is impossible to avoid moral impressions. No inference to the prejudice of moral order can be drawn from this, "because," says a writer, "the marked and regular development of the understanding almost inevitably carries with it an elevated moral character;" virtue and intelligence are vigorously synonymous. I believe the soul to live in all parts of the body. It is omnipresent, like the blood, the nervous system, the life, or matter itself.

That the mind operates through certain physical organs of the brain, and that there are as many diverse moral qualities as there are organs of the brain, is a physiological absurdity; though the mind is made up of many different faculties most utterly unlike. We may search among the protuberances of the skull for ages, and we are still ignorant of the wondrous working of the soul within. A general outline of the contour is the only reliable data from which we can derive a correct idea of the nature and character of the individual. The peculiarities common to certain temperamental conditions of an individual, have been determined by long observation, and have almost been reduced to a certain science. The mental temperament is perhaps the most desirable, other things being equal, which gives a

DELICATE SUSCEPTIBILITY

to vivid and strong impressions, rapidity of conception, retentive memory, capacity for profound attention, clear and sound judgment, bold and fertile imagination. These are the characteristics of a vast intellect; and such is, perhaps, the standard measure of a superior man.

THE PRINCIPAL NERVE CENTRES.

Now these traits, which compose the three fold capacity of feeling, knowing, and expressing, are allied with a highly susceptible, active, and energetic nervous system. A preponderance of this system may co-exist with a preponderance in the vascular, or any other organic apparatus, and in proportions infinitely varied in the scale of organic energy.

It is then in these constitutional differences that we must seek for the origin of moral inclinations, of talents and faculties, and not exclusively in this or that partial or isolated development of the brain; although the influence of this, among all the organs, is most direct upon the mind.

It is of great importance to study these constitutional differences early, if we would give to the moral and intellectual faculties a direction accordant with the aims of nature. A man of genius, who puts his heart and soul into what he creates, obeys unconsciously the impulse of organic tendencies; and in this sense he is always himself. "Let us not force our talent," said the Fabulist; and this principle of the purest taste is at the same time the exact expression of a physiologic truth.

These different constitutions are modified by age, habit, and disease. We observe a corresponding variation in the faculties of the mind, and the talents that spring from them. Life is short, but the life of talent is still more brief. As we have remarked, an author's age is recognized by the quality of the productions of his pen. Who does not understand what is meant by the "good time" of the artist? But this period of his life is more or less limited. It is not given to every one to say, as did Necker to Suard "How fine for literary labor is the age of seventy years!"

As it is beyond question that the predominance of the nervous element, with a greater or less diminution of the contractility, is the special characteristic of the temperament of celebrated men, it will not be amiss to consider its principal agents. The nervous system is one. It confines and interlocks the several parts of the corporeal organism in a vast net-work of sympathetic irradiations; yet, anatomically considered, it consists of several divisions. Physiologists agree in distinguishing at least two. The first, known under the name of ganglionic, nervous, or visceral apparatus, has its real seat in the viscera, and its centre in the epigastrium. The second is the cerebro-spinal apparatus. It is upon the nervous, visceral, or splanchnis apparatus that the excitations of the brain take effect. It first receives and transmits them to the viscera. In its turn it re-acts upon the brain by perceptions frequently dull and confused, but at times so vivid, energetic, and engrossing, as to involve that organ itself in the re-action. It is to this division of the nervous system that physiologists ancient and modern, with the exception of Gall, have assigned the instinctive impulses, the affections and spasms. Their doctrine has been: Man knows and judges through the brain : he hates or loves with the nervous visceral apparatus.

Whatever may be true of this opinion, in our day combated with more or less success, it is always true, on the one hand, that impressions made upon the brain pass with such rapidity to the viscera, that it is impossible to appreciate the time of the transition; and, on the other hand, that active stimuli and an extreme and sometimes morbid visceral sensibility have a direct and positive effect upon the brain, particularly when certain emotions of the soul are called out. To have "bowels of compassion" is not, then, a simple metaphorical expression; and when La Rochefoucauld said that the head is often the dupe of the heart, he stated a physical fact as well as a moral truth,—a truth all the more exact and profound, as it has its root in the physical organization itself.

The cerebro-spinal nervous apparatus consists of that mass which fills the whole cranium and extends through the vertebral canal. This is, in truth, the sole nervous centre. It animates and vivifies every portion of the body. It is everywhere present and active, by means of the forty-two pairs of nerves which issue from it. In it terminate all the impressions produced upon the extremities of the nerves in all their ramifications, and from it depart all the innumerable decisions that originate in the brain. Excited by the energy of the cerebral influx, the functions of the body are executed, and the organism lives and moves. Thence springs our health and disease, our pains and pleasures, our existence and our end.

Whoever gazes for the first time upon the brain, after the removal of the bony covering, can not but experience a lively emotion of surprise and admiration. Contemplate this magnificent ruin of the self, the residence of a varnished soul! behold this royal organ in which dwells the consciousness of existence, the mental man, the *me;*—a vessel a thousand times frailer than clay, and which yet holds the treasure of thought! In that soft, whitish, corruptible pulp, the combination of an hour, are found the empire and the asylum of reason, the work-shop in which human knowledge is stored and elaborated, and where immortal conceptions take shape! It is in the space comprised between the *crista galli* and the internal occipital crest—that is to say, within the compass of a few inches—that are conceived the ideas of God, infinity, and eternity! In truth, the brain, the real *siliqua mentis immortalis*—shell of the immortal mind, as says Van Helmont—forms the indispensable condition of intelligence. The tabernacle of the soul, in it alone is found the evident manifestation of the immortal being in the perishable. Sublime illustration of the nothingness and the greatness of man.

But after the first gush of emotion, we desire to know the structure of this marvelous instrument. We study with curiosity its two hemispheres so happily conjoined; its lobes, its prominences, its windings and circumvolutions; its cavities and ventricles; its varieties of color; the triple membranes that envelop it, press upon, and penetrate it, to protect and support it by nicely adjusted foldings. A mild and warm vapor, moreover, bathes these parts, softens them, and facilitates their action and play.

We must also notice the prodigious number of blood vessels, their admirable interlacement and their extreme divisibility, that every cerebral molecule may be fed with highly vitalized blood. Physiologists, indeed, have estimated that the brain received a sixth part of the blood of the body. But how is the delicate substance of this organ to resist the impetuous movement of this fluid? Everything has been foreseen. The arterial vessels exhibit curves and bends skillfully devised to break and diminish the projectile force of the blood; these arteries, moreover, are reduced to capillary vessels before penetrating the tissue of the brain. The veins from sinuses or venous reservoirs, which receive the excess of blood, and cause it to pass gradually into the main current of the circulation. In order to secure the noble functions of the brain, nature has multiplied her functions to such an extent, that nothing short of the wildest excess on the part of man can render them vain; hence, death or frightful maladies are the inevitable consequence of such excess.

The curiosity of the philosopher, however, far from being satisfied, is only stimulated the more. After the most minute anatomical inspection, he desires to penetrate still further. He would know the intimate structure of the cerebral pulp, and the function of every portion of the encephalon. He desires to know the scale of proportion between the modified form and substance of the brain and the variations of intelligence; to establish a plain, accurate, and measurable correlation between the organ and its functions, between the cause and its effects. He desires to know in what consists the movement that generates ideas; how is framed that material base of so little solidity; when thought, in its varied forms and with its vivid illuminations, arises; in fine, where the *me*, that point to which all conceptions converge, resides, and where thought having become flesh and soul in its powerful indivisibility awaits the action of the will alone, to manifest itself externally.

For three thousand years the solution of this great problem has been sought, but it is an equation containing so many unknown quantities that it seems forever insoluble to the human mind. All attempts toward its solution are only monuments of the weakness of our faculties. After having traveled the field of hypothesis in the wildest sense of that word, men have returned to the pure and simple observation of facts. Experimental physiology, in our day, has made incredible exertions to raise the veil. A few glimpses, and some uncertain gleams of light, with purely general results, have been thus far the reward of these protracted researches. We shall speak of them presently; but unless we hit upon new methods of investigation, and particularly obtain instruments more perfect than those we now possess, men of science will never be able to pass the limits of the possible and the known; and yet the science of man depends entirely upon a perfect knowledge of the brain, at least if we are to make a true study of man and not invent him. As long as this important secret shall be withheld from us, the human being, except in some respects, will remain for us an insoluble problem. Shall we some day penetrate this profound mystery of our organization? who knows? Time, chance, genius—are they not omnipotent? By the aid of this threefold lever do we not wrest some secrets from nature?—we who appear condemned to the eternal necessity of seeking truth and to a like incapacity to discover it.

THE ADVANTAGES OF THE TEMPERAMENT IN WHICH THE NERVOUS SYSTEM PREDOMINATES.

There are physicians who, viewing the question

only in one aspect, observe in the temperament under consideration the liability to danger and disease which is inherent in it. Others, on the contrary, have been struck with its advantages merely. They have carried their respective views indeed to paradoxical extremes.

The error of both parties appears to be plain. Let us, then, endeavor to distinguish between the good and the bad, which are almost always mingled; to discover the truth as it is ordinarily to be found, by observing a strict impartiality.

A lofty stature; a vast, bony frame, clothed with compact and rugged masses of muscle; an ample chest; brawny shoulders; the arms of a Hercules,—all may be the attributes of physical strength, but they furnish no guaranty for inviolable health. Such an organism only demonstrates that the muscular system is highly developed,—that contractility predominates. But what is the indispensable condition for preserving health and prolonging life? It is this: a perfect harmony of the functions, a just equilibrium of the vital forces, a precise and duly proportioned balance between the several organic acts; but these conditions are not always to be found in bodies of athletic mould. Nature, in the robust man, always triumphs by energy of movement; but if an obstacle intervene which he can not surmount, this energy becomes the enemy of its possessor. The constitutional intensity of the vital forces, then, should be estimated by their regularity and by their mutual balance; never by their excess.

If extreme sensibility predisposes to a multitude of

pathological affections, the contractile energy out of proportion to the other functions, will exhibit the same results. Exuberant health is ever on the verge of its own decline. Too much blood, too much flesh, too much life, is an inevitable source of disease. Celsus, in speaking of the athletæ, observes that bodies so plethoric as theirs are exposed to sudden attacks of disease and speedily grow old. But be the reason what it may, these bodies, so vigorous in appearance, possess an energy in some sort merely deceptive. Real strength is lacking in them, that which originates in the nervous principle.

Moreover, one of two things will happen; either the man of physical vigor is indolent—in which case, neglecting to exercise his body, a plethoric condition supervenes, and disease is always imminent —or, as it often happens, trusting imprudently to his strength which has so many times proved reliable, he runs into excesses which, sooner or later, have the same issue. If the disease be slight, the equilibrium is speedily restored; but the morbific cause may resist the effort to dislodge it, and then the violence and impetuosity of the organic movements are so great that art and nature are powerless; the malady grows worse, the physical derangements become irreparable, the gravity of the symptoms rapidly augments, the storm bursts, and the proud oak, torn up by the roots, is cast upon the ground.

The man of letters, the savant and the artist, but too often of frail and feeble constitutions, are not readily seduced into excesses: they husband their health, so easily impaired by the least mishap. Reflective, continent, and reserved, they act with prudence and circumspection, at least when they know how to lay down rules for the conduct of life. Moreover, the sensibility with which they are so liberally endowed by nature preserves them from innumerable perils. Excited at every moment, it rapidly makes the round of all organs, warns them of the slightest shock, of the least accident injurious to their delicate mechanism. A vigilant sentinel, it suffers no cause of destruction to take root in the system, as it is easily aroused in every organ that maintains a contest with disease; from the very fact that the constitution is weak, advances with less intensity or more tardiness; the patient and the physician have time to concert measures to combat it; in fine, accidents with them are less rapid in their tendencies to fatal issues, the struggle with them less intense—*the reed bends but does not break.*

Thus we may consider it certain that individuals endowed with a nervous temperament, attended with a diminution of the contractility, as is the case with most thinkers, are generally little liable to severe diseases if they listen to the will of nature. If they pass the bounds of moderation, they are soon brought back through the very weakness of their organs. Wisdom here has its source in physical necessity, but we must admit that temperament is that form and shape to practical philosophy.

Moreover, temperance in the scientific man, and in the artist who has reflected on his own nature, is a virtue which costs little and produces a great deal. This happy inability of his to deviate from the laws of hygiene is the source of his happiness—often, indeed, of his glory, because in consequence of it he is able to devote himself to the labors which secure glory. Let us add that the more one has cultivated his mind, the less does he seek to be a man merely in and by his physical organs. Yes, whatever may be said, the cultivation of the intellect simplifies our wants, diminishes the greediness for gain, and deprives material wealth of a part of its importance. Doubtless a man of a delicate, nervous, and extremely sensitive temperament should study himself, attend to his style of living, and strive to ascertain to what extent it is permitted to satisfy his desires; but he at least enjoys the absence of ill, if not very exquisite pleasures; he keeps the counters constantly in his hand. No person more than he is conscious of the value of health, which disposes him to make the utmost possible sacrifice to preserve it. Is he not every hour and moment rewarded? Does he not know that the future is the fruit of the present? He neglects, then, no attention, no care or precaution, to attain his end. To him who would censure his conduct, this is his reply: "Nature has refused me the strength to resist the cause of disease. I supply this want by my prudence. I was born feeble, and yet I live; moreover I live almost exempt from the ills of the flesh, and with some chances of longevity." Indeed, in some men of weak constitutions there is an amazing tenacity of life; but the reason of this is found when we perceive with what art they sustain the struggle against the agents destructive of life.

If we now compare the chances of the delicate constitution when suffering from disease with those of the robust and muscular we shall see that the advantage is often with the former. Whilst nature, in the weak constitution, as I have said, does not hurry forward the different stages of the malady and its inevitable shocks,—such a constitution bends to it readily. It waits and hopes; and the benign influence of this mood rarely fails to make itself felt, and even if the malady be obstinate, it can make terms with it. It consents to give it right of domicil, and makes over to it, so to speak, its share of tyranny, on condition of keeping some share of freedom for itself; and often ends by nullifying and subduing it by a diet of care and patience. Valetudinarians and creatures, particularly women, furnish to physicians frequent illustrations of the truth of this remark. Certain literary characters, of frail and sickly habits, have likewise verified it. Such a one has nothing to envy other mortals. His life has enchantments of its own, notwithstanding the vigor of nature and the illusions of fortune. They are happy through the very circumstance which ordinarily renders existence a burden—the possession of a feeble constitution. In the first place, this organization enjoys an indescribable pleasure unknown to others. Then the very toils of thought contribute greatly to this kind of felicity, which consists in enjoying the present, and even the homage of posterity in advance. The hope that bronze shall perpetuate his memory, that he shall leave behind him a name and a few truths to be delivered down from age to age, certainly gives to life a peculiar charm. The presentiment of glory is already a draft on the happiness which it promises, and so far, at least, that happiness is sure. There is a deep inward delight in creating, in thinking, in imagining, and meditating, of which the vulgar have no conception. The slightest difficulties overcome in these labors enhance enjoyment.

One can not conceive why Madame de Stael should have called glory the "glittering mourning garb of happiness." This assertion is, at least, too general. No! this dream of immortality which enables us here below to suffer and to die is not always the enemy of our peace. We should look at it philosophically, that is, estimate it at what it is worth, neither make too much nor too little of it. And even considering glory in relation to health, which is our particular object, we should be deceived were we to suppose the latter always compromised by the pursuit of the former. There is in the man who desires or possesses an honorable celebrity an active principle, which animates and sustains the vital force, enabling its possessor to live, and to live well. That self-satisfaction which one experiences in the conception of the noble and beautiful is not without its value as regards health. A good work that meets with success infuses balm into the blood. For proof, refer to the artists and most renowned poets. Furthermore, the energetic and manly exercise of the mental faculties, when we do not force nature,—let me be clearly understood,—would alone suffice to impress upon the system an activity advantageous to health. When this is preserved, who can doubt that the feeling of comfort that always attends health in its turn reacts beneficially on the imagination,—the chief source of our happiness and of our misfortunes? Celebrity is not always that which profound thinkers most want; they often need in retirement a work to which, in order to enjoy their repose, they can confide the thoughts that oppress them; for the brain is not always the master of these that are ripe for utterance. It is known that Metastasis was early in life attacked with a serious nervous disease, and that he lived to the age of eighty. Palipot, who was quite feeble in his childhood and youth, received the degree of Master of Arts at twelve, and of Bachelor of Theology at sixteen. At nineteen he was married, and became the father of a family, and the author of two tragedies; and at eighty, in spite of a very agitated life, his health was still sound and his mind full of vigor. In our day, have we not seen Andrieux, a man of letters, by care protect his days, notwithstanding his miserable health? Be this as it may, the thinker in infirm health in some measure adapts himself to his ills, and grows familiar with them. He and his maladies are wont to keep up a long acquaintance. The case is otherwise with the man of vigorous health. Disease always takes him by surprise, being a stranger who terrifies him; for it is with good health as with long-continued prosperity,—we feel all the more deeply the misfortune of losing it, in proportion to the length of time we have enjoyed it. The man in whom the animal predominates, who is consequently healthy and robust, feels extreme confidence in the strength of his constitution. He entertains an exaggerated estimate of it, accustomed as he is to look upon himself as the spoiled child of nature. But no sooner is he stricken down by sickness than he is overcome by amazement,—is indignant that it should dare to assail *him*. His moral strength fails entirely, and hence the origin of the ancient simile: "as foolish as a sick athlete." Indeed, if the malady be obstinate, gloomy reflections succeed. This robust man thinks that the cause of the evil is unquestionably extremely violent, since it has succeeded in prostrating him; that art can be of no avail, as the attack has been so severe and overwhelming. Thence come discouragement, a yielding to melancholy, a prostration of strength, so prejudicial to the restoration of the natural play of the functions. The daily practice of physicians attests the truth of the assertion.

Thus, even as regards health, sickness, and longevity, many chances are in favor of the constitution in which the nervous element predominates—that of artists and men of letters. Meanwhile we should be careful not to consider these disadvantages as first in importance. There are others, immense and incontestible, which are equal, the result of this constitution: they are those of thought. If the mind is the real man; if through the intellect man is severed from the merely animal kingdom; if the physical life is of little value in itself, and the sphere of existence is measured by the moral sphere,—beyond contradiction, it is to the development of the nervous system that we owe this prerogative; but when this boon is conferred in its perfection, is it then a gift to be despised?

Every individual endowed with a gross physical organization has necessarily a limited intellect. It might be said that the very vigor of its impelling forces is incompatible with delicacy and refinement in those forces. Such an one is a slave, and born to obey. Let him not find fault with nature. Frequently, on the contrary, in a frail and wasted body, whence life seems ready to exhale every instant, there is observed an energetic organic apparatus which endows its possessor with a refinement of the mora nature, and in this very circumstance gives him a superiority which it is vain to contest. He who has the light, and the mission to enlighten and guide mankind; he whose thought rises beyond the range of vulgar conceptions; who rouses the world by his opinions, and constrains it to yield attention; who has the ability to charm away our dejection, lift us above ourselves, and dissipate the power they possess of easing themselves of the burden—he is to give utterance to them in language. After expression has been given them, the repose and calm of the system is restored. "Were it not for mental exercise," says Byron, "I should have already sunk under the weight of my imagination and of reality." We must remember, also, that with others the discovery of that which *is*, is sufficient for their happiness. Did not the illustrious Bennet maintain that the felicity of the future life would consist solely in knowing? "If I were to conceive of a nature consisting of pure mind," says Bossuet, "it seems to me that I should give it only the attributes of understanding and loving the truth; and that alone would render it happy."

Even supposing there is a lack of that restless, bold, and persevering genius, which agonizes while it produces, is not the love of study a happy privilege bestowed upon this organization? It is an error to assert that the age is entirely utilitarian; that physical industrialism rules foremost in our day. How many are there who still devote their lives to science, art, and poetry? How many take refuge in philosophy through their extreme desire for peace of soul, or flee to science through their insatiable craving for knowledge? The delicious fragrance of the honey of the muses attracts them, and confines them in peaceful seclusion. Whether it be contempt of glory, which costs so much time to those who confer and those who attain it, or whether that interior charm, that mastery over one's self, inseparable from studious pursuits, has seduced them, they soon forget the world, its errors and its social inequalities—so absurd and so revolting. Everything interests in the grand system of nature. Here the most vigorous truths still excel in attracting the most agreeable illusions. The most lowly flower, a grain of sand, the winding streamlet, the spider's webb, the buzzing insect, a raindrop on the wing of a bird, possess their scientific interest and their poetic ideality. It is often in the study of minute objects that a vigorous and penetrating mind soars toward that world of ideas which things represent. Everything depends upon the vision exerted, and upon the mind that studies. Here are innumerable pleasures for him who has the skill to find them.

APPENDIX I.

HANGING AS A MEANS OF GRACE

Eloquent Discourse by W. H. Ryder, D. D.

DOES HANGING QUALIFY A MURDERER FOR HEAVEN?

If it is a Means of Grace, the More of it the Better.

How the Condemned should be Treated.

THE MATERIAL IDEA OF HEAVEN AND HELL.

By special permit, we here publish a practical and sensible sermon preached by the eminent Rev. Dr. Ryder, on the subject of Capital Punishment, which will be read with great interest, and is in strong support of the principles set forth in this volume. The discourse, which is given in full, was preached March 30th, and phonographically reported by the Chicago *Tribune:*

BIBLE TEXT.

Whither shall I go from thy spirit? or whither shall I flee from thy presence? If I ascend up into heaven, thou art there. If I make my bed in hell, behold thou art there. If I take the wings of the morning, and dwell in the uttermost parts of the sea, even there shall thy hand lead me, and thy right hand shall hold me. 139 Psalm; 7, 8, 9, 10.

THE SERMON.

One is surely acting in harmony with the spirit of the gospel when he interests himself in the welfare of the criminal classes. No man can be so low as to be entirely shut out from human sympathy. It matters not of what offense against the law one may be guilty, he is to be treated as a human being, and to be subjected to no needless torture. God's mercy is extended to the vilest; His grace is free to all. So should man's sympathy be; and we ought all to be actuated by a desire to do the worst of our race as much good as we conveniently can. I do not hold, therefore, that a man should be suffered to go to the gallows, as if by the act of murder he had shut himself out from all human regard.

By common consent, the civilization of our time has pronounced against many of the forms of torture formerly employed to deprive one of his life,—such as quartering a man, burning him in the use of green wood, pouring heated lead and oil into his ears and eyes. All such instruments of death are utterly set aside as inhuman, and, even when we employ hanging, we demand of the sheriff that he shall apply that penalty without needless torture. This much I say on the side of humanity.

And I think, also, that one is acting in the name of religion who seeks to offer to the culprit the benefits of religion, and, as far as possible, bring him into a proper temper to enter the eternal world. Far be it from me to condemn the efforts of clergymen in this behalf. I commend them for it. But this sympathy which is offered to the criminals, especially those of a particular class, may be injudiciously expressed, and so harmful to the public morals; as may be also the efforts to promote the spiritual welfare of the criminal, and so injurious to the cause of religion. Under the former head I place all attempts to pardon criminals out of regard for them or for their families, or on the ground that the penalty is severe. I condemn all such interposition in behalf of criminals as that employed by Dr. Tyng, of New York, in the case of Foster. It is no matter whether Foster went to Dr. Tyng's church or not. It is no matter whether he belonged to a respectable family or not. It is not at all pertinent to the case that his family were the friends of the pastor, and the pastor wished to be the friend of the family. The simple fact in the case is that the man Foster was notoriously guilty of murder, and, being so, deserved the penalty of the law. It is mistaken compassion and mistaken sympathy that leads a clergyman to try to save from the gallows a man clearly guilty of murder, who may happen to belong to a family in whose welfare he is interested. On the other hand, we are not to seek to save one from the just condemnation of the law, because, in our judgment, the penalty of the law is needlessly severe. Because some of you may believe that imprisonment for life is a proper penalty for murder, and not hanging, you are not therefore to oppose the execution of the law so long as hanging is the penalty; but rather remember that your judgment with regard to what ought to be the penalty is not to interfere with the just execution of the law, so long as hanging is the penalty. The like is true in the case of a recent murderer in this city; and in the case of almost every murderer there is an earnest effort made to save the man from his just deserts. Petitions are signed; benevolent Christian men and women, well-disposed, sign the papers. I think all such attempts, unless there is some reason for it outside of sympathy, outside of one's objection to the death penalty, outside of the fact that it is a terrible thing to take a man's life in that way, are hurtful to the public morals, and ought not to be encouraged. This injudicious attempt to get murderers pardoned is rightly quoted, I see, latterly, in favor of capital punishment; and I am frank to say that unless you regulate the pardoning power, hanging seems to be the only sure penalty,—and that is not very sure,—not because as some of our preachers say God said to Noah, "Whosoever sheddeth man's blood, by man shall his blood be shed," but because the safety of society requires it. God also said to Noah (and he said it before he said the other; in the record it stands two or three verses before), "But flesh with the life thereof, which is the blood thereof, shall ye not eat." But as most persons, including clergymen, consider animal food necessary to the health, they leave this command to Noah unenforced. But one is just as authoritative as the other, and neither has any more to do with our time than a communication that may have been made to the antediluvians.

Personally, I prefer, if I could have everything as I would wish it, imprisonment for life to the death penalty. But, if a man condemned for murder is to be pardoned and set at liberty in the community again, whatever may be my personal preference, I am obliged to place myself on the side of those who defend capital punishment. The dignity and majesty of the law must be maintained. That is a fundamental proposition. No matter what I may like or dislike, the law must be upheld, for we are all of us dependent upon the enforcement of law, and nothing is reliable unless the criminal classes are made to understand that the law means what it says, and must be respected. The penalties of law should not, therefore, be set aside to please an individual, for the welfare of millions should never be jeopardized to gratify a few. I, and the persons of my household, and the members of my church, may wish to save some one from the gallows, but shall I and they be gratified to the detriment of the whole community?

The exercise of the pardoning power in some cases seems necessary; but, after the courts have pronounced against a criminal the penalty of death, it ought not to be competent for the governor to set aside the verdict, unless facts which are developed subsequent to the trial justify it. The criminal, as a criminal, deserves no sympathy; pity, but not sympathy. The wrong-doer has a claim upon our humanity, but not the wrong-doing. And I am satisfied that sometimes sympathy is exercised in this connection so indiscriminately that it really aids and abets crime.

But this leads me to the next topic—the injudicious application of religion to the criminal. It is not for me, Christian friends, to limit the divine mercy. That forgiveness in any way lessens or removes the punishment, I do not stand here to say; but it is clear that, in the providence of God, forgiveness is mainly applied to the sin rather than to the punishment, and that Christ did not come into this world so much to take away punishment due to mankind for their sins as he did to take away the sinfulness of man. And it is also clear that the only effect of such gallow's spectacles as we have had of late in this city and in other cities is to lessen the enormity of sinfulness and to take away something of the sanctity of religion. The more I think about these things the more they distress me,—the more I am satisfied that, as the case now stands, the criminal classes are not affected favorably by these hanging spectacles.

I want first of all, now to call your attention briefly, and yet with due respect to those from whom I differ theologically, to the theological errors involved in all this. About every man who has been hung within my remembrance, has been, subsequent to the commission of the crime, and ordinarily a day or two days before, made ready for the eternal world; and the announcement has been given through the press, and frequently by the criminal himself when he stands upon the very verge of eternity—"I have made my peace with God; I am on the Lord's side; I am going straight to Heaven." I do not say these men are not sincere, but I say, when a clergyman takes hold of a case of that kind he has a case to make out; and when a man is taken hold of, it seems to be for his interest to yield to the appeal. That there is any deception practised in the case, of course I say nothing about, one way or the other; but it looks so much like a business transaction that, if applied to anything *but* religion, I should call it a "sham." To me it is psychologically impossible for a man who has been sinful, corrupt, wicked all his life, an hour, or two hours, or a day, or two days before he dies, to be made ready to enter the eternal world and to rise up into grandeur and perfectness of a saintly man. I concede that the *worst* criminal may repent, and be sincere in his repentance; I consider that the last moment before he goes out of the world he may ejaculate those sentences which it is pleasant for us to hear; but to carry the idea to the community that a man, by anything done for him, or by him, in that short time, takes rank with the angels in glory, is to me not only absurd, but to my mind, is making little less than a mockery of religion. Let me relate to you a brief incident. A brother, who has been at my house during the past week, told me of the following circumstance that came within his own personal observation. In the city where he preaches, a good man, while in the performance of his ordinary business, was shot and instantly killed. He was not the person the murderer intended to kill, but was mistaken for the individual the murderer wanted to dispose of. The murdered man attended the Universalist Church, and was a correct and exemplary person of good standing in the community. My friend, after the murderer had had his trial and been condemned, a day or two before his execution, called upon him in his cell. He asked him how he felt with regard to the fate before him, and he said, "I am all right. I have made my peace with God. I am all ready to die. I expect to be in heaven in forty-eight hours." "Well," said the clergyman, "what do you think is the condition of the man you killed?" Said he, "That bothers me a good deal. I have been thinking about that since I was converted; how it will seem for me when I get to heaven, to look down upon him in hell?" "What makes you think he is in hell?" "Why, because I shot him so quickly he hadn't a chance to repent. Just as quick as the pistol went off he fell, and couldn't think about it."

Here you have emotional piety set over against solid character. You all know which is the higher; you all know which society rests on; you all know which is best in your sons, in your daughters, in business men, in citizens generally,—a wild impulse of religion or solid morality ingrained into the very fibre of one's manhood. And yet emotional piety takes a man to heaven (and so little of it that I think it is mostly froth), and solid character lets him down the other way. Now, mark you, I recommend and plead for emotional piety. Better that a man should show a religious interest, as did Nicodemus at the burial of his Lord, than not at all. Better for the wayward son to say, the last hour before he dies, "Father, I renounce this wicked living of mine; I ask your pardon for the wrong done." There is comfort in that; but when you come to say that the prodigal son deserves more at the hands of his God than the son who had lived faithfully, and nobly, and generously all the while, you utterly pervert the New Testament. In the parable of the Prodigal Son, the father shows his gratitude by many expressive acts that the wayward son has come home, but do you think he put that son in his affection and confidence above that other son who had remained faithfully by him and been dutiful all the while?

Furthermore, such spectacles as I am considering, as educational influences, are mischievous. As if a man should say, "Well, now, if I murder another I shall probably be hung. So far as human law is concerned, I shall have to suffer the penalty, but so far as the divine law is concerned, I know how to get rid of that. I can manage that part. I can live forty and nine years in sin, and wipe away the consequences, but I can not do anything against man's law without, in all probability, being arrested. These detectives are so terribly searching in their inquiries that it is pretty hard to get rid of them; but so far as God is concerned, I know how to elude his law, and shirk the penalty of it. I am not troubled about that." Now, I contend that everything of that kind is demoralizing. It is not giving a man his deserts. I maintain that the conviction ought to rest upon your heart and mine, that, if we go through the world in opposition to God, he will hold us answerable for those things, not only while we live, but after we pass out of this body as well; and that the character ingrained into the human organization can not be wiped out by any ejaculatory sentences uttered at any time.

I am reminded here of what Jesus said to the thief on the cross. It seems, in the judgment of many, to stand in opposition to what I am teaching. In reference to what our Lord said to the man who was crucified by his side, there are two facts to be stated:

FIRST—It is confessedly difficult to determine how much the robber understood about the mission of Christ. For it hardly seems probable that he understood that Christ had set up a spiritual kingdom when his disciples supposed he was setting up a material kingdom. If the Apostles, when they found our Lord was crucified, supposing his work had come to an end, went their way, it is not likely that this criminal understood much about Christ's spiritual kingdom.

SECOND—Precisely what is meant by the word "Paradise" is not clear, and perhaps never can be now. Some individuals say it means "state of the dead," as if our Lord meant to say, "You ask me to remember you when I come into my kingdom. Why this day both of us are to be in the state of the dead, and, therefore, what can you expect in my kingdom?" Others understand it to include something more than the state of the dead—to include what the Greeks meant by the word Elysium. In view of all the facts, it seems to me that our Lord referred to the spiritual world into which they were both soon to pass, and that he meant in some way to speak approvingly of the condition of the penitent thief in connection with that reference. But, as already said, the precise meaning it is difficult to affirm. There is, however, no reason to suppose that our Lord meant to say, "This day you will be a perfect human being; this day you will be an angel of light; or this day you will be with me in heaven;" because that is contradictory of what our Lord says subsequently. For after his resurrection, when Mary met him in the garden, near the tomb in which his body had been placed, as recorded in the 17th verse of the 20th chapter of John, we are told that Jesus said to Mary, when she addressed him: "Touch me not, for I am not yet ascended to my Father." This was the third day after the crucifixion. Jesus, therefore, could not have meant that the repentant robber would be that day with him in heaven, because what our Lord afterwards says of himself shows that he himself had not been there. His reference probably was to the spiritual realm.

I do not wish, Christian friends, in what I say in opposition to the material conception with which this whole subject is shrouded, to discourage any individual, in connection with any church, from laboring earnestly in behalf of the conversion and restoration of the criminal classes, but I beg that they so conduct their affairs that their efforts shall not be detrimental to the cause of religion, and so that these gallows speeches, in the estimation of many right-minded and law-observing citizens, shall not seem a burlesque on religion. For, if the gallows can thus be made a means of grace; if almost every one who goes out of the world by hanging goes straight to glory, and would hardly get there but by that process, it might be well for us to consider whether it would not be useful to employ hanging as a means of grace on very many other occasions. I do not know but it would be well to apply it to some of our aldermen and members of the Board of Trade, and directors of insurance companies, and congressmen; and now and then a minister, and a merchant, and so on all the way through, thus making their salvation sure. If a bad man commits a murder the matter of his future destiny seems to be quite sure. Oh! brethren, this is not the Gospel. Christ in his word does not talk to the human heart in that way. It is the old material conception of things, that has come down into the age, and still lingers among the people. In many of our leading churches, or what we call orthodox, to-day, there are taught the most excellent, valuable spiritual doctrines, and the religion of the New Testament is interpreted in the light of the age, but among the common people that old, material idea of heaven as a locality, and of hell as a locality and place of torment, and, for aught I know, of liquid fire and brimstone, still lingers. Some of you remember that a fortnight ago to-day I referred to this general subject. At the close of my sermon, there came up to this desk a young man, and he said to me, "I am not accustomed to hearing Universalist preaching, so I would like to ask you a question." "Talk on, my young friend," said I. "There are only two places spoken of in the Bible after death into which the dead go; one is heaven and the other is hell. Now, if the murderer don't go to heaven, must he not go to the other place?" That seems logical, does it not? What is the root error? It is that there is no *place* in the universe that deserves to be called heaven; and there is no *place* in the universe that deserves to be called hell. Heaven is a *state* and a condition; hell is a *state* and a condition, and no place at all. It is the old material conception of a beautiful garden, with running streams, or a great city with golden streets fixed up grandly, and people are going up there, and they are going to knock at the gates, and the gates are to be opened, and they are to walk in and live in fine houses. That is the idea still prevailing with the less intelligent portion of our community. The right view is, the good man is in heaven to-day, and all the heaven there is for him, of which we have any knowledge. The bad man is in hell to-day, and he will be in hell so long as he remains a bad man. Heaven is a state. And good men, truth-seeking and God-fearing people, are in that state. They are known by many names, and live in many lands, but they are united by a common bond in their devotion to the good and true. Put away, therefore, this idea of locality, and remember that heaven is a condition—a state, not a locality, as if men and women are to be separated from each other by a sort of isothermal line, as if on one side is Illinois and on the other is Minnesota; as if a kind of Mississippi River is to separate heaven from hell. It is the old Jewish conception of the end of the world that has worked its way down to our time, and the old pagan conception corrupted, even by grosser, nominally, Christian ideas. It is time the religion of Christ were free of these errors.

"And now, Christian friends, all that remains for me to say this morning is that the language of our text is applicable to us all— to the criminal classes, to all conditions and phases of society. "Whither shall I go from thy spirit? or whither shall I flee from thy presence? If I ascend up into heaven, God is there; if I make my bed in hell, behold, God is there. If I take the wings of the morning, and dwell in the uttermost parts of the sea, even there shall thy hand lead me, and thy right hand shall hold me." God is everywhere present. We are judged according to our deserts. Character is that which we all ought to strive to obtain. It is our privilege to enjoy what I have called emotional piety; but it is a great deal more important for us to have substantial character than to put, now and then, a religious interjection into our talk. I commend these interjections; I believe in these pious, religious services. Those who know me need scarcely be told this; but I beg you not to suppose that God can be deceived by these pious phrases. I beg you not to think that a man can live forty years in iniquity, and throw off his bad character as he would an old coat. Character is a part of the man. Wherever the man goes the character goes. As long as a man lives, his identity and character live. Changing day by day, becoming better as he rises higher, but always under the eye of God, and always rewarding him and punishing him according to his deserts. Young man, be not deceived by the idea that, in any manner or way, God can be "mocked." God's verdict can not be set aside. I tell you that if you go into the ocean, God is there; if you go to California or Europe, God is there: in the light, in the darkness, wherever you are, the judgment seat is before you and you before it.

And now, brethren and friends, I would like, in a very few words, to put by the side of this representation as to the manner in which culprits are often treated and regarded, my own idea of what is sound doctrine. If I were called to administer to a man who was to be hung to-morrow, I would not say to him, "If you repent of your sins and are sorry, the consequences of all your guilt will be wiped away, and you stand abreast with the most valiant soldier of the cross of Christ." I could not say that, because it is a misrepresentation and a great untruth. I would say to him, "My brother, I am sorry for you; you are in a bad condition; you are scarred all over with sin, but God is your father and friend. He sent his Son to die for sinners. Put yourself in the best frame of mind you can; begin to retrace your steps; walk toward Zion the few day that remain, and every step you take this side of the grave is so much ground re-won, and you are all the better prepared to go home." That, I think, is Christian morality; and as I would say it to the worst culprit, so I would say it to myself and to you. "Be not deceived; God is not mocked. For whatever a man soweth that shall he also reap." This, I believe, is the teaching of the New Testament, and is illustrated and verified by every sound maxim in moral philosophy.

APPENDIX II.

TO HANG OR NOT TO HANG.

We copy the following from the *Christian Union*, to show that the abolition of the death penalty is fast becoming the sentiment of the people:

The fairest morning of this spring was made horrible to a whole city by the black shadow of the gallows which stretched across it and seemed to put out the sunshine. All imaginations turned to the prison-yard, seeing a pallid, shuddering wretch snatch one hungry, hopeless look at the brilliant day, then hide his face with his shaking hand, while the sheriffs shortened the ceremonies of the dreadful waiting lest he should die of fear on the very drop, and so affront the majesty of the law. It was the anticipated horror of that spectacle which roused much of the morbid sympathy with Foster. It is the sickening remembrance of it which will withhold future juries from convicting. A juror, solemnized by his oath, moved too often to pity by the black-robed, woeful presence of the prisoner's wife or mother or child, touched by the appeals of cunning counsel, cannot be made to remember that he is to pronounce upon the evidence regardless of the penal consequences it may entail. In effect, he becomes the judge, and he will not condemn a fellow-man to death save in phenomenal instances.

If it can be proven that the gallows represses murder, then press and pulpit must unite to overcome this sentimental weakness in the community. If, on the other hand, it is shown that the fear of the gibbet does not restrain the homicidal mind, then public opinion must be aroused to demand its abolition. For society can punish only for the well-being of society. Any other notion of the functions of penal law is simple barbarism.

In the city of New York alone there have occurred one hundred and forty-one known murders within three years. There have also occurred precisely two executions. It is estimated that one-half of the doers of murder escape arrest, and that four-fifths of the captive moiety escape conviction. There are now in the tombs fifteen murderers of ascertained guilt, with several more whose crime is not yet proven. All of these fifteen expect to escape punishment through a disagreement of the jury or through technicalities of law. Their hope is doubtless well founded. It seems clear that if the death-rate is to be two in one hundred and forty-one, the scaffold is a lax and careless guardian of public safety.

In Massachusetts, perhaps the most law-abiding of the states, there are fifty-one homicides in the Charlestown prison, twenty-two of them being under life-sentence. Within the last nineteen years Massachusetts has permitted herself, we think, twelve executions, the result being that the ratio of murders has increased faster than that of population. In 1865, sixteen persons were committed for murder and twelve for manslaughter. In 1872, several executions having intervened, thirty-eight commitments for murder and twenty-two for manslaughter were recorded, the number having doubled in the seven years. Of these, four men were convicted of murder and eleven of manslaughter; three times as many as in 1865. If it be said that, had these men suffered hanging instead of imprisonment, lawless violence would have been checked, it may be answered that it was the opinion of the closest legal observers that Alley really gained his acquittal because McElhaney lay under sentence of imminent death in the jail close at hand. The jury could not forget that threatening scaffold.

Rhode Island, next neighbor to Massachusetts, decided, twenty years ago, that the death-penalty was a mistake, and changed the punishment for murder to imprisonment for life. Her governors, state officers, supreme judges, and prison wardens agree that life is made safer thereby. Her chief justice testifies that he opposed the passage of the act, but adds that "conviction for murder is far more certain now, in proper cases, than when death was the punishment for it." The warden of the State Prison testified in 1868: "The crime of murder has not been more frequent since the abolition of the death-penalty. On the contrary, considering the increase of population, it has diminished."

It is twenty-seven years since Michigan abrogated capital punishment. During the first thirteen years thereafter there were thirty convictions for murder in a population of six hundred thousand. In the fourteen years next succeeding, there were but twenty-six convictions in a population of nine hundred thousand.

Wisconsin gave up the gallows in 1853. In his recent report Governor Washburne says: "There can be no doubt that the change in the law has rendered punishment more certain," but for which change, "at least one-half of those heretofore convicted would have escaped all punisnment, so difficult is conviction where the penalty is death. From 1848 to 1853, I have no knowledge of more than one person having suffered the extreme penalty of the law. This was not because of lack of offenses, but of the extreme difficulty of conviction." Other competent testimony declares the old law to have been practically a nullity in Wisconsin for ten years before its abolition.

Maine, while recognizing capital punishment, forbids its infliction for one year after conviction, and then empowers the governor to order the murderer to execution or to detain him in prison, as the well-being of the State seems to demand. The result is that there have been but two executions in forty years, while conviction is nearly certain. The law of Vermont and that of Kansas are similar, and show like results. Iowa abolished hanging last spring, and, of course, no relative statistics yet justify or condemn the innovation. Indiana, Minnesota, and Illinois already begin to consider the expediency of like action.

We have purposely ignored consideration of the criminal and the Scriptural plea for the death-penalty. The remorseless fact is that murders multiply and that convictions decrease. The instant need is the protection of society. A law that cannot be enforced provokes lawlessness. Not only common-sense but public safety demands its repeal. If the punishment of murder were imprisonment for life; if the pardoning power were vested only in a high court of pardons, and hedged about with difficult conditions; if no new trial could be granted on technicalities, but only upon new and vital evidence tending to acquittal, who doubts that half the murders of the past three years would have been left undone? The penalties that God affixes to outraged law are not vengeful nor bloody. They are logical, swift, awful through their certainty. When our human legislation shall discriminate between certain penalty and fitful punishment, murder will not walk abroad unhindered in our streets, nor fools make a mock at sin.

APPENDIX III.

PAUPERISM AND COMPULSORY EDUCATION.

[From the National Independent of Philadelphia, Pa.]

"And if it were done, what pleasure shall the compelled party have of the compellor, or what trust can the compellor have of the compelled."—*Life of Sir T. Smith.*

The subject of compulsory education is again agitated in the board of education, of our public schools. An act of the legislature making it universal without provision made for a class, or classes, whose associations, antecedents, and habits are diametrically opposite to those who now enjoy the benefit of our public schools, would not only be improper, but highly injurious.

Compulsion here would be to strike at the moral root of our public schools, and at once sap the foundation of their purity and usefulness. Such a law would be wrong in principle, impolitic; and one to which the people would not willingly submit. The parents of those children for whom the law more particularly applies, are, or at least many of them, paupers, incapable of supplying their families with the common necessaries of life, but relying in a great measure on their children for support. Our city is filled with a vast number of this class, for whose moral training there is no one responsible. Is it not, therefore, the great duty of the city to take charge of them, provide for and educate them without the consent of their drunken, disreputable parents? Keep them away from the influences which are gradually preparing them for crime, and if a parent should resist these tendencies of the law, place him in the house of correction, for his reform is just as essential as is that of his children. If something of this kind is not done for this class, they will grow up as thieves and vagabonds. It is said there are now 5,000 children anxious to get into our public schools, but, owing to their already crowded state, they must "abide their time." Then come those classes for which compulsory education is demanded, the whole numbers of which is estimated at 20,000! The greater portion of these are idlers, vagrants, and thieves; others, again, accustomed to a sort of Bohemian life, are ungovernable, willful, and whose parents are as ready to encourage them in idleness, as they would disregard the rules and regulations of our schools. Such parents will be the antagonists to any law compelling them to send their children to school on compulsion. Enforcement of such a law, would be to send the father to prison, for the non-payment of the fine, and give his children up to starvation!

That education is essential to the welfare of all classes, as it is one of the main pillars of a government and a permanent source of blessing, there can not be a question of doubt, but the mode of imparting such education to all classes has not been established.

When we look at the condition of our country—when we see cities overflowing with population, with dens of vice and misery multiplying and becoming more and more crowded with the children of misery, want and crime, when we observe how poor humanity is thrust into holes to live in poverty and die in destitution because the surface of the land can afford no better resting-place, when we see thousands huddled together with pestilence, filth and dirt surrounding them, and eddying into one common center, and then diffused to contaminate others, when these things meet our eye is it not natural that we should ask: "Are they necessary evils in the world?" What is the cause? And if they are not necessary, why do we not seek for some preventive—some cure—some remedy? *They are not necessary.* It is a blasphemous imputation on Providence to say that God made the earth so full of beauty, comfort and plenty for his children, that these outcasts, these miserable destitute wretches, should live and die amid such scenes as described. It were a gross impiety to assert that the world was made for sin and suffering, and that crime in high places, hypocrisy in the temples, usurped the rights of the moral and the just.

OFFICIAL CORRUPTION.

The manifest and total disregard of good faith and integrity on the part of public officers is now attracting general attention and considerable comment among the people. What mode of redress may be resorted to, it is impossible to say; but one thing is certain, and that is if we wait for the present race of office-holders to enforce the law and apply the corrective, we will be sadly disappointed. "Dog won't eat dog," and, as all public men are tainted with the same odor, and under the same bad influence, and are affected by the same depravity, they cannot—nay, they dare not—pursue the offenders to conviction.

Each act of the officials in regard to the recent disclosures in the treasury, tax receivers and in councils, clearly indicate a prevailing disposition to effect a full and complete discharge of all the offenders, and thereby punish the tax-payers (!). Is this not true in relation to all official plunders, county, state and national? Can we account for this obliquity of morals? Let us see: has not the teaching of the whole nation for the last eight years been marked with an obvious tendency toward a relaxing of morals, and at the same time to promote corruption, and a want of political fidelity, so that our office-holders have become men "without understanding, covenant breakers, without natural affection, implacable, unmerciful." They have been led, if not encouraged, to this, by men in high places. It has been justified, if not directly taught, in our schools; preached from the sacred desk, and proclaimed from the political rostrum. The people, the source of all power, have become effeminate, and the natural result of all this is that our "princes are rebellious and companions of thieves; every one loveth gifts and followeth after reward." While this is so, we can only pray that our judge may be restored as at the first.

We would not be cynical, nor would we set down ought in malice, but the ore is so deep, the rottenness so thorough, that the remedy must be radical, the language plain, and of undoubted purport. The wrong-doers have become a host; society is permeated with loose notions of moral obligations, and false theories of the rights and duties of a citizen. All politicians, from the president down to street supervisors, are the consorts of thieves. In no other way can we account for the fact that men are appointed to great public trusts, who are utterly deficient in every attribute of a gentleman; hence we read daily of nothing but frauds and peculation on the part of those, their appointees. History teaches that in time of public agitation and tumult the worst of men arise to power. Is this not pre-eminently true in our case? and has not the late war raised to official positions, dignity, and pride men of the baser sort—men who have been notorious for nothing but profligate lives, a mean truckling to party dictation, and panderers to wrong and crime? Such are our rulers, and the people mourn.

If there be virtue enough left in the body politic to found a hope upon, let it be brought forth, for except we stop now, at once, in our mad career, and hold every man who is guilty of official malfeasance or misfeasance personally to a strict accountability for their misdoings, we as a nation will be utterly ruined, and so degraded in public estimation that we will become a "perpetual hissing,"—every one that passeth thereby shall be astonished and wag their heads. They will say that no people ever paid so dearly for their liberties and parted with them so cheaply.*

---

*The New York *Tribune* complains that a man convicted of pilfering a money-letter from the mail, in Chicago, has been pardoned, and seeks to draw public attention to its consequences. We have no more sympathy with petty crime than we have with large ones, but we suggest that it is small business to complain of this particular pardon so soon after the adjournment of the Credit Mobilier Congress, and while eminent and distinguished statesmen are contending in the United States Senate that successful bribery is not a disqualifying offense. So long as Senators can boast that they purchased their seats in the Senate at a cost of from $50,000 to $80,000 each, and so long as the House refuses to expel those who offered and paid bribes to its members, refuses to censure even those who accepted the bribes, it is a small business to talk about the escape of a man convicted of taking a few dollars from the mails. Is it not straining at a gnat and swallowing a camel to be demanding that a man be placed ten years in the penitentiary for stealing ten dollars, and at the same time

But there is a remedy, and that remedy, is education. And yet the skeptic will say, what has education done for those who swindle the community—What has education done for the corrupt legislator, the politicians, and the financier? An educated rogue is the most dangerous to society. The poor man who steals a loaf of bread to save his children from starvation finds no mercy, while the well dressed speculator filches millions, is dined by his accomplices, wined by his tools, and his felony compromised, after conviction.

Now we contend that to compel these 20,000 pauper children to attend our public schools without undergoing some reformatory process is perfect nonsense. It would be like placing Satan in paradise, or turning the waters of the "Dead Sea" (if it could be done geographically) into the pure water of the river Schuylkill. What is the remedy?

RESCUE AND REFORMATORY SCHOOLS.

Rescue schools is one of the means for "Suppressing Juvenile Depravity." Will our public schools open their doors for the

---

give an "ovation" and a public dinner to the chief of a gang that stole thirty-five millions of dollars, and with it debauched the legislation of Congress and the veracity of its members? It has been but a few months when an entire political party either demanded or applauded the pardon of a person convicted of robbing the city of Philadelphia, the election of a president seeming to depend on the release of this convict. Three months later, a man convicted of illegal voting and perjury was promptly pardoned by the President. There has been no person convicted, during the last four years, of robbing the United States Treasury, who has not been pardoned. Why complain of the escape of a man convicted of a comparatively petty offense, when three hundred members of Congress each took $5,000 from the Public Treasury without any warrant of law other than their own votes? Public sentiment upon the subject of crimes against the United States Treasury has been debauched; even among the religious classes in New York there are found those who defraud the revenue by false oaths and forged invoices, and who, when caught, expect, as a matter of right, to escape punishment for the crime by paying the money back, and are allowed to go free. The attempted robbery in the Chorpenning case, and the actual fraud upon the Treasury in the Secor case, have been condoned by the reappointments of Creswell and Robeson to the Cabinet, and the whole Civil Service of the country has been advised that there is no really degrading crime that a public officer can commit, except stealing money out of a letter, or opposing the re-election of the member of Congress from his district.—*Chicago Tribune.*

classes named? No! unless by *legislative compulsion*. Will those men, and legislators who advocate "Compulsory Education" clothe these 20,000 children, so that they could appear in their proper places at school, or would they drag them in by main force in all their dirt and filth to startle, astonish and drive the better class out? When we say better class, it is not making a distinction between rich and poor, but between vice and virtue. That class they now attempt to force into our schools are, as we have said, the children of the lost and abandoned, their condition is one that calls forth all our sympathies. Their drunken parents maltreat them—starve, and drive them to begging. Often without a home, without clothes, without food, they beg and steal from necessity. Give them food and clothing first; educate them afterwards. Our police reports place on the criminal records many instances of children sent to prison for petty crimes. The novelty of a prison, instead of reforming them, suits the Bohemian notion of life in prison. They recall the story of Jack Sheppard,* Paul Clifford, and other celebrated highwaymen. Thus repeated short imprisonments prepare them for the patient endurance of a longer; and, having served three or four short and one or two long ones, they are considered eligible for a sentence of still a much longer period. Thus, we have the "School for Rogues," established under a mistaken notion that children of a tender age are rogues in grain and should be punished.

---

* When the drama of Jack Sheppard was first played in this city, one of the city magistrates informed us that he had committed thirty young Jack Sheppards (so calling themselves) during the first two months of its representation. The stage has a powerful influence on the morals of youth, either for good or evil.

www.ingramcontent.com/pod-product-compliance
Lightning Source LLC
Chambersburg PA
CBHW051728300426
44115CB00007B/503